GMAT™
Focus Edition

Where do you see yourself in 6 weeks?

You can prep for the GMAT Focus Edition in less time than it takes to catch up on your favorite television shows. Get your FREE 6-Week Study Planner: **mba.com/6-weeks**

- ⊙ **Start** your prep on the right foot
- ⊙ **Track** your progress as you learn
- ⊙ **Keep focused** on your business school journey
- ⊙ **Gain tools and tips** to achieve your dream score

Graduate Management Admission Council™

GMAT™
Focus Edition

For the GMAT™
Focus Edition

GMAT™ Official Guide Quantitative Review
2023 - 2024

Add additional Quantitative questions to your practice.

The only source of real GMAT questions

What's Included:

✓ Over 150 Practice Questions
✓ Math Review Chapter
✓ Answer Explanations

Plus! Online Exclusive:

✓ **Mobile App** - Study on the Go
✓ Flashcards
✓ Track Your Progress

 Book + Online + Mobile

GMAT™ Official Guide Quantitative Review 2023–2024

For general information on our other products and services or to obtain technical support please contact our Customer Care Department within the U.S. at (877) 762-2974, outside the U.S. at (317) 572-3993 or fax (317) 572-4002.

Wiley also publishes its books in a variety of electronic formats. Some content that appears in print may not be available in electronic books. For more information about Wiley products, please visit our Web site at www.wiley.com.

ISBN 978-1-394-16995-5 (pbk); ISBN 978-1-394-16998-6 (ePub)

Printed in the United States of America

SKY10038553_032323

Table of Contents

Dear GMAT™ Test Taker,

Thank you for your interest in graduate management education. Today more than 7,700 graduate programs around the world use the GMAT exam to establish their MBA, business master's, and other graduate-level management degree programs as hallmarks of excellence. Seven out of ten candidates apply to business school with their GMAT exam score.*

By using the *GMAT™ Official Guide* to prepare for the GMAT Focus Edition, you're taking a very important step toward achieving your goals and pursuing admission to the MBA or business master's program that is the best fit for you.

The *GMAT™ Official Guide Quantitative Review 2023–2024*, is designed to help you prepare for and build confidence to do your best on exam day. It's the only guide that features real GMAT questions published by the Graduate Management Admission Council (GMAC™), the makers of the GMAT exam. This guide and the other print and digital GMAT™ Official Prep products available at **mba.com** will give you the confidence to achieve your personal best on the GMAT exam and launch or reinvigorate a rewarding career.

For 70 years, the GMAT exam has helped candidates like you demonstrate their command of the skills needed for success in the classroom and showcase to schools their commitment to pursuing a graduate business degree. Schools use and trust the GMAT exam as part of their admissions process because it's a proven predictor of classroom success and your ability to excel in your chosen program.

The mission of GMAC is to ensure no talent goes undiscovered. We are driven to provide you with the tools and information you need to guide you through your journey in graduate management education, continuously improve the GMAT exam, and help you find and connect with the best-fit schools and programs for you.

We applaud your commitment to educational success and wish you the best on all your future educational and professional endeavors.

Sincerely,

Joy J. Jones
CEO, Graduate Management Admission Council

GMAT™ Official Guide
Quantitative Review 2023–2024

1.0 What Is the GMAT™ Exam?

1.0 What Is the GMAT™ Exam?

The Graduate Management Admission Test™ (GMAT™) is used in admissions decisions by more than 7,700 graduate management programs at about 2,400 business schools worldwide. It helps both you and these schools gauge how well you can do in graduate-level management studies. Unlike undergraduate grades and courses, whose meanings vary across regions and institutions, your GMAT scores are a standardized, statistically valid, and reliable measure of how well you are likely to do in the core courses of a graduate management program. This guide is for the **GMAT™ Focus Edition**.

The exam has three sections, which test your Verbal Reasoning, Quantitative Reasoning, and Data Insights skills. These skills include critical thinking, data analysis, and problem-solving, which all call for complex judgments. Management faculty and admissions professionals have found that incoming graduate students need these skills. And employers worldwide need their professional staff to have these skills as well.

This chapter gives more details about the GMAT Focus Edition below. You will take the exam on a computer either online or at a test center, always in English. It is not a test of business knowledge, subject mastery, English vocabulary, or advanced computing skills. Nor does it measure other factors helpful in business, such as job experience, leadership ability, motivation, or social skills. Your GMAT score is meant to be an objective, numeric measure of your ability and potential for success. Business schools will use it as part of their holistic admissions processes, which may also consider recommendation letters, essays, interviews, work experiences, and other signs of social and emotional intelligence as well as leadership.

1.1 Why Take the GMAT Exam?

Taking the exam helps you stand out as an applicant and show you're ready for and committed to graduate management education. Schools use GMAT scores in choosing the most qualified applicants. They know an applicant who has taken the exam is serious about earning a graduate business degree, and they know the exam scores reliably predict how well applicants can do in graduate business programs.

No matter how you do on the exam, you should contact schools that interest you to learn more about them and to ask how they use GMAT scores and other criteria in admissions decisions. School admissions offices, websites, and publications are key sources of information when you are researching business schools. Note that schools' published GMAT scores are averages of the scores of their admitted students, not minimum scores needed for admission.

Myth -vs- **FACT**

M – **If I don't get a high GMAT score, I won't get into my top-choice schools.**

F – **There are great schools for students with any GMAT score.**

Few people taking the GMAT exam will get a perfect score of 805, yet many will get into top business-school programs around the world. Admissions officers will use GMAT scores as one factor in admissions decisions along with undergraduate records, application essays, interviews, letters of recommendation, and other information. Visit Program Finder on **mba.com** to learn which programs and schools are right for you.

To learn more about the exam, test preparation materials, registration, and how to use your GMAT scores in applying to business schools, please visit **mba.com/gmatfocus**.

1.2 GMAT™ Focus Edition Format

The GMAT™ Focus Edition has three separately timed sections (see the table on the following page). The Data Insights section includes multiple-choice questions along with other kinds of graphical and data analysis questions. The Quantitative Reasoning section and the Verbal Reasoning section have only multiple-choice questions.

All three GMAT sections are computer adaptive. This means the test chooses from a large bank of questions to adjust itself to your ability level, so you will not get many questions that are too hard or too easy for you. The first question will be of medium difficulty. As you answer each question, the computer uses your answer, along with your responses to earlier questions, to choose the next question with the right difficulty level.

Computer-adaptive tests get harder as you answer more questions right. But getting a question that seems easier than the last one doesn't always mean your last answer was wrong. The test must ask you many types of questions on different subjects, so it will not always give you a question of the perfect difficulty level.

A new feature in the GMAT is a bookmark you can use to mark any questions you feel unsure about during the exam. Another new feature lets you review and edit your answers at the end of each section. You can review and edit answers even to questions you have not bookmarked, but bookmarking a question helps you find it again quickly. You can bookmark as many questions as you like. You can review all questions whether or not they are bookmarked, but you can only change your answers to three questions per section. You must finish all your bookmarking, reviewing, and editing within each section's time limit. No extra time is given to use these new features.

Because the computer uses your answers to choose your next question, you cannot skip questions. But at the end of each section, you can go back, review all questions, and edit your answers for up to three questions. If you don't know how to answer a question, try to rule out as many wrong answer choices as possible. Then pick the answer choice you think is best.

Though each test taker gets different questions, the mix of question types is always the same. Your score depends on the difficulty and statistical traits of the questions you answer, as well as on which of your answers are right. By adapting to each test taker, the exam can accurately and efficiently gauge a full range of skill levels, from very high to very low.

The practice questions in this book and the online question bank accessed via **mba.com/my-account** are formatted and presented differently than questions on the actual exam. The practice questions are organized by question type and from easiest to hardest. But on the test, you may see different types of questions in any order within each section.

Myth -vs- FACT

M – Getting an easier question means I answered the last one wrong.

F – Worrying that a question seems too easy isn't helpful.

Many factors may make the questions easier or harder, so don't waste time worrying if some questions seem easy.

To make sure every test taker gets equivalent content, the test gives specific numbers of questions of each type and about each kind of subject. But sometimes no available question perfectly meets these constraints. In this case, the test chooses the best available question, which may be slightly harder or easier than your next question would normally be. Also, remember you will be stronger in some subjects than in others. Since the test covers the same kinds of subjects for everyone, some items may be harder or easier for you than for other test takers.

Here are six things to know about GMAT questions:

(1) The computer screen shows only one question or question prompt at a time, except for some types of Data Insights questions.

(2) Radio buttons, rather than letters, mark the answer choices for multiple-choice questions.

(3) The Data Insights section gives questions of different types in random order.

(4) You must choose an answer and confirm your choice before moving on to the next question.

(5) You can bookmark questions to remind yourself to review them at the end of the section.

(6) Once you answer all of a section's questions, you may revisit any questions, whether bookmarked or not, and edit up to three answers in the section.

Format of the GMAT™ Focus Edition		
	Questions	Timing
Data Insights Data Sufficiency Multi-Source Reasoning Table Analysis Graphics Interpretation Two-Part Analysis	20	45 min.
Quantitative Reasoning	21	45 min.
Verbal Reasoning Reading Comprehension Critical Reasoning	23	45 min.
	Total Time	135 min.

On exam day, right before you start the exam, you can choose any order in which you will take the three sections. For example, you can choose to start with Verbal Reasoning, then do Quantitative Reasoning, and end with Data Insights. Or, you can choose to do Data Insights first, followed by Verbal Reasoning and then Quantitative Reasoning. Between sections, you can take one optional ten-minute break after either the first section or the second section.

1.3 What Is the Test Experience Like?

You can take the exam either online or at a test center—whichever you prefer. You may feel more comfortable at home with the online delivery format. Or you may prefer the uninterrupted, secure environment of a test center. It is your choice. Both options have the same content, structure, optional ten-minute break, scores, and score scales.

At the Test Center: Over 700 test centers worldwide administer the GMAT exam under standardized conditions. Each test center has proctored testing rooms with individual computer workstations that let you take the exam in a peaceful, quiet setting, with some privacy. You must not take notes or scratch paper into the testing room, but you will get an erasable notepad and marker to use during the test. To learn more about exam day, visit **mba.com/gmatfocus**.

Online: The GMAT exam delivered online is proctored remotely, so you can take it in the comfort of your home or office. You will need a quiet workspace with a desktop or laptop computer that meets minimum system requirements, a webcam, and a reliable internet connection. For more information about exam day, visit **mba.com/gmatfocus**.

To learn more about available accommodations for the exam, visit **mba.com/accommodations**.

1.4 What Is the Test Content Like?

The GMAT exam measures several types of analytical reasoning. The Data Insights section asks you to use diverse reasoning skills to solve realistic problems involving data. It also asks you to interpret and combine data from different sources and in different formats to reach conclusions. The Quantitative Reasoning section gives you basic arithmetic and algebra problems. Some are abstract, while others are realistic word problems.

The test questions are about various subjects, but the exam tells you everything you need to know to answer the questions. You do not need detailed outside knowledge of the subjects. The exam does not test business knowledge, vocabulary, or advanced computer skills. You will need basic math and English skills to do well on the test, but it mainly measures analytical and critical thinking skills.

Myth -vs- FACT

M – My GMAT score does not predict my success in business school.

F – False. The GMAT exam measures your critical thinking skills, which you will need in business school and your career.

Hundreds of studies across hundreds of schools have proven the GMAT's validity. Together, these studies have shown that performance on the GMAT predicts success in business school even better than undergraduate grades do.

The exam measures how well you reason, solve problems, and analyze data. Some employers may even use the exam to judge your skills in these areas. Even if your program does not require GMAT scores, you can stand out from the crowd by doing well on the exam to show you have the skills to succeed in business school.

1.5 Data Insights Section

The GMAT Data Insights section highlights skills that today's business managers need to analyze intricate data and solve complex problems. It tests how well you can assess multiple sources and types of information—graphic, numeric, and verbal—as they relate to one another. It also tests how well you can analyze a practical math problem to tell if enough data is given to solve it. This section asks you to use math, data analysis, and verbal reasoning to analyze complex problems and solve related problems together.

The Data Insights section has five types of questions:

- Multi-Source Reasoning
- Table Analysis
- Graphics Interpretation
- Two-Part Analysis
- Data Sufficiency

Data Insights questions may require math, data analysis, verbal reasoning, or all three. You will have to interpret graphs and sort data tables to answer some questions, but you won't need advanced statistics or spreadsheet skills. For both online and test center exam delivery, you will have access to an on-screen calculator with basic functions for the Data Insights section, but **not** for the Quantitative Reasoning section.

1.6 Quantitative Reasoning Section

The GMAT Quantitative Reasoning section measures how well you solve math problems and interpret graphs. All questions in this section require solving problems using basic arithmetic, algebra, or both. Some are practical word problems, while others are pure math.

To review the basic mathematical concepts that you will need to answer Quantitative Reasoning questions, see the "Math Review" in Chapter 3. For test-taking tips specific to the question types asked in the Quantitative Reasoning section, practice questions, and answer explanations, see Chapter 4.

1.7 Verbal Reasoning Section

The GMAT Verbal Reasoning section measures how well you reason, understand what you read, and evaluate arguments. The Verbal Reasoning section includes passages about many topics. Neither the passages nor the questions assume you already know much about the topics discussed. Mingled throughout the section are multiple-choice questions of two main types: Reading Comprehension and Critical Reasoning.

1.8 How Are Scores Calculated?

The Verbal Reasoning, Quantitative Reasoning, and Data Insights sections are each scored on a scale from 60 to 90, in 1-point increments. You will get four scores: a Data Insights section score, a Verbal Reasoning section score, a Quantitative Reasoning section score, and a Total GMAT Score based on your three section scores. The Total GMAT Score ranges from 205 to 805. Your scores depend on:

- Which questions you answered right
- How many questions you answered
- Each question's difficulty and other statistical characteristics

An algorithm finds your scores based on the factors above. After you answer easier questions correctly, you will get harder questions to answer, letting you earn a higher score. The computer calculates your scores after you finish the exam or when your time runs out.

The following table shows the different types of scores, the scales, and the increments.

Type of Score	Scale	Increments
Total Score	205–805	10
Quantitative Reasoning	60–90	1
Verbal Reasoning	60–90	1
Data Insights	60–90	1

Your GMAT scores are valid for five years from your exam date. Your Total GMAT Score includes a predicted percentile ranking, which shows the percentage of tests taken with scores lower than your score. Visit **mba.com** to view the most recent predicted percentile rankings tables.

To register for the GMAT™ exam go to www.mba.com/register

2.0 How to Prepare

2.0 How to Prepare

2.1 How Should I Prepare for the Test?

The GMAT™ Focus Edition has several unique question
formats. You should at least know about the test format
and these question formats before you take the test.
Because the exam is timed, you should also try answering
the practice questions in this book. By practicing, you'll
learn to pace yourself so that you can finish each section
during the exam. You'll also learn about the question
formats and the skills you need.

Because the exam assesses reasoning rather than
knowledge, memorizing facts probably won't help you. You
don't need to study advanced math, but you should know
some basic arithmetic and algebra. Likewise, you don't
need to study advanced vocabulary words, but you should
know English well enough to understand writing at an
undergraduate level.

> *Myth* -vs- **FACT**
>
> *M* – **You need advanced math skills to get a high GMAT score.**
>
> *F* – **The exam measures your reasoning ability rather than your advanced math skills.**
>
> The exam only requires basic math. You should review the math skills in chapter 3 of this guide. GMAT Quantitative Reasoning questions are challenging mainly because of the reasoning skills needed to solve the problems, not the underlying math skills.

2.2 Getting Ready for Exam Day

Whether you take the test online or in a test center, knowing what to expect will help you feel confident
and succeed.

Test Center

While checking into a test center, be ready to:

- Show proper identification.
- Give your palm vein scan (where permitted by law).
- Give your digital signature to show that you understand and agree to the Test-Taker Rules and Agreement.
- Have a digital photograph taken.

For more information, visit **mba.com/gmatfocus**.

Online

At least a day before you take your exam online:

- Check your computer—make sure your computer meets the minimum system requirements to run the exam.
- Prepare your workspace—find a quiet place to take your exam, clean your workspace, and remove all objects except your computer and whiteboard.
- Plan ahead—be ready to begin checking in 30 minutes before your scheduled exam time.

For more information, visit **mba.com/gmatfocus**.

2.3 How to Use the *GMAT™ Official Guide Quantitative Review 2023–2024*

The *GMAT™ Official Guide Quantitative Review* is designed for those who have completed the Quantitative Reasoning questions in the *GMAT™ Official Guide 2023–2024* and are looking for additional practice questions in Quantitative Reasoning. Questions are organized by difficulty level from easy to hard, so if you are new to studying, we recommend starting at the beginning of each chapter and working your way through the questions sequentially. Some "easy" questions may seem hard to you, and some "hard" questions may seem easy. This is common. Different questions often seem harder to some people and easier to others.

You may also find the questions in this book generally easier or harder than questions you see on the Official Practice Exams or the actual exam. This is expected because, unlike the Official Practice Exams and the actual exam, this guidebook doesn't adjust to your abilities. In this book, about a third of the practice questions are easy, a third are medium, and a third are hard. However, on the actual exam and the Official Practice Exams, you probably won't find such an even mix of difficulty levels. Also, the proportions of questions about different content areas in this book don't reflect the proportions in the actual exam. To find questions of a specific type and difficulty level, use the index of questions in chapter 5.

> **TIP**
>
> Since the exam is given on a computer, we suggest you practice the questions in this book using the **Online Question Bank** accessed via **mba.com/my-account**. It includes all the questions in this book, and it lets you create practice sets and track your progress more easily. The Online Question Bank is also available on your mobile device through the GMAT™ Official Practice mobile app. To access the Online Question Bank on your mobile device, first, create an account at **mba.com**, and then sign into your account on the mobile app.

2.4 How to Use Other GMAT Official Prep Products

We recommend using our other GMAT Official Prep products along with this guidebook.

- **For a realistic simulation of the exam:** GMAT™ Official Practice Exams 1–6 are the only practice exams that use real exam questions along with the scoring algorithm, user interface, and online whiteboard tool from the real exam. The first two practice exams are free to all test takers at **mba.com/gmatprep**.

- **For more practice questions:** *GMAT™ Official Guide Data Insights Review 2023–2024* and *GMAT™ Official Guide Verbal Review 2023–2024* offer more practice questions not included in this book.

For the best results:

1. Learn about the exam and the question types by reading the *GMAT™ Official Guide 2023–2024*.

2. Take the Diagnostic evaluation in the Online Question Bank (access via **mba.com/my-account**) to gauge your strengths and weaknesses.

3. Practice the questions in the *GMAT™ Official Guide 2023–2024*, focusing on skills you need to improve.

4. Take GMAT™ Focus Official Practice Exam 1. Do not worry about your score on this first practice exam! The goal is to become familiar with the exam and get a baseline score so that you can gauge your progress.

5. As you keep practicing, take more GMAT™ Focus Official Practice Exams to gauge your progress.

6. Before your actual GMAT exam, take a final GMAT™ Official Practice Exam to simulate the real test and see how you score.

The first two GMAT™ Official Practice Exams are in the free GMAT™ Official Starter Kit, which has free practice questions and is available to everyone with an **mba.com** account. You can buy GMAT™ Focus Official Practice Exams 3 through 6, more GMAT™ Focus Official Practice Questions, and other Official Prep products through **mba.com/gmatprep**.

2.5 Tips for Taking the Exam

Tips for answering questions of the different types are given later in this book. Here are some general tips to help you do your best on the test.

1. **Use your time wisely.**
Although the exam stresses accuracy over speed, you should use your time wisely. On average, you have just under 2 minutes per Verbal Reasoning question, about 2 minutes, 9 seconds per Quantitative Reasoning question, and 2 minutes, 15 seconds per Data Insights question. Once you start the test, an on-screen clock shows how much time you have left. You can hide this display if you want, but by checking the clock periodically, you can make sure to finish in time.

2. **Before the actual exam, decide in what order to take the sections.**
The exam lets you choose in which order you'll take the sections. Use the GMAT™ Official Practice Exams to practice and find your preferred order. No order is "wrong." Just practice each order and see which one works best for you.

3. **Try the practice questions ahead of time.**
Timing yourself as you answer the practice questions can give you a sense of how long you will have for each question on the actual test, and whether you are answering them fast enough to finish in time.

Myth -vs- **FACT**

M – Avoiding wrong answers is more important than finishing the test.

F – Not finishing can lower your score a lot.

Pacing is important. If a question stumps you, just pick the answer choice that seems best and move on. If you guess wrong, the computer will likely give you an easier question, which you're more likely to answer right. Soon the computer will return to giving you questions matched to your ability. You can bookmark questions you get stuck on, then return to change up to three of your answers if you still have time left at the end of the section. But if you don't finish the section, your score will be reduced. Failing to answer five verbal questions, for example, could lower your score from the 91st percentile to the 77th percentile.

TIP

After you've learned about all the question types, use the practice questions in this book and practice them online at **mba.com/my-account** to prepare for the actual test. Note that most types of Data Insights practice questions are available only online.

4. **Study all test directions.**

    The directions explain exactly what you need to do to answer questions of each type. Study the directions so that you don't miss anything you need to know to answer properly. To review directions during the test, click on the Help icon. But note that your time spent reviewing directions counts against your available time for that section of the test.

5. **Study each question carefully**

    Before you answer a question, understand exactly what it says. Then pick the best answer choice. Never skim a question or the answer choices. Skimming may make you miss important details or nuances.

6. **Do not spend too much time on any one question.**

    If finding the right answer is taking too long, try to rule out answer choices you know are wrong. Then pick the best of the remaining choices and move on to the next question.

    Not finishing sections or randomly guessing answers can lower your score significantly. As long as you've worked on each section, you will get a score even if you didn't finish one or more sections in time. You don't earn points for questions you never get to see.

7. **Confirm your answers ONLY when you are ready to move on.**

    In the Quantitative Reasoning and Verbal Reasoning sections, once you choose your answer to a question, you are asked to confirm it. As soon as you confirm your response, the next question appears. You can't skip questions. In the Data Insights section, several questions based on the same prompt may appear at once. When more than one question is on a single screen, you can change your answers to any questions on that screen before moving on to the next screen. But until you've reached the end of the section, you can't navigate back to a previous screen to change any answers.

Myth -vs- FACT

M – The first ten questions are critical, so you should spend the most time on them.

F – All questions count.

The test uses each answered question to *initially* estimate how hard your questions should be. As you keep answering questions, the test adjusts by updating the estimate based on all your answers so far. It then chooses questions that closely match its new estimate of your ability. Your final score depends on all your responses and on how hard all the questions you answered were. Taking extra time on the first ten questions won't game the system and might make you run out of time.

This book and other study materials from the Graduate Management Admission Council (GMAC) are the ONLY sources of real GMAT questions. All questions that appear or have appeared on the exam are copyrighted and owned by GMAC, which doesn't license them to be reprinted elsewhere. Accessing live GMAT questions in advance or sharing test content while or after you take the test is a serious violation. It could cause your scores to be canceled and schools to be notified. For serious violations, you may be banned from future testing, and other legal remedies may be pursued.

3.0   Math Review

3.0 Math Review

This chapter reviews the math you need to answer GMAT™ Quantitative Reasoning questions and some GMAT Data Insights questions. This is only a brief overview, so if you find unfamiliar terms, consult other resources to learn more.

Unlike some math problems you may have solved in school, GMAT math questions ask you to *apply* your math knowledge. For example, rather than asking you to list a number's prime factors to show you understand prime factorization, a GMAT question may ask you to *use* prime factorization and exponents to simplify an algebraic expression with a radical.

To prepare for the GMAT Quantitative Reasoning section and the Data Insights section, first review basic math to make sure you know enough to answer the questions. Then practice using GMAT questions from past exams.

Section 3.1, "Value, Order, and Factors," includes:

1. Numbers and the Number Line
2. Factors, Multiples, Divisibility, and Remainders
3. Exponents
4. Decimals and Place Value
5. Properties of Operations

Section 3.2, "Algebra, Equalities, and Inequalities," includes:

1. Algebraic Expressions and Equations
2. Linear Equations
3. Factoring and Quadratic Equations
4. Inequalities
5. Functions
6. Graphing
7. Formulas and Measurement Conversion

Section 3.3, "Rates, Ratios, and Percents," includes:

1. Ratio and Proportion
2. Fractions
3. Percents
4. Converting Decimals, Fractions, and Percents
5. Working with Decimals, Fractions, and Percents
6. Rate, Work, and Mixture Problems

Section 3.4, "Statistics, Sets, Counting, Probability, Estimation, and Series," includes:

1. Statistics
2. Sets
3. Counting Methods
4. Probability
5. Estimation
6. Sequences and Series

Section 3.5, Reference Sheets

3.1 Value, Order, and Factors

1. Numbers and the Number Line

A. All ***real numbers*** correspond to points on ***the number line***, and all points on the number line represent real numbers.

The figure below shows the number line with labeled points standing for the real numbers $-\frac{3}{2}$, 0.2, and $\sqrt{2}$.

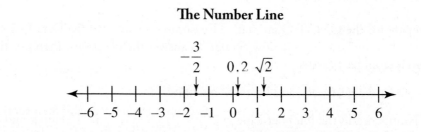

The Number Line

B. On a number line, points to the left of zero stand for ***negative*** numbers, and points to the right of zero stand for ***positive*** numbers. All real numbers except zero are either positive or negative.

C. For any two numbers on the number line, the number to the left is less than the number to the right. So, as the figure above shows, $-4 < -3 < -\frac{3}{2} < -1$, and $1 < \sqrt{2} < 2$.

D. If a number n is between 1 and 4 on the number line, then $n > 1$ and $n < 4$; that is, $1 < n < 4$. If n is "between 1 and 4, inclusive," then $1 \le n \le 4$.

E. The ***absolute value*** of a real number x, written as $|x|$, is x if $x \ge 0$ and $-x$ if $x < 0$. A number's absolute value is the distance between that number and zero on the number line. Thus, -3 and 3 have the same absolute value, since each is three units from zero on the number line. The absolute value of any nonzero number is positive.

Examples:

$|-5| = |5| = 5$, $|0| = 0$, and

$\left|\frac{-7}{2}\right| = \frac{7}{2}$.

For any real numbers x and y, $|x + y| \le |x| + |y|$.

Example:

If $x = 10$ and $y = 2$, then $|x + y| = |12| = 12 = |x| + |y|$.

If $x = 10$ and $y = -2$, then $|x + y| = |8| = 8 < 12 = |x| + |y|$.

---

2. Factors, Multiples, Divisibility, and Remainders

A. An *integer* is any number in the set $\{\ldots -3, -2, -1, 0, 1, 2, 3, \ldots\}$. For any integer n, the numbers in the set $\{n, n + 1, n + 2, n + 3, \ldots\}$ are *consecutive integers*.

B. If x and y are integers and $x \neq 0$, then x is a *divisor* or *factor* of y if $y = xn$ for some integer n. Then y is *divisible* by x and is called a *multiple* of x.

> *Example:*
>
> Since $28 = (7)(4)$, both 4 and 7 are divisors or factors of 28.
>
> But 8 isn't a divisor or factor of 28, since n isn't an integer if $28 = 8n$.

C. Dividing a positive integer y by a positive integer x, and then rounding down to the nearest nonnegative integer, gives the *quotient* of the division.

To find the *remainder* of the division, multiply x by the quotient, then subtract the result from y. The quotient and the remainder are the unique positive integers q and r, respectively, such that $y = xq + r$ and $0 \leq r < x$.

> *Example:*
>
> When 28 is divided by 8, the quotient is 3 and the remainder is 4, because $28 = (8)(3) + 4$.

The remainder r is 0 if and only if y is *divisible* by x. Then x is a divisor or factor of y, and y is a multiple of x.

> *Example:*
>
> Since 32 divided by 8 has a remainder of 0, 32 is divisible by 8. So 8 is a divisor or factor of 32, and 32 is a multiple of 8.

When a smaller integer is divided by a larger integer, the quotient is 0 and the remainder is the smaller integer.

> *Example:*
>
> When 5 is divided by 7, the quotient is 0 and the remainder is 5, since $5 = (7)(0) + 5$.

D. Any integer divisible by 2 is *even*; the set of even integers is $\{\ldots -4, -2, 0, 2, 4, 6, 8, \ldots\}$. Integers not divisible by 2 are *odd*, so $\{\ldots -3, -1, 1, 3, 5, \ldots\}$ is the set of odd integers. For any integer n, the numbers in the set $\{2n, 2n + 2, 2n + 4, \ldots\}$ are *consecutive even integers*, and the numbers in the set $\{2n + 1, 2n + 3, 2n + 5, \ldots\}$ are *consecutive odd integers*.

If a product of integers has at least one even factor, the product is even; otherwise, it's odd. If two integers are both even or both odd, their sum and their difference are even. Otherwise, their sum and their difference are odd.

E. A *prime* number is a positive integer with exactly two positive divisors, 1 and itself. That is, a prime number is divisible by no integer but itself and 1.

> *Example:*
>
> The first six prime numbers are 2, 3, 5, 7, 11, and 13.
>
> But 15 is not a prime number, because it has four positive divisors: 1, 3, 5, and 15.
>
> Nor is 1 a prime number, because it has only one positive divisor: itself.

Every integer greater than 1 is either prime or a product of a unique set of prime factors. A *composite number* is an integer greater than 1 that's not prime.

> *Example:*
>
> 14 = (2)(7), 81 = (3)(3)(3)(3), and
>
> 484 = (2)(2)(11)(11) are composite numbers.

3. Exponents

A. An expression of the form k^n means the nth *power* of k, or k raised to the nth power, where n is the *exponent* and k is the *base*.

B. A positive integer exponent shows how many instances of the base are multiplied together. That is, when n is a positive integer, k^n is the product of n instances of k.

> *Examples:*
>
> x^5 is $(x)(x)(x)(x)(x)$; that is, the product in which x is a factor 5 times and no other factors. We can also say x^5 is the 5th power of x, or x raised to the 5th power.
>
> The 2nd power of 2, also called 2 *squared*, is $2^2 = 2 \times 2 = 4$. The 3rd power of 2, also called 2 *cubed*, is $2^3 = 2 \times 2 \times 2 = 8$.

Squaring a number greater than 1, or raising it to any power greater than 1, gives a larger number.

Squaring a number between 0 and 1 gives a smaller number.

> *Examples:*
>
> $3^2 = 9$, and $9 > 3$.
>
> $(0.1)^2 = 0.01$, and $0.01 < 0.1$.

C. A **square root** of a number n is a number x such that $x^2 = n$. Every positive number has two real square roots, one positive and the other negative. The positive square root of n is written as $\sqrt{n}$ or $n^{\frac{1}{2}}$.

> *Example:*
>
> The two square roots of 9 are $\sqrt{9} = 3$ and $-\sqrt{9} = -3$.

For any x, the nonnegative square root of x^2 equals the absolute value of x; that is, $\sqrt{x^2} = |x|$.

The square root of a negative number is not a real number and is called an **imaginary number**.

D. Every real number r has exactly one real **cube root**, which is the number s such that $s^3 = r$. The real cube root of r is written as $\sqrt[3]{r}$ or $r^{\frac{1}{3}}$.

> *Examples:*
>
> Since $2^3 = 8$, $\sqrt[3]{8} = 2$.
>
> Likewise, $\sqrt[3]{-8} = -2$ because $(-2)^3 = -8$.

4. Decimals and Place Value

A. A **decimal** is a real number written as a series of digits, often with a period called a **decimal point**. The decimal point's position sets the **place values** of the digits.

> *Example:*
>
> The digits in the decimal 7,654.321 have these place values:
>
> | Thousands | | Hundreds | Tens | Ones or units | | Tenths | Hundredths | Thousandths |
> |---|---|---|---|---|---|---|---|---|
> | 7 | , | 6 | 5 | 4 | . | 3 | 2 | 1 |

B. In **scientific notation**, a decimal is written with only one nonzero digit to the decimal point's left, multiplied by a power of 10. To convert a number from scientific notation to regular decimal notation, move the decimal point by the number of places equal to the absolute value of the exponent on the 10. Move the decimal point to the right if the exponent is positive or to the left if the exponent is negative.

Examples:

In scientific notation, 231 is written as 2.31×10^2, and 0.0231 is written as 2.31×10^{-2}.

To convert 2.013×10^4 to regular decimal notation, move the decimal point 4 places to the right, giving 20,130.

Likewise, to convert 1.91×10^{-4} to regular decimal notation, move the decimal point 4 places to the left, giving 0.000191.

C. To add or subtract decimals, line up their decimal points. If one decimal has fewer digits to the right of its decimal point than another, insert zeros to the right of its last digit.

Examples:

To add 17.6512 and 653.27, insert zeros to the right of the last digit in 653.27 to line up the decimal points when the numbers are in a column:

$$\begin{array}{r} 17.6512 \\ + 653.2700 \\ \hline 670.9212 \end{array}$$

Likewise for 653.27 minus 17.6512:

$$\begin{array}{r} 653.2700 \\ -17.6512 \\ \hline 635.6188 \end{array}$$

D. Multiply decimals as if they were integers, then insert the decimal point in the product so that the number of digits to the right of the decimal point is the sum of the numbers of digits to the right of the decimal points in the numbers being multiplied.

Example:

To multiply 2.09 by 1.3, first multiply the integers 209 and 13 to get 2,717. Since $2 + 1 = 3$ digits to the right of the decimal points in 2.09 and 1.3, put 3 digits in 2,717 to the right of the decimal point to find the product:

$$\begin{array}{r} 2.09 \quad \text{(2 digits to the right)} \\ \times 1.3 \quad \text{(1 digit to the right)} \\ \hline 627 \\ 2090 \\ \hline 2.717 \quad (2+1=3 \text{ digits to the right}) \end{array}$$

E. To divide a number (the ***dividend***) by a decimal (the ***divisor***), move the divisor's decimal point to the right to make the divisor an integer. Then move the dividend's decimal point the same number of places to the right. Then divide as you would integers. The decimal point in the quotient goes directly above the decimal point in the new dividend.

Example:

To divide 698.12 by 12.4, first move the decimal points in both the divisor 12.4 and the dividend 698.12 one place to the right to make the divisor an integer. That is, replace 698.12/12.4 with 6981.2/124. Then do the long division normally:

$$
\begin{array}{r}
56.3 \\
124\overline{)6981.2} \\
\underline{620} \\
781 \\
\underline{744} \\
372 \\
\underline{372} \\
0
\end{array}
$$

5. Properties of Operations

Here are some basic properties of arithmetical operations for any real numbers x, y, and z.

A. Addition and Subtraction

$x + 0 = x = x - 0$

$x - x = 0$

$x + y = y + x$

$x - y = -(y - x) = x + (-y)$

$(x + y) + z = x + (y + z)$

If x and y are both positive, then $x + y$ is also positive.

If x and y are both negative, then $x + y$ is negative.

B. Multiplication and Division

$x \times 1 = x = \dfrac{x}{1}$

$x \times 0 = 0$

If $x \neq 0$, then $\dfrac{x}{x} = 1$

$\dfrac{x}{0}$ is undefined.

$xy = yx$

If $x \neq 0$ and $y \neq 0$, then $\dfrac{x}{y} = \dfrac{1}{\left(\frac{y}{x}\right)}$.

$(xy)z = x(yz)$

$xy + xz = x(y + z)$

If $y \neq 0$, then $\left(\dfrac{x}{y}\right) + \left(\dfrac{z}{y}\right) = \dfrac{(x + z)}{y}$.

If x and y are both positive, then xy is also positive.

If x and y are both negative, then xy is positive.

If x is positive and y is negative, then xy is negative.

If $xy = 0$, then $x = 0$ or $y = 0$, or both.

C. Exponentiation

$x^1 = x$

$x^0 = 1$

If $x \neq 0$, then $x^{-1} = \frac{1}{x}$

$(x^y)^z = x^{yz} = (x^z)^y$

$x^{y+z} = x^y x^z$

If $x \neq 0$, then $x^{y-z} = \frac{x^y}{x^z}$.

$(xz)^y = x^y z^y$

If $z \neq 0$, then $\left(\frac{x}{z}\right)^y = \frac{x^y}{z^y}$.

If $z \neq 0$, then $x^{\frac{y}{z}} = (x^y)^{\frac{1}{z}} = \left(x^{\frac{1}{z}}\right)^y$.

3.2 Algebra, Equalities, and Inequalities

1. Algebraic Expressions and Equations

A. Algebra is based on arithmetic and on the concept of an **unknown quantity**. Letters like **x** or **n** are **variables** that stand for unknown quantities. Numerical expressions called **constants** stand for known quantities. A combination of variables, constants, and arithmetical operations is an **algebraic expression**.

Solving word problems often requires translating words into algebraic expressions. The table below shows how some words and phrases can be translated as math operations in algebraic expressions:

3.2 Translating Words into Math Operations				
$x + y$	$x - y$	xy	$\frac{x}{y}$	x^y
x added to y / x increased by y / x more than y / x plus y / the sum of x and y / the total of x and y	x decreased by y / difference of x and y / y fewer than x / y less than x / x minus y / x reduced by y / y subtracted from x	x multiplied by y / the product of x and y / x times y	x divided by y / x over y / the quotient of x and y / the ratio of x to y	x to the power of y / x to the yth power
		If $y = 2$: double x / twice x	If $y = 2$: half of x / x halved	If $y = 2$: x squared
		If $y = 3$: triple x		If $y = 3$: x cubed

B. In an algebraic expression, a **_term_** is a constant, a variable, or a product of simpler terms that are each a constant or a variable. A variable in a term may be raised to an exponent. A term with no variables is a **_constant term_**. A constant in a term with one or more variables is a **_coefficient_**.

> *Example:*
>
> Suppose Pam has 5 more pencils than Fred has. If F is the number of pencils Fred has, then the number of pencils Pam has is $F + 5$. The algebraic expression $F + 5$ has two terms: the variable F and the constant term 5.

C. A **_polynomial_** is an algebraic expression that's a sum of terms and has exactly one variable. Each term in a polynomial is a variable raised to some power and multiplied by some coefficient. If the highest power a variable is raised to is 1, the expression is a **_first degree_** (or **_linear_**) **_polynomial_** in that variable. If the highest power a variable is raised to is 2, the expression is a **_second degree_** (or **_quadratic_**) **_polynomial_** in that variable.

> *Examples:*
>
> $F + 5$ is a linear polynomial in F, since the highest power of F is 1.
>
> $19x^2 - 6x + 3$ is a quadratic polynomial in x, since the highest power of x is 2.
>
> $\dfrac{3x^2}{(2x - 5)}$ is not a polynomial, because it's not a sum of powers of x multiplied by coefficients.

D. You can simplify many algebraic expressions by factoring or combining **_like_** terms.

> *Example:*
>
> The expression $6x + 5x$ is equivalent to $(6 + 5)x$, or $11x$.
>
> In the expression $9x - 3y$, 3 is a factor common to both terms: $9x - 3y = 3(3x - y)$.
>
> The expression $5x^2 + 6y$ has no like terms and no common factors.

E. In a fraction $\dfrac{n}{d}$, n is the **_numerator_** and d is the **_denominator_**. In an algebraic expression's numerator and denominator, you can divide out any common factors not equal to zero.

> *Example:*
>
> If $x \neq 3$, then $\dfrac{(x - 3)}{(x - 3)} = 1$.
>
> So $\dfrac{(3xy - 9y)}{(x - 3)} = \dfrac{3y(x - 3)}{(x - 3)} = 3y(1) = 3y$.

F. To multiply two algebraic expressions, multiply each term of one expression by each term of the other.

> *Example:*
>
> $$(3x - 4)(9y + x) = 3x(9y + x) - 4(9y + x)$$
> $$= 3x(9y) + 3x(x) - 4(9y) - 4(x)$$
> $$= 27xy + 3x^2 - 36y - 4x$$

G. To evaluate an algebraic expression, replace its variables with constants.

> *Example:*
>
> If $x = 3$ and $y = -2$, we can evaluate $3xy - x^2 + y$ as
>
> $3(3)(-2) - (3)^2 + (-2) = -18 - 9 - 2 = -29$.

H. An *algebraic equation* is an equation with at least one algebraic expression. An algebraic equation's *solutions* are the sets of assignments of constant values to its variables that make it true, or "satisfy the equation." An equation may have no solution, one solution, or more than one solution. For equations solved together, the solutions must satisfy all the equations at once. An equation's solutions are also called its *roots*. To confirm the roots are correct, you can substitute them into the equation.

I. Two equations with the same solution or solutions are *equivalent*.

> *Examples:*
>
> The equations $2 + x = 3$ and $4 + 2x = 6$ are equivalent, because each has the unique solution $x = 1$. Notice the second equation is the first equation multiplied by 2.
>
> Likewise, the equations $3x - y = 6$ and $6x - 2y = 12$ are equivalent, although each has infinitely many solutions. For any value given to x, giving the value $3x - 6$ to y satisfies both these equations. For example, $x = 2$ with $y = 0$ is a solution to both equations, and so is $x = 5$ with $y = 9$.

2. Linear Equations

A. A *linear equation* has a linear polynomial on one side of the equals sign and either a linear polynomial or a constant on the other side—or can be converted to that form. A linear equation with only one variable is a *linear equation with one unknown*. A linear equation with two variables is a *linear equation with two unknowns*.

> *Examples:*
>
> $5x - 2 = 9 - x$ is a linear equation with one unknown.
>
> $3x + 1 = y - 2$ is a linear equation with two unknowns.

B. To solve a linear equation with one unknown (that is, to find what value of the unknown satisfies the equation), isolate the unknown on one side of the equation by doing the same operations on both sides. Adding or subtracting the same number from both sides of the equation doesn't change the equality. Likewise, multiplying or dividing both sides by the same nonzero number doesn't change the equality.

Example:

To solve the equation $\frac{5x-6}{3} = 4$, isolate the variable x like this:

$$5x - 6 = 12 \quad \text{multiply both sides by 3}$$

$$5x = 18 \quad \text{add 6 to both sides}$$

$$x = \frac{18}{5} \quad \text{divide both sides by 5}$$

To check the answer $\frac{18}{5}$, substitute it for x in the original equation to confirm it satisfies that equation:

$$\frac{\left(5\left(\frac{18}{5}\right) - 6\right)}{3} = \frac{(18 - 6)}{3} = \frac{12}{3} = 4$$

So $x = \frac{18}{5}$ is the solution.

C. If two linear equations with the same two unknowns are equivalent, they have infinitely many solutions, as in the example of the equivalent equations $3x - y = 6$ and $6x - 2y = 12$ in section 3.2.1.I above. But if two linear equations with the same two unknowns aren't equivalent, they have at most one solution.

Two linear equations with two unknowns can be solved in several ways. If in solving them you reach a trivial equation like $0 = 0$, the equations are equivalent and have infinitely many solutions. But if you reach a contradiction, the equations have no solution.

Example:

Consider the two equations $3x + 4y = 17$ and $6x + 8y = 35$. Note that $3x + 4y = 17$ implies $6x + 8y = 34$, contradicting the second equation. So, no values of x and y can satisfy both equations at once.

If neither a trivial equation nor a contradiction is reached, a unique solution can be found.

D. To solve two linear equations with two unknowns, you can use one of the equations to express one unknown in terms of the other unknown. Then substitute this result into the second equation to make a new equation with only one unknown. Next, solve this new equation. Substitute the value of its unknown into either of the original equations to find the value of the remaining unknown.

Example:

Let's solve these two equations for x and y:

$$(1) \quad 3x + 2y = 11$$
$$(2) \quad x - y = 2$$

In equation (2), $x = 2 + y$. So, in equation (1), substitute $2 + y$ for x:

$$3(2 + y) + 2y = 11$$
$$6 + 3y + 2y = 11$$
$$6 + 5y = 11$$
$$5y = 5$$
$$y = 1$$

Since $y = 1$, we find $x - 1 = 2$, so $x = 2 + 1 = 3$.

E. Another way to remove one unknown and solve for x and y is to make the coefficients of one unknown the same in both equations (ignoring the sign). Then either add the equations or subtract one from the other.

Example:

Let's solve the equations:

$$(1) \quad 6x + 5y = 29 \text{ and}$$
$$(2) \quad 4x - 3y = -6$$

Multiply equation (1) by 3 and equation (2) by 5 to get

$$18x + 15y = 87 \text{ and}$$
$$20x - 15y = -30$$

Add the two equations to remove y. This gives us $38x = 57$, or $x = \frac{3}{2}$.

Substituting $\frac{3}{2}$ for x in either original equation gives $y = 4$. To check these answers, substitute both values into both the original equations.

3. Factoring and Quadratic Equations

A. Some equations can be solved by *factoring*. To do this, first add or subtract to bring all the expressions to one side of the equation, with 0 on the other side. Then try to express the nonzero side as a product of factors that are algebraic expressions. When that's possible, setting any of these factors equal to 0 makes a simpler equation, because for any x and y, if $xy = 0$, then $x = 0$ or $y = 0$ or both. The solutions of the simpler equations made this way are also solutions of the factored equation.

Example:

Factor to find the solutions of the equation $x^3 - 2x^2 + x = -5(x-1)^2$:

$$x^3 - 2x^2 + x + 5(x-1)^2 = 0$$
$$x(x^2 - 2x + 1) + 5(x-1)^2 = 0$$
$$x(x-1)^2 + 5(x-1)^2 = 0$$
$$(x+5)(x-1)^2 = 0$$
$$x + 5 = 0 \text{ or } x - 1 = 0$$
$$x = -5 \text{ or } x = 1.$$

So, $x = -5$ or $x = 1$.

B. When factoring to solve equations with algebraic fractions, note that a fraction equals 0 if and only if its numerator equals 0 and its denominator doesn't.

Example:

Find the solutions of the equation $\dfrac{x(x-3)(x^2+5)}{x-4} = 0$

The numerator must equal 0: $x(x-3)(x^2+5) = 0$.

Thus, $x = 0$, or $x - 3 = 0$, or $x^2 + 5 = 0$. So, $x = 0$, or $x = 3$, or $x^2 + 5 = 0$.

But $x^2 + 5 = 0$ has no real solution, because $x^2 + 5 = 0$ for every real number x. So, the original equation's solutions are 0 and 3.

C. A *quadratic equation* has the standard form $ax^2 + bx + c = 0$, where a, b, and c are real numbers and $a \neq 0$.

Examples:

$$x^2 + 6x + 5 = 0$$
$$3x^2 - 2x = 0, \text{ and}$$
$$x^2 + 4 = 0$$

D. Some quadratic equations are easily solved by factoring.

Example (1):
$$x^2 + 6x + 5 = 0$$
$$(x+5)(x+1) = 0$$
$$x + 5 = 0 \text{ or } x + 1 = 0$$
$$x = -5 \text{ or } x = -1$$

Example (2):
$$3x^2 - 3 = 8x$$
$$3x^2 - 8x - 3 = 0$$
$$(3x+1)(x-3) = 0$$
$$3x + 1 = 0 \text{ or } x - 3 = 0$$
$$x = -\frac{1}{3} \text{ or } x = 3$$

E. A quadratic equation has at most two real roots but may have just one or even no root.

Examples:

The equation $x^2 - 6x + 9 = 0$ can be written as $(x - 3)^2 = 0$ or $(x - 3)(x - 3) = 0$. So, its only root is 3.

The equation $x^2 + 4 = 0$ has no real root. Since any real number squared is greater than or equal to zero, $x^2 + 4$ must be greater than zero if x is a real number.

F. An expression of the form $a^2 - b^2$ can be factored as $(a - b)(a + b)$.

Example:

We can solve the quadratic equation $9x^2 - 25 = 0$ like this:

$$(3x - 5)(3x + 5) = 0$$
$$3x - 5 = 0 \text{ or } x + 5 = 0$$
$$x = \frac{5}{3} \text{ or } x = -\frac{5}{3}$$

G. If a quadratic expression isn't easily factored, we can still find its roots with the **quadratic formula:**
If $ax^2 + bx + c = 0$ and $a \neq 0$, the roots are

$$x = \frac{-b + \sqrt{b^2 - 4ac}}{2a} \text{ and } x = \frac{-b - \sqrt{b^2 - 4ac}}{2a}$$

These roots are two distinct real numbers unless $b^2 - 4ac \leq 0$.

If $b^2 - 4ac = 0$, the two root expressions both equal $-\frac{b}{2a}$, so the equation has only one root.

If $b^2 - 4ac < 0$, then $\sqrt{b^2 - 4ac}$ is not a real number, so the equation has no real root.

4. Inequalities

A. An *inequality* is a statement with one of these symbols:

$\neq$ is not equal to

$>$ is greater than

$\geq$ is greater than or equal to

$<$ is less than

$\leq$ is less than or equal to

Example:

$5x - 3 < 9$ and $6x \geq y$

B. Solve a linear inequality with one unknown like you solve a linear equation: isolate the unknown on one side. As with an equation, the same number can be added to or subtracted from both sides of the inequality. And you can multiply or divide both sides by a positive number without changing the order of the inequality. However, multiplying or dividing an inequality by a negative number reverses the order of the inequality. Thus, $6 > 2$, but $(-1)(6) < (-1)(2)$.

Example (1):

To solve the inequality $3x - 2 > 5$ for x, isolate x:

$3x - 2 > 5$

$3x > 7$ (add 2 to both sides)

$x > \dfrac{7}{3}$ (divide both sides by 3)

Example (2):

To solve the inequality $\dfrac{5x - 1}{-2} < 3$ for x, isolate x:

$\dfrac{5x - 1}{-2} < 3$

$5x - 1 > -6$ (multiply both sides by -2)

$5x > -5$ (add 1 to both sides)

$x > -1$ (divide both sides by 5)

---

5. Functions

A. An algebraic expression in one variable can define a ***function*** of that variable. A function is written as a letter like f or g along with the variable in the expression. Function notation is a short way to express a value's substitution for a variable.

Examples:

(i) The expression $x^3 - 5x^2 + 2$ can define a function f written as $f(x) = x^3 - 5x^2 + 2$.

(ii) The expression $\dfrac{2z + 7}{\sqrt{z + 1}}$ can define a function g written as $g(z) = \dfrac{2z + 7}{\sqrt{z + 1}}$.

In these examples, the symbols "$f(x)$" and "$g(z)$" don't stand for products. Each is just a symbol for an algebraic expression, and is read "f of x" or "g of z."

The substitution of 1 for x in the first expression can be written as $f(1) = -2$. Then $f(1)$ is called the "value of f at $x = 1$."

Likewise, in the second expression the value of g at $z = 0$ is $g(0) = 7$.

B. Once a function $f(x)$ is defined, think of x as an input and $f(x)$ as the output. In any function, any one input gives at most one output. But different inputs can give the same output.

Example:

If $h(x) = |x + 3|$, then $h(-4) = 1 = h(-2)$.

C. The set of all allowed inputs for a function is the function's ***domain***. In the examples in section 3.2.5.A above, the domain of f is the set of all real numbers, and the domain of g is the set of all numbers greater than -1.

Any function's definition can restrict the function's domain. For example, the definition "$a(x) = 9x - 5$ for $0 \leq x \leq 10$" restricts the domain of a to real numbers greater than or equal to 0 but less than or equal to 10. If the definition has no restrictions, the domain is the set of all values of x that each give a real output when input into the function.

D. The set of a function's outputs is the function's **range**.

Examples:

(i) For the function $h(x) = |x + 3|$ in the example in section 3.2.5.B above, the range is the set of all numbers greater than or equal to 0.

(ii) For the function $a(x) = 9x - 5$ for $0 \leq x \leq 10$ defined in section 3.2.5.C above, the range is the set of every value y such that $-5 \leq y \leq 85$.

---

6. Graphing

A. The figure below shows the rectangular **coordinate plane.** The horizontal line is the **x–axis** and the vertical line is the **y-axis**. These two axes intersect at the **origin**, called O. The axes divide the plane into four quadrants, I, II, III, and IV, as shown.

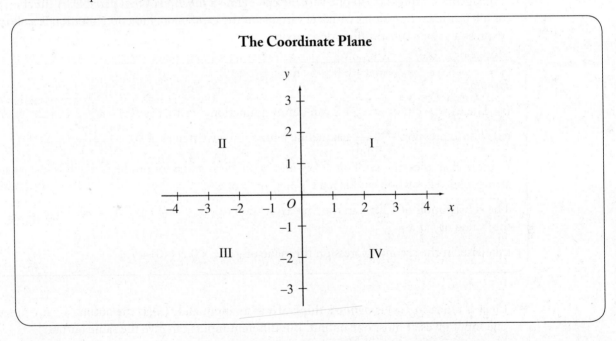

The Coordinate Plane

B. Any ordered pair (x, y) of real numbers defines a point in the coordinate plane. The point's **x-coordinate** is the first number in this pair. It shows how far the point is to the right or left of the y-axis. If the x-coordinate is positive, the point is to the right of the y-axis. If it's negative, the point is to the left of the y-axis. If it's 0, the point is on the axis. The point's **y-coordinate** is the second number in the ordered pair. It shows how far the point is above or below the x-axis. If the y-coordinate is positive, the point is above the x-axis. If it's negative, the point is below the x-axis. If it's 0, the point is on the axis.

Example:

In the graph below, the (x,y) coordinates of point P are (2,3). P is 2 units to the right of the y-axis, so $x = 2$. Since P is 3 units above the x-axis, $y = 3$.

Likewise, the (x,y) coordinates of point Q are (−4,−3). The origin O has coordinates (0,0).

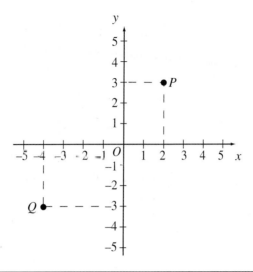

C. The coordinates of each point on a line in the coordinate plane satisfy a linear equation of the form $y = mx + b$ (or the form $x = a$ if the line is vertical).

In the equation $y = mx + b$, the coefficient m is the line's ***slope***, and the constant term b is the line's ***y-intercept***.

The y-intercept is the y-coordinate of the point where the line intersects the y-axis. Likewise, the ***x-intercept*** is the x-coordinate of the point where the line intersects the x-axis.

For any two points on the line, the slope is the ratio of the difference in their y-coordinates to the difference in their x-coordinates. To find the slope, subtract one point's y-coordinate from that of the others. Then subtract the former point's x-coordinate from the latter's—not the other way around!

If a line's slope is negative, the line slants down from left to right.

If its slope is positive, the line slants up.

If the slope is 0, the line is horizontal. A horizontal line's equation has the form $y = b$, since $m = 0$.

For a vertical line, the slope is not defined.

Example:

In the graph below, each point on the line satisfies the equation $y = -\frac{1}{2}x + 1$. To check this for the points $(-2, 2)$, $(2, 0)$, and $(0, 1)$, substitute each point's coordinates for x and y in the equation.

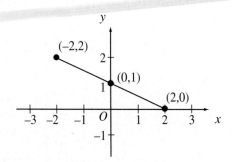

You can use the points $(-2, 2)$ and $(2, 0)$ to find the line's slope:

$$\frac{\text{the difference in the } y\text{-coordinates}}{\text{the difference in the } x\text{-coordinates}} = \frac{0 - 2}{2 - (-2)} = \frac{-2}{4} = -\frac{1}{2}.$$

The y-intercept is 1. That's the value of y when x is set to 0 in $y = -\frac{1}{2}x + 1$.

To find the x-intercept, set y to 0 in the same equation:

$$-\frac{1}{2}x + 1 = 0$$
$$-\frac{1}{2}x = -1$$
$$x = 2.$$

Thus, the x-intercept is 2.

D. You can use the definition of slope to find the equation of a line through two points (x_1, y_1) and (x_2, y_2) with $x_1 \neq x_2$. The slope is $m = \frac{y_2 - y_1}{x_2 - x_1}$. Given the known point (x_1, y_1) and the slope m, any other point (x, y) on the line must satisfy the equation $m = \frac{(y - y_1)}{(x - x_1)}$, or equivalently $(y - y_1) = m(x - x_1)$. Using (x_2, y_2) instead of (x_1, y_1) as the known point gives an equivalent equation.

Example:

The graph below shows points (−2,4) and (3,−3).

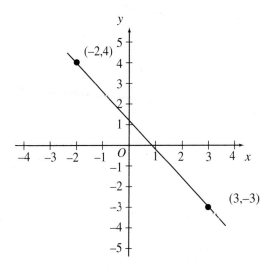

The line's slope is $\dfrac{(-3-4)}{(3-(-2))} = \dfrac{-7}{5}$. To find an equation of this line, let's use the point (3,−3):

$$y - (-3) = \left(-\frac{7}{5}\right)(x - 3)$$

$$y + 3 = \left(-\frac{7}{5}\right)x + \frac{21}{5}$$

$$y = \left(-\frac{7}{5}\right)x + \frac{6}{5}$$

So, the *y*-intercept is $\dfrac{6}{5}$.

Find the *x*-intercept like this:

$$0 = -\frac{7}{5}x + \frac{6}{5}$$

$$\frac{7}{5}x = \frac{6}{5}$$

$$x = \frac{6}{7}$$

The graph shows both these intercepts.

E. If two linear equations with unknowns *x* and *y* have a unique solution, their graphs are two lines intersecting at the point that is the solution.

   If two linear equations are equivalent, they both stand for the same line and have infinitely many solutions.

   Two linear equations with no solution stand for parallel lines that don't intersect.

F. Graph any function $f(x)$ in the coordinate plane by equating *y* with the function's value: $y = f(x)$. For any *x* in the function's domain, the point $(x, f(x))$ is on the function's graph. For every point in the graph, the *y*-coordinate is the function's value at the *x*-coordinate.

Example:

Consider the function $f(x) = -\dfrac{7}{5}x + \dfrac{6}{5}$.

If $f(x)$ is equated with the variable y, the function's graph is the graph of the equation $y = -\dfrac{7}{5}x + \dfrac{6}{5}$ in the example above.

G. For any function f, the x-intercepts are the solutions of the equation $f(x) = 0$. The y-intercept is the value $f(0)$.

Example:

To see how a quadratic function $f(x) = x^2 - 1$ relates to its graph, let's plot some points $(x, f(x))$ in the coordinate plane:

x	$f(x)$
-2	3
-1	0
0	-1
1	0
2	3

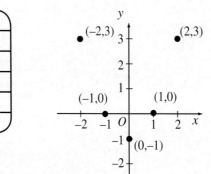

The graph below shows all the points for $-2 \leq x \leq 2$:

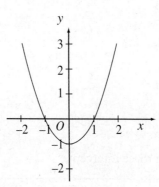

The roots of this equation $f(x) = x^2 - 1 = 0$ are $x = 1$ and $x = -1$. They match the x-intercepts, since x-intercepts are found by setting $y = 0$ and solving for x.

The y-intercept is $f(0) = -1$, because that's the value of y for $x = 0$.

7. Formulas and Measurement Conversion

A. A *formula* is an algebraic equation whose variables have specific meanings. To use a formula, assign quantities to its variables to match these meanings.

Example:

In the physics formula $F = ma$, the variable F stands for force, the variable m stands for mass, and the variable a stands for acceleration. The standard metric unit of force, the newton, is just enough force to accelerate a mass of 1 kilogram by 1 meter/second^2.

So, if we know a rock with a mass of 2 kilograms is accelerating at 5 meters/second^2, we can use the formula $F = ma$ by setting the variable m to 2 kilograms, and the variable a to 5 meters/second^2. Then we find that 10 newtons of force F are pushing the rock.

Note: You don't need to learn physics formulas or terms like this to prepare for the GMAT, but some specific GMAT questions may give you the formulas and terms you need to solve them.

B. Any quantitative relationship between units of measure can be written as a formula.

Examples:

(i) Since 1 kilometer is 1,000 meters, the formula $m = 1000k$ can stand for the relationship between kilometers (k) and meters (m).

(ii) The formula $C = \frac{5}{9}(F - 32)$ can stand for the relationship between temperature measurements in degrees Celsius (C) and degrees Fahrenheit (F).

C. Except for units of time, a GMAT question that requires converting one unit of measure to another will give the relationship between those units.

Example:

A train travels at a constant 25 meters per second. How many kilometers does it travel in 5 minutes? (1 kilometer = 1,000 meters)

Solution: In 1 minute the train travels $(25)(60) = 1,500$ meters, so in 5 minutes it travels 7,500 meters. Since 1 kilometer = 1,000 meters, we find 7,500 meters = 7.5 kilometers.

3.3 Rates, Ratios, and Percents

1. Ratio and Proportion

A. The *ratio* of a number x to a nonzero number y may be written as $x : y$, or $\frac{x}{y}$, or x to y. The order of a ratio's terms is important. Unless the absolute values of x and y are equal, $\frac{x}{y} \neq \frac{y}{x}$.

Examples:

The ratio of 2 to 3 may be written as 2:3, or $\frac{2}{3}$, or 2 to 3.

The ratio of the number of months with exactly 30 days to the number of months with exactly 31 days is 4:7, not 7:4.

B. A *proportion* is an equation between two ratios.

Example:

2:3 = 8:12 is a proportion.

C. One way to solve for an unknown in a proportion is to cross multiply, then solve the resulting equation.

Example:

To solve for n in the proportion $\frac{2}{3} = \frac{n}{12}$, cross multiply to get $3n = 24$, then divide both sides by 3 to find $n = 8$.

D. Some word problems can be solved using ratios.

Example:

If 5 shirts cost a total of $44, then what is the total cost of 8 shirts at the same cost per shirt?

Solution: If c is the cost of the 8 shirts, then $\frac{5}{44} = \frac{8}{c}$. Cross multiplying gives $5c = 8 \times 44 = 352$, so $c = \frac{352}{5} = 70.4$. Thus, the 8 shirts cost a total of $70.40.

2. Fractions

A. In a fraction $\frac{n}{d}$, n is the **numerator** and d is the **denominator**. A fraction's denominator can never be 0, because division by 0 is undefined.

B. *Equivalent* fractions stand for the same number. To check whether two fractions are equivalent, divide each fraction's numerator and denominator by the largest factor common to that numerator and that denominator, their **greatest common divisor** (gcd). This is called **reducing each fraction to its lowest terms**. Two fractions are equivalent if and only if reducing each to its lowest terms makes them identical.

> *Example:*
>
> To check whether $\frac{8}{36}$ and $\frac{14}{63}$ are equivalent, first reduce each to its lowest terms. In the first fraction, 4 is the gcd of the numerator 8 and the denominator 36. Dividing both the numerator and the denominator of $\frac{8}{36}$ by 4 gives $\frac{2}{9}$. In the second fraction, 7 is the gcd of the numerator 14 and the denominator 63. Dividing both the numerator and the denominator of $\frac{14}{63}$ by 7 also gives $\frac{2}{9}$. Since reducing $\frac{8}{36}$ and $\frac{14}{63}$ to their lowest terms makes them identical, they're equivalent.

C. To add or subtract two fractions with the same denominator, just add or subtract the numerators, leaving the denominators the same.

> *Example:*
>
> $$\frac{3}{5} + \frac{4}{5} = \frac{3+4}{5} = \frac{7}{5} \text{ and}$$
>
> $$\frac{5}{7} - \frac{2}{7} = \frac{5-2}{7} = \frac{3}{7}$$

D. To add or subtract two fractions with different denominators, first express them as fractions with the same denominator.

> *Example:*
>
> To add $\frac{3}{5}$ and $\frac{4}{7}$, multiply the numerator and denominator of $\frac{3}{5}$ by 7 to get $\frac{21}{35}$. Then multiply the numerator and denominator of $\frac{4}{7}$ by 5 to get $\frac{20}{35}$. Since both fractions now have the same denominator 35, you can easily add them: $\frac{3}{5} + \frac{4}{7} = \frac{21}{35} + \frac{20}{35} = \frac{41}{35}$

E. To multiply two fractions, multiply their numerators, and also multiply their denominators.

> *Example:*
>
> $$\frac{2}{3} \times \frac{4}{7} = \frac{2 \times 4}{3 \times 7} = \frac{8}{21}$$

F. The *reciprocal* of a fraction $\frac{n}{d}$ is $\frac{d}{n}$ if n and d are not 0.

> *Example:*
>
> The reciprocal of $\frac{4}{7}$ is $\frac{7}{4}$

G. To divide by a fraction, multiply by its reciprocal.

Example:

$$\frac{2}{3} \div \frac{4}{7} = \frac{2}{3} \times \frac{7}{4} = \frac{14}{12} = \frac{7}{6}$$

H. A *mixed number* is written as an integer next to a fraction. It equals the integer plus the fraction.

Example:

The mixed number $7\frac{2}{3} = 7 + \frac{2}{3}$

I. To write a mixed number as a fraction, multiply the integer part of the mixed number by the denominator of the fractional part. Add this product to the numerator. Then put this sum over the denominator.

Example:

$$7\frac{2}{3} = \frac{(7 \times 3) + 2}{3} = \frac{23}{3}$$

3. Percents

A. The word *percent* means *per hundred* or *number out of 100*.

Example:

Saying that 37 percent, or 37%, of the houses in a city are painted blue means that 37 houses per 100 in the city are painted blue.

B. A percent may be greater than 100.

Example:

Saying that the number of blue houses in a city is 150% of the number of red houses means the city has 150 blue houses for every 100 red houses. Since 150:100 = 3:2, this is the same as saying the city has 3 blue houses for every 2 red houses.

C. A percent need not be an integer.

> *Example:*
>
> Saying that the number of pink houses in a city is 0.5% of the number of blue houses means the city has 0.5 of a pink house for every 100 blue houses. Since 0.5:100 = 1:200, this is the same as saying the city has 1 pink house for every 200 blue houses.
>
> Likewise, saying that the number of orange houses is 12.5% of the number of blue houses means the ratio of orange houses to blue houses is 12.5:100 = 1:8. Therefore, there is 1 orange house for every 8 blue houses.

4. Converting Decimals, Fractions, and Percents

A. Decimals can be rewritten as fractions or sums of fractions.

> *Examples:*
>
> $$0.321 = \frac{3}{10} + \frac{2}{100} + \frac{1}{1,000} = \frac{321}{1,000}$$
>
> $$0.0321 = \frac{0}{10} + \frac{3}{100} + \frac{2}{1,000} + \frac{1}{10,000} = \frac{321}{10,000}$$
>
> $$1.56 = 1 + \frac{5}{10} + \frac{6}{100} = \frac{156}{100}$$

B. To rewrite a percent as a fraction, write the percent number as the numerator over a denominator of 100. To rewrite a percent as a decimal, move the decimal point in the percent two places to the left and drop the percent sign. To rewrite a decimal as a percent, move the decimal point two places to the right, then add a percent sign.

> *Examples:*
>
> $$37\% = \frac{37}{100} = 0.37$$
>
> $$300\% = \frac{300}{100} = 3$$
>
> $$0.5\% = \frac{0.5}{100} = 0.005$$

C. To find a certain percent of a number, multiply the number by the percent expressed as a fraction or decimal.

Examples:

20% of $90 = 90\left(\dfrac{20}{100}\right) = 90\left(\dfrac{1}{5}\right) = \dfrac{90}{5} = 18$

20% of $90 = 90(0.2) = 18$

250% of $80 = 80\left(\dfrac{250}{100}\right) = 80(2.5) = 200$

0.5% of $12 = 12\left(\dfrac{0.5}{100}\right) = 12(0.005) = 0.06$

5. Working with Decimals, Fractions, and Percents

A. To find the percent increase or decrease from one quantity to another, first find the amount of increase or decrease. Then divide this amount by the original quantity. Write this quotient as a percent.

Examples:

Suppose a price increases from \$24 to \$30. To find the percent increase, first find the amount of increase: \$30 − \$24 = \$6. Divide this \$6 by the original price of \$24 to find the percent increase: $\dfrac{6}{24} = 0.25 = 25\%$.

Now suppose a price falls from \$30 to \$24. The amount of decrease is \$30 − \$24 = \$6. So, the percent decrease is $\dfrac{6}{30} = 0.20 = 20\%$.

Notice the percent **increase** from 24 to 30 (25%) doesn't equal the percent **decrease** from 30 to 24 (20%).

A percent increase or decrease may be greater than 100%.

Example:

Suppose a house's price in 2018 was 300% of its price in 2003. By what percent did the price increase?

Solution: If n is the price in 2003, the percent increase is $\left|\dfrac{(3n - n)}{n}\right| = \left|\dfrac{2n}{n}\right| = 2$, or 200%.

B. A price discounted by n percent is $(100 - n)$ percent of the original price.

Example:

A customer paid $24 for a dress. If the customer got a 25% discount off the original price of the dress, what was the original price before the discount?

Solution: The discounted price is $(100 - 25 = 75)$% of the original price. So, if p is the original price, $0.75p = \$24$ is the discounted price. Thus, $p = (\$24 / 0.75) = \$32$, the original price before the discount.

Two discounts can be combined to make a larger discount.

Example:

A price is discounted 20%. Then this reduced price is discounted another 30%. These two discounts together make an overall discount of what percent?

Solution: If p is the original price, then $0.8p$ is the price after the first discount. The price after the second discount is $(0.7)(0.8)\,p = 0.56p$. The overall discount is $100\% - 56\% = 44\%$.

C. *Gross profit* equals revenues minus expenses, or selling price minus cost.

Example:

A certain appliance costs a merchant $30. At what price should the merchant sell the appliance to make a gross profit of 50% of the appliance's cost?

Solution: The merchant should sell the appliance for a price s such that $s - 30 = (0.5)(30)$. So, $s = \$30 + \$15 = \$45$.

D. *Simple annual interest* on a loan or investment is based only on the original loan or investment amount (the ***principal***). It equals (principal) × (interest rate) × (time).

Example:

If $8,000 is invested at 6% simple annual interest, how much interest is earned after 3 months?

Solution: Since the annual interest rate is 6%, the interest for 1 year is $(0.06)(\$8,000) = \$480$.

A year has 12 months, so the interest earned in 3 months is $\left(\dfrac{3}{12}\right)(\$480) = \$120$.

E. *Compound interest* is based on the principal plus any interest already earned.

Compound interest over n periods = (principal) × (1 + interest per period)^n − principal.

Example:

If $10,000 is invested at 10% annual interest, compounded every 6 months, what is the balance after 1 year?

Solution: Since the interest is compounded every 6 months, or twice a year, the interest rate for each 6-month period is 5%, half the 10% annual rate. So, the balance after the first 6 months is $10,000 + (10,000)(0.05) = \$10,500$.

For the second 6 months, the interest is based on the $10,500 balance after the first 6 months. So, the balance after 1 year is $10,500 + (10,500)(0.05) = \$11,025$.

The balance after 1 year can also be written as $10,000 \times \left(1 + \frac{0.10}{2}\right)^2$ dollars.

F. To solve some word problems with percents and fractions, you can organize the information in a table.

Example:

In a production lot, 40% of the toys are red, and the rest are green. Half of the toys are small, and half are large. If 10% of the toys are red and small, and 40 toys are green and large, how many of the toys are red and large?

Solution: First make a table to organize the information:

	Red	Green	Total
Small	10%		50%
Large			50%
Total	40%	60%	100%

Then fill in the missing percents so that the "Red" and "Green" percents in each row add up to that row's total, and the "Small" and "Large" percents in each column add up to that column's total:

	Red	Green	Total
Small	10%	40%	50%
Large	30%	20%	50%
Total	40%	60%	100%

The number of large green toys, 40, is 20% of the total number of toys (n), so $0.20n = 40$. Thus, the total number of toys $n = 200$. So, 30% of the 200 toys are red and large. Since $(0.3)(200) = 60$, we find that 60 of the toys are red and large.

6. Rate, Work, and Mixture Problems

A. The distance an object travels is its average speed multiplied by the time it takes to travel that distance. That is, ***distance = rate × time.***

> *Example:*
>
> How many kilometers did a car travel in 4 hours at an average speed of 70 kilometers per hour?
>
> *Solution:* Since distance = rate × time, multiply 70 km/hour × 4 hours to find that the car went 280 kilometers.

B. To find an object's average travel speed, divide the total travel distance by the total travel time.

> *Example:*
>
> On a 600-kilometer trip, a car went half the distance at an average speed of 60 kilometers per hour (kph), and the other half at an average speed of 100 kph. The car didn't stop between the two halves of the trip. What was the car's average speed over the whole trip?
>
> *Solution:* First find the total travel time. For the first 300 kilometers, the car went at 60 kph, taking $\frac{300}{60} = 5$ hours. For the second 300 kilometers, the car went at 100 kph, taking $\frac{300}{100} = 3$ hours. So, the total travel time was 5 + 3 = 8 hours. The car's average speed was $\frac{600 \text{ kilometers}}{8 \text{ hours}} = 75$ kph.
>
> Notice the average speed was not $\frac{(60 + 100)}{2} = 80$ kph.

C. A ***work problem*** usually says how fast certain individuals work and asks you to find how fast they work together, or vice versa.

The basic formula for work problems is $\frac{1}{r} + \frac{1}{s} = \frac{1}{h}$, where r is how long an amount of work takes a certain individual, s is how long that much work takes a different individual, and h is how long that much work takes both individuals working at the same time.

> *Example:*
>
> Suppose one machine takes 4 hours to make 1,000 bolts, and a second machine takes 5 hours to make 1,000 bolts. How many hours do both machines working at the same time take to make 1,000 bolts?
>
> *Solution:*
>
> $$\frac{1}{4} + \frac{1}{5} = \frac{1}{h}$$
> $$\frac{5}{20} + \frac{4}{20} = \frac{1}{h}$$
> $$\frac{9}{20} = \frac{1}{h}$$
> $$9h = 20$$
> $$h = \frac{20}{9} = 2\frac{2}{9}$$
>
> Working together, the two machines can make 1,000 bolts in $2\frac{2}{9}$ hours.

Use the same formula to find how long it takes one individual to do an amount of work alone.

Example:

Suppose Art and Rita both working at the same time take 4 hours to do an amount of work, and Art alone takes 6 hours to do that much work. Then how many hours does Rita alone take to do that much work?

Solution:

$$\frac{1}{6} + \frac{1}{R} = \frac{1}{4}$$

$$\frac{1}{R} = \frac{1}{4} - \frac{1}{6} = \frac{1}{12}$$

$$R = 12$$

Rita alone takes 12 hours to do that much work.

D. In ***mixture problems***, substances with different properties are mixed, and you must find the mixture's properties.

Example:

If 6 kilograms of nuts that cost $1.20 per kilogram are mixed with 2 kilograms of nuts that cost $1.60 per kilogram, how much does the mixture cost per kilogram?

Solution: The 8 kilograms of nuts cost a total of 6($1.20) + 2($1.60) = $10.40. So, the cost per kilogram is $\frac{\$10.40}{8}$ = $1.30.

Some mixture problems use percents.

Example:

How many liters of a solution that is 15% salt must be added to 5 liters of a solution that is 8% salt to make a solution that is 10% salt?

Solution: Let n be the needed number of liters of the 15% solution. The amount of salt in n liters of 15% solution is $0.15n$. The amount of salt in the 5 liters of 8% solution is $(0.08)(5)$. These amounts add up to the amount of salt in the 10% mixture, which is $0.10(n + 5)$. So,

$$0.15n + 0.08(5) = 0.10(n + 5)$$

$$15n + 40 = 10n + 50$$

$$5n = 10$$

$$n = 2 \text{ liters}$$

So, 2 liters of the 15% salt solution must be added to the 8% solution to make the 10% solution.

3.4 Statistics, Sets, Counting, Probability, Estimation, and Series

1. Statistics

A. A common statistical measure is the ***average*** or ***(arithmetic) mean,*** a type of center for a set of numbers. The average or mean of n numbers is the sum of the n numbers divided by n.

> *Example:*
>
> The average of the 5 numbers 6, 4, 7, 10, and 4 is $\dfrac{(6 + 4 + 7 + 10 + 4)}{5} = \dfrac{31}{5} = 6.2$.

B. The ***median*** is another type of center for a set of numbers. To find the median of n numbers, order the numbers from least to greatest. If n is odd, the median is the middle number in the list. But if n is even, the median is the average of the two middle numbers. The median may be less than, equal to, or greater than the mean of the same numbers.

> *Example:*
>
> To find the median of the 5 numbers 6, 4, 7, 10, and 4, order them from least to greatest: 4, 4, 6, 7, 10. The median is 6, the middle number in this list.
>
> The median of the 6 numbers 4, 6, 6, 8, 9, 12 is $\dfrac{(6 + 8)}{2} = 7$. But the mean of these 6 numbers is $\dfrac{(4 + 6 + 6 + 8 + 9 + 12)}{6} = \dfrac{45}{6} = 7.5$.

Often about half the numbers in a set are less than the median, and about half are greater than the median. But not always.

> *Example:*
>
> For the 15 numbers 3, 5, 7, 7, 7, 7, 7, 7, 8, 9, 9, 9, 9, 10, and 10, the median is 7. Only $\dfrac{2}{15}$ of the numbers are less than the median.

C. The ***mode*** of a list of numbers is the number that occurs most often in the list.

> *Example:*
>
> The mode of the list of numbers 1, 3, 6, 4, 3, 5 is 3, since 3 is the only number that occurs more than once in the list.

A list of numbers may have more than one mode.

> *Example:*
>
> The list 1, 2, 3, 3, 3, 5, 7, 10, 10, 10, 20 has two modes, 3 and 10.

D. There are many ways to measure how spread out or dispersed numerical data are. The simplest measure of dispersion is the *range*, which is the greatest value in the data minus the least value.

> *Example:*
>
> The range of the 5 numbers 11, 10, 5, 13, 21 is 21 − 5 = 16. Notice the range depends on only 2 of the numbers.

E. Another common measure of dispersion is the *standard deviation.* Generally, the farther the numbers spread away from the mean, the greater the standard deviation. To find the standard deviation of *n* numbers:

(1) Find their arithmetic mean,

(2) Find the differences between the mean and each of the *n* numbers,

(3) Square each difference,

(4) Find the average of the squared differences, and

(5) Take the nonnegative square root of this average.

> *Examples:*
>
> Let's use the table below to find the standard deviation of the 5 numbers 0, 7, 8, 10, 10, which have the mean 7.
>
> | x | $x - 7$ | $(x - 7)^2$ |
> |-----|---------|-------------|
> | 0 | −7 | 49 |
> | 7 | 0 | 0 |
> | 8 | 1 | 1 |
> | 10 | 3 | 9 |
> | 10 | 3 | 9 |
> | | Total | 68 |
>
> The standard deviation is $\sqrt{\dfrac{68}{5}} \approx 3.7$
>
> The standard deviation depends on every number in the set, but more on those farther from the mean. This is why the standard deviation is smaller for a set of data grouped closer around its mean.
>
> As a second example, consider the numbers 6, 6, 6.5, 7.5, 9, which also have the mean 7. These numbers are grouped closer around the mean 7 than the numbers in the first example. That makes the standard deviation in this second example only about 1.1, far below the standard deviation of 3.7 in the first example.

F. How many times a value occurs in a data set is its *frequency* in the set. When different data values have different frequencies, a *frequency distribution* can help show how the values are distributed.

Example:

Consider this data set of 20 numbers:

$$-4 \quad 0 \quad 0 \quad -3 \quad -2 \quad -1 \quad -1 \quad 0 \quad -1 \quad -4$$
$$-1 \quad -5 \quad 0 \quad -2 \quad 0 \quad -5 \quad -2 \quad 0 \quad 0 \quad -1$$

We can show its frequency distribution in a table listing each data value x and x's frequency f:

Data Value x	Frequency f
−5	2
−4	2
−3	1
−2	3
−1	5
0	7
Total	20

This frequency distribution table makes computing statistical measures easier:

Mean: $= \dfrac{(-5)(2) + (-4)(2) + (-3)(1) + (-2)(3) + (-1)(5) + (0)(7)}{20} = -1.6$

Median: −1 (the average of the 10th and 11th numbers)

Mode: 0 (the number that occurs most often)

Range: $0 - (-5) = 5$

Standard deviation: $\sqrt{\dfrac{(-5 + 1.6)^2(2) + (-4 + 1.6)^2(2) + \ldots + (0 + 1.6)^2(7)}{20}} \approx 1.7$

---

2. Sets

A. In math, a *set* is a collection of numbers or other things. The things in the set are its *elements*. A list of a set's elements in a pair of braces stands for the set. The list's order doesn't matter.

Example:

$\{-5, 0, 1\}$ is the same set as $\{0, 1, -5\}$. That is, $\{-5, 0, 1\} = \{0, 1, -5\}$.

B. The number of elements in a finite set S is written as $|S|$.

> *Example:*
>
> $S = \{-5, 0, 1\}$ is a set with $|S| = 3$.

C. If all the elements in a set S are also in a set T, then S is a **subset** of T. This is written as $S \subseteq T$ or $T \supseteq S$.

> *Example:*
>
> $\{-5, 0, 1\}$ is a subset of $\{-5, 0, 1, 4, 10\}$. That is, $\{-5, 0, 1\} \subseteq \{-5, 0, 1, 4, 10\}$.

D. The **union** of two sets A and B is the set of all elements that are each in A or in B or both. The union is written as $A \cup B$.

> *Example:*
>
> $\{3, 4\} \cup \{4, 5, 6\} = \{3, 4, 5, 6\}$

E. The **intersection** of two sets A and B is the set of all elements that are each in **both** A and B. The intersection is written as $A \cap B$.

> *Example:*
>
> $\{3, 4\} \cap \{4, 5, 6\} = \{4\}$

F. Two sets sharing no elements are **disjoint** or **mutually exclusive.**

> *Example:*
>
> $\{-5, 0, 1\}$ and $\{4, 10\}$ are disjoint.

G. A **Venn diagram** shows how two or more sets are related. Suppose sets S and T aren't disjoint, and neither is a subset of the other. The Venn diagram below shows their intersection $S \cap T$ as a shaded area.

A Venn Diagram of Two Intersecting Sets

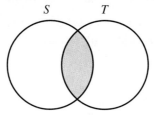

A Venn diagram of sets S and T, with their intersection $S \cap T$ shaded.

H. The number of elements in the union of two finite sets S and T is the number of elements in S, plus the number of elements in T, minus the number of elements in the intersection of S and T. That is, $|S \cup T| = |S| + |T| - |S \cap T|$. This is the ***general addition rule for two sets.***

Example:

$$|\{3, 4\} \cup \{4, 5, 6\}| = |\{3, 4\}| + |\{4, 5, 6\}| - |\{3, 4\} \cap \{4, 5, 6\}| =$$

$$|\{3, 4\}| + |\{4, 5, 6\}| - |\{4\}| = 2 + 3 - 1 = 4.$$

If S and T are disjoint, then $|S \cup T| = |S| + |T|$, since $|S \cap T| = 0$.

I. You can often solve word problems involving sets by using Venn diagrams and the general addition rule.

Example:

Each of 25 students is taking history, mathematics, or both. If 20 of them are taking history and 18 of them are taking mathematics, how many of them are taking both history and mathematics?

Solution: Separate the 25 students into three disjoint sets: the students taking history only, those taking mathematics only, and those taking both history and mathematics. This gives us the Venn diagram below, where n is the number of students taking both courses, $20 - n$ is the number taking history only, and $18 - n$ is the number taking mathematics only.

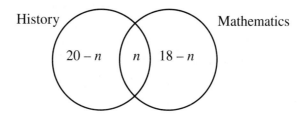

Since there are 25 students total, $(20 - n) + n + (18 - n) = 25$, so $n = 13$. So, 13 students are taking both history and mathematics. Notice $20 + 18 - 13 = 25$ is an example of the general addition rule for two sets.

3. Counting Methods

A. To count sets of elements without listing them, you can sometimes use this ***multiplication principle***:

If an object will be chosen from a set of m objects, and another object will be chosen from a different set of n objects, then mn different choices are possible.

> *Example:*
>
> Suppose a meal at a restaurant must include exactly 1 entree and 1 dessert. The entree can be any 1 of 5 options, and the dessert can be any 1 of 3 options. Then $5 \times 3 = 15$ different meals are available.

B. Here is a more general version of the multiplication principle: the number of possible choices of 1 object apiece out of any number of sets is the product of the numbers of objects in those sets. For example, when choosing 1 object apiece out of 3 sets with x, y, and z elements, respectively, xyz different choices are possible. The general multiplication principle also means that when choosing 1 object apiece out of n different sets of exactly m objects apiece, m^n different choices are possible.

> *Example:*
>
> Each time a coin is flipped, the 2 possible results are heads and tails. In a set of 8 consecutive coin flips, think of each flip as a set of those 2 possible results. The 8 flips give us 8 of these 2-element sets. So, the set of 8 flips has a total of 2^8 possible results.

C. A concept often used with the multiplication principle is the ***factorial***. For any integer $n > 1$, n factorial is written as $n!$ and is the product of all the integers from 1 through n. Also, by definition, $0! = 1! = 1$.

> *Examples:*
>
> $2! = 2 \times 1 = 2$
>
> $3! = 3 \times 2 \times 1 = 6$
>
> $4! = 4 \times 3 \times 2 \times 1 = 24$, etc.

Two other useful equations for working with factorials are $n! = (n-1)!(n)$ and $(n+1)! = (n!)(n+1)$.

D. Any sequential ordering of a set's elements is a ***permutation*** of the set. A permutation is a way to choose elements one by one in a certain order.

The factorial is useful for finding how many permutations a set has. If a set of n objects is being ordered from 1st to nth, there are n choices for the 1st object, $n-1$ choices left for the 2nd object, $n-2$ choices left for the 3rd object, and so on, until only 1 choice is left for the nth object. So, by the multiplication principle, a set of n objects has $n(n-1)(n-2) \ldots (3)(2)(1) = n!$ permutations.

> *Example:*
>
> The set of letters A, B, and C has $3! = 6$ permutations: ABC, ACB, BAC, BCA, CAB, and CBA.

E. When $0 \leq k \leq n$, each possible choice of k objects out of n objects is a **combination** of n objects taken k at a time. The number of these combinations is written as $\binom{n}{k}$. This is also the number of k-element subsets of a set with n elements, since the combinations simply are these subsets. It can be calculated as $\binom{n}{k} = \dfrac{n!}{k!(n-k)!}$. Note that $\binom{n}{k} = \binom{n}{n-k}$.

Example:

The 2-element subsets of $S = \{A, B, C, D, E\}$ are the combinations of the 5 letters in S taken 2 at a time. There are $\binom{5}{2} = \dfrac{5!}{2!3!} = \dfrac{120}{(2)(6)} = 10$ of these subsets: $\{A, B\}, \{A, C\}, \{A, D\}, \{A, E\}, \{B, C\}, \{B, D\}, \{B, E\}, \{C, D\}, \{C, E\}$, and $\{D, E\}$.

For each of its 2–element subsets, a 5-element set also has exactly one 3-element subset containing the elements not in that 2-element subset. For example, in S the 3-element subset $\{C, D, E\}$ contains the elements not in the 2-element subset $\{A, B\}$, the 3-element subset $\{B, D, E\}$ contains the elements not in the 2-element subset $\{A, C\}$, and so on. This shows a 5-element set like S has exactly as many 2-element subsets as 3-element subsets, so $\binom{5}{2} = 10 = \binom{5}{3}$.

---

4. Probability

A. Sets and counting methods are also important to **discrete probability.** Discrete probability involves **experiments** with finitely many possible **outcomes.** An **event** is a set of an experiment's possible outcomes.

Example:

Rolling a 6-sided die with faces numbered 1 to 6 is an experiment with 6 possible outcomes. Let's call these outcomes 1, 2, 3, 4, 5, and 6, each number being the one facing up after the roll. One event in this experiment is that the outcome is 4. This event is written as $\{4\}$.

Another event in the experiment is that the outcome is an odd number. This event has the three outcomes 1, 3, and 5. It is written as $\{1, 3, 5\}$.

B. The probability of an event E is written as $P(E)$ and is a number between 0 and 1, inclusive. If E is an empty set of no possible outcomes, then E is **impossible**, and $P(E) = 0$. If E is the set of all possible outcomes of the experiment, then E is **certain**, and $P(E) = 1$. Otherwise, E is possible but uncertain, and $0 < P(E) < 1$. If F is a subset of E, then $P(F) \leq P(E)$.

C. If the probabilities of two or more outcomes of an experiment are equal, those outcomes are **equally likely.** For an experiment whose outcomes are all equally likely, the probability of an event E is

$$P(E) = \frac{\text{the number of outcomes in } E}{\text{the total number of possible outcomes}}$$

Example:

In the earlier example of a 6-sided die rolled once, suppose the die is fair so that all 6 outcomes are equally likely. Then each outcome's probability is $\dfrac{1}{6}$. The probability that the outcome is an odd number is $P(\{1, 3, 5\}) = \dfrac{|\{1, 3, 5\}|}{6} = \dfrac{3}{6} = \dfrac{1}{2}$.

D. Given two events E and F in an experiment, these further events are defined:

(i) "not E" is the set of outcomes not in E;

(ii) "E or F" is the set of outcomes in E or F or both, that is, $E \cup F$;

(iii) "E and F" is the set of outcomes in both E and F, that is, $E \cup F$.

The probability that E doesn't occur is $P(\text{not } E) = 1 - P(E)$.

The probability that "E or F" occurs is $P(E \text{ or } F) = P(E) + P(F) - P(E \text{ and } F)$. This is based on the general addition rule for two sets, given above in section 3.4.2.H.

Example:

In the example above of a 6-sided die rolled once, let E be the event $\{1, 3, 5\}$ that the outcome is an odd number. Let F be the event $\{2, 3, 5\}$ that the outcome is a prime number. Then

$P(E \text{ and } F) = P(E \cap F) = P(\{3, 5\}) = \dfrac{|\{3, 5\}|}{6} = \dfrac{2}{6} = \dfrac{1}{3}$. So $P(E \text{ or } F) = P(E) + P(F) -$

$P(E \text{ and } F) = \dfrac{3}{6} + \dfrac{3}{6} - \dfrac{2}{6} = \dfrac{4}{6} = \dfrac{2}{3}$.

The event "E or F" is $E \cup F = \{1, 2, 3, 5\}$, so $P(E \text{ or } F) = \dfrac{|\{1, 2, 3, 5\}|}{6} = \dfrac{4}{6} = \dfrac{2}{3}$.

Events E and F are ***mutually exclusive*** if no outcomes are in $E \cap F$. Then the event "E and F" is impossible: $P(E \text{ and } F) = 0$. The special addition rule for the probability of two mutually exclusive events is $P(E \text{ or } F) = P(E) + P(F)$.

E. Two events A and B are ***independent*** if neither changes the other's probability. The multiplication rule for independent events E and F is $P(E \text{ and } F) = P(E)P(F)$.

Example:

In the example above of the 6-sided die rolled once, let A be the event $\{2, 4, 6\}$ and B be the

event $\{5, 6\}$. Then A's probability is $P(A) = \dfrac{|A|}{6} = \dfrac{3}{6} = \dfrac{1}{2}$. The probability of A occurring **if B**

occurs is $\dfrac{|A \cap B|}{|B|} = \dfrac{|\{6\}|}{|\{5, 6\}|} = \dfrac{1}{2}$, the same as $P(A)$.

Likewise, B's probability is $P(B) = \dfrac{|B|}{6} = \dfrac{2}{6} = \dfrac{1}{3}$. The probability of B occurring **if A occurs**

is $\dfrac{|B \cap A|}{|A|} = \dfrac{\{6\}}{|\{2, 4, 6\}|} = \dfrac{1}{3}$, the same as $P(B)$.

So, neither event changes the other's probability. Thus, A and B are independent. Therefore, by the multiplication rule for independent events, $P(A \text{ and } B) = P(A)P(B) = \left(\dfrac{1}{2}\right)\left(\dfrac{1}{3}\right) = \dfrac{1}{6}$.

Notice the event "A and B" is $A \cap B = \{6\}$, so $P(A \text{ and } B) = P(\{6\}) = \dfrac{1}{6}$.

The general addition rule and the multiplication rule discussed above provide that if E and F are independent, $P(E \text{ or } F) = P(E) + P(F) - P(E)P(F)$.

F. An event A is ***dependent*** on an event B if B changes the probability of A.

The probability of A occurring if B occurs is written as $P(A|B)$. So, the statement that A is dependent on B can be written as $P(A|B) \neq P(A)$.

A general multiplication rule for any dependent or independent events A and B is $P(A \text{ and } B) = P(A \mid B)P(B)$.

Example:

In the example of the 6-sided die rolled once, let A be the event $\{4, 6\}$ and B be the event $\{4, 5, 6\}$.

Then the probability of A is $P(A) = \dfrac{|A|}{6} = \dfrac{2}{6} = \dfrac{1}{3}$. But the probability that A occurs **if B occurs** is $P(A|B) = \dfrac{|A \cap B|}{|B|} = \dfrac{|\{4, 6\}|}{|\{4, 5, 6\}|} = \dfrac{2}{3}$. Thus, $P(A|B) \neq P(A)$, so A is dependent on B.

Likewise, the probability that B occurs is $P(B) = \dfrac{|B|}{6} = \dfrac{3}{6} = \dfrac{1}{2}$. But the probability that B occurs **if A occurs** is $P(B|A) = \dfrac{|B \cap A|}{|A|} = \dfrac{|\{4, 6\}|}{|\{4, 6\}|} = 1$. Thus, $P(B|A) \neq P(B)$, so B is dependent on A.

In this example, by the general multiplication rule for events,

$P(A \text{ and } B) = P(A|B)P(B) = \left(\dfrac{2}{3}\right)\left(\dfrac{1}{2}\right) = \dfrac{1}{3}$. Likewise, $P(A \text{ and } B) = P(B|A)P(A) = (1)\left(\dfrac{1}{3}\right) = \dfrac{1}{3}$.

Notice the event "A and B" is $A \cap B = \{4, 6\} = A$, so $P(A \text{ and } B) = P(\{4, 6\}) = \dfrac{1}{3} = P(A)$.

G. The rules above can be combined for more complex probability calculations.

Example:

In an experiment with events A, B, and C, suppose $P(A) = 0.23$, $P(B) = 0.40$, and $P(C) = 0.85$. Also suppose events A and B are mutually exclusive, and events B and C are independent. Since A and B are mutually exclusive, $P(A \text{ or } B) = P(A) + P(B) = 0.23 + 0.40 = 0.63$.

Since B and C are independent, $P(B \text{ or } C) = P(B) + P(C) - P(B)P(C) = 0.40 + 0.85 - (0.40)(0.85) = 0.91$.

$P(A \text{ or } C)$ and $P(A \text{ and } C)$ can't be found from the information given. But we can find that $P(A) + P(C) = 1.08 > 1$. So $P(A) + P(C)$ can't equal $P(A \text{ or } C)$, which like any probability must be less than or equal to 1. This means that A and C can't be mutually exclusive, and that $P(A \text{ and } C) \geq 0.08$.

Since $A \cap B$ is a subset of A, we can also find that $P(A \text{ and } C) \leq P(A) = 0.23$.

And C is a subset of $A \cup C$, so $P(A \text{ or } C) \geq P(C) = 0.85$.

Thus, we've found that $0.85 \leq P(A \text{ or } C) \leq 1$ and that $0.08 \leq P(A \text{ and } C) \leq 0.23$.

---

5. Estimation

A. Calculating exact answers to complex math questions is often too hard or too slow. Estimating the answers by simplifying the questions may be easier and faster.

One way to estimate is to **round** the numbers in the original question: replace each number with a nearby number that has fewer digits. Often a number is rounded to a nearby multiple of some power of 10.

For any integer n and real number m, you can **round m down** to a multiple of 10^n by deleting all of m's digits to the right of the digit that stands for multiples of 10^n.

To **round m up** to a multiple of 10^n, first add 10^n to m, then round the result down.

To **round m to the nearest** 10^n, first find the digit in m that stands for a multiple of 10^{n-1}. If this digit is 5 or higher, round m up to a multiple of 10^n. Otherwise, round m down to a multiple of 10^n.

Examples:

(i) To round 7651.4 to the nearest hundred (multiple of 10^2), first notice the digit standing for tens (multiples of 10^1) is 5.

Since this digit is 5 or higher, round up:

First add 100 to the original number: 7651.4 + 100 = 7751.4.

Then drop all the digits to the right of the one standing for multiples of 100 to get 7700.

Notice that 7700 is closer to 7651.4 than 7600 is, so 7700 is the nearest 100.

(ii) To round 0.43248 to the nearest thousandth (multiple of 10^{-3}), first notice the digit standing for ten-thousandths (multiples of 10^{-4}) is 4. Since 4 < 5, round down: just drop all the digits to the right of the digit standing for thousandths to get 0.432.

B. Rounding can simplify complex arithmetical calculations and give rough answers. If you keep more digits of the original numbers, the answers are usually more exact, but the calculations take longer.

Example:

You can roughly estimate the value of $\dfrac{(298.534 + 58.296)}{1.4822 + 0.937 + 0.014679}$ by rounding the numbers in the dividend to the nearest 10 and the numbers in the divisor to the nearest 0.1:

$$\frac{(298.534 + 58.296)}{1.4822 + 0.937 + 0.014679} \approx \frac{300 + 60}{1.5 + 0.9 + 0} = \frac{360}{2.4} = 150$$

C. Sometimes it is easier to estimate by rounding to a multiple of a number other than 10, like the nearest square or cube of an integer.

Examples:

(i) You can roughly estimate the value of $\frac{2447.16}{11.9}$ by noting first that both the dividend and the divisor are near multiples of 12: 2448 and 12. So $\frac{2447.16}{11.9} \approx \frac{2448}{12} = 204.$

(ii) You can roughly estimate the value of $\sqrt{\frac{8.96}{24.82 \times 4.057}}$ by noting first that each decimal number in the expression is near the square of an integer: $8.96 \approx 9 = 3^2, 24.82 \approx 25 = 5^2,$

and $4.057 \approx 4 = 2^2.$ So $\sqrt{\frac{8.96}{24.82 \times 4.057}} \approx \sqrt{\frac{3^2}{5^2 \times 2^2}} = \sqrt{\frac{3^2}{10^2}} = \frac{3}{10}.$

D. Sometimes finding a *range* of possible values for an expression is more useful than finding a single estimated value. The range's *upper bound* is the smallest number found to be greater than (or greater than or equal to) the expression's value. The range's *lower bound* is the largest number found to be less than (or less than or equal to) the expression's value.

Example:

In the equation $x = \frac{2.32^2 - 2.536}{2.68^2 + 2.79}$, each decimal is greater than 2 and less than 3. So, $\frac{2^2 - 3}{3^2 + 3} < x < \frac{3^2 - 2}{2^2 + 2}.$ Simplifying these fractions, we find that x is in the range $\frac{1}{12} < x < \frac{7}{6}.$ The range's lower bound is $\frac{1}{12}$, and the upper bound is $\frac{7}{6}.$

6. Sequences and Series

A. A *sequence* is an algebraic function whose domain includes only positive integers. A function $a(n)$ that is a sequence can be written as a_n. The domain of an *infinite sequence* is the set of all positive integers. For any positive integer n, the domain of a *finite sequence of length* n is the set of the first n positive integers.

Example:

(i) The function $a(n) = n^2 + \left(\frac{n}{5}\right)$ is an infinite sequence a_n whose domain is the set of all positive integers $n = 1, 2, 3, \ldots.$ Its value at $n = 3$ is $a_3 = 3^2 + \frac{3}{5} = 9.6.$

(ii) The same function $a(n) = n^2 + \left(\frac{n}{5}\right)$ restricted to the domain $\{1, 2, 3\}$ is a finite sequence of length 3 whose range is $\{1.2, 4.4, 9.6\}.$

(iii) An infinite sequence like $b_n = (-1)^n(n!)$ can be written out by listing its values in the order $b_1, b_2, b_3, \ldots, b_n, \ldots$: that is, $-1, 2, -6, \ldots, (-1)^n(n!), \ldots$

The value $(-1)^n(n!)$ is the nth term of the sequence.

B. A *series* is the sum of a sequence's terms.

For an infinite sequence $a(n)$, the **infinite series** $\sum\limits_{n=1}^{\infty} a(n)$ is the sum of the sequence's infinitely many terms, $a_1 + a_2 + a_3 + \ldots$

The sum of the first k terms of sequence a_n is called a **partial sum**. It is written as $\sum\limits_{i=1}^{k} a_i$, or $a_1 + \ldots + a_k$.

Example:

The infinite series based on the function $a(n) = n^2 + \left(\dfrac{n}{5}\right)$ is $\sum\limits_{i=1}^{\infty} n^2 + \left(\dfrac{n}{5}\right)$. It's the sum of the infinitely many terms $\left(1^2 + \dfrac{1}{5}\right) + \left(2^2 + \dfrac{2}{5}\right) + \left(3^2 + \dfrac{3}{5}\right) + \ldots$

The partial sum of the first three terms of the same function $a(n) = n^2 + \left(\dfrac{n}{5}\right)$ is

$\sum\limits_{i=1}^{3} a_i = \left(1^2 + \dfrac{1}{5}\right) + \left(2^2 + \dfrac{2}{5}\right) + \left(3^2 + \dfrac{3}{5}\right) = 1.2 + 4.4 + 9.6 = 15.2.$

3.5   Reference Sheets

Arithmetic and Decimals

ABSOLUTE VALUE:

$|x|$ is x if $x \geq 0$ and $-x$ if $x < 0$.

For any x and $y, |x + y| \leq |x| + |y|$.

$\sqrt{x^2} = |x|$.

EVEN AND ODD NUMBERS:

Even × Even = Even	Even × Odd = Even
Odd × Odd = Odd	Even + Even = Even
Even + Odd = Odd	Odd + Odd = Even

ADDITION AND SUBTRACTION:

$x + 0 = x = x - 0$

$x - x = 0$

$x + y = y + x$

$x - y = -(y - x) = -y + x$

$(x + y) + z = x + (y + z)$

If x and y are both positive, then $x + y$ is also positive.

If x and y are both negative, then $x + y$ is negative.

DECIMALS:

Add or subtract decimals by lining up their decimal points:

17.6512	653.2700
+ 653.2700	−17.6512
670.9212	635.6188

To multiply decimal A by decimal B:

First, ignore the decimal points, and multiply A and B as if they were integers.

Next, if decimal A has n digits to the right of its decimal point, and decimal B has m digits to the right of its decimal point, place the decimal point in $A \times B$ so it has $m + n$ digits to its right.

To divide decimal A by decimal B, first move the decimal points of A and B equally many digits to the right until B is an integer, then divide as you would integers.

QUOTIENTS AND REMAINDERS:

The quotient q and the remainder r of dividing positive integer x by positive integer y are unique positive integers such that

$y = xq + r$ and $0 \leq r < x$.

The remainder r is 0 if and only if y is divisible by x. Then x is a factor of y.

MULTIPLICATION AND DIVISION:

$x \times 1 = x = \dfrac{x}{1}$

$x \times 0 = 0$

If $x \neq 0$, then $\dfrac{x}{x} = 1$.

$\dfrac{x}{0}$ is undefined.

$xy = yx$

If $x \neq 0$ and $y \neq 0$, then $\dfrac{x}{y} = \dfrac{1}{\left(\dfrac{y}{x}\right)}$.

$(xy)z = x(yz)$

$xy + xz = x(y + z)$

If $y \neq 0$, then $\left(\dfrac{x}{y}\right) + \left(\dfrac{z}{y}\right) = \dfrac{(x + z)}{y}$

If x and y are both positive, then xy is also positive.

If x and y are both negative, then xy is positive.

If x is positive and y is negative, then xy is negative.

If $xy = 0$, then $x = 0$ or $y = 0$, or both.

SCIENTIFIC NOTATION:

To convert a number in scientific notation $A \times 10^n$ into regular decimal notation, move A's decimal point n places to the right if n is positive, or $|n|$ places to the left if n is negative.

To convert a decimal to scientific notation, move the decimal point n spaces so that exactly one nonzero digit is to its left. Multiply the result by 10^n if you moved the decimal point to the left or by 10^{-n} if you moved it to the right.

Exponents

SQUARES, CUBES, AND SQUARE ROOTS:

Every positive number has two real square roots, one positive and the other negative. The table below shows the positive square roots rounded to the nearest hundredth.

n	n^2	n^3	$\sqrt{n}$
1	1	1	1
2	4	8	1.41
3	9	27	1.73
4	16	64	2
5	25	125	2.24
6	36	216	2.45
7	49	343	2.65
8	64	512	2.83
9	81	729	3
10	100	1,000	3.16

EXPONENTIATION:

Formula	Example
$x^1 = x$	$2^1 = 2$
$x^0 = 1$	$2^0 = 1$
If $x \neq 0$, then $x^{-1} = \frac{1}{x}$.	$2^{-1} = \frac{1}{2}$
If $x > 1$ and $y > 1$, then $x^y > x$.	$2^3 = 8 > 2$
If $0 < x < 1$ and $y > 1$, then $x^y < x$.	$0.2^3 = 0.008 < 0.2$
$(x^y)^z = x^{yz} = (x^z)^y$	$(2^3)^4 = 2^{12} = (2^4)^3$
$x^{y+z} = x^y x^z$	$2^7 = 2^3 2^4$
If $x \neq 0$, then $x^{y-z} = \frac{x^y}{x^z}$.	$2^{5-3} = \frac{2^5}{2^3}$
$(xz)^y = x^y z^y$	$6^4 = 2^4 3^4$
If $z \neq 0$, then $\left(\frac{x}{z}\right)^y = \frac{x^y}{z^y}$	$\left(\frac{3}{4}\right)^2 = \frac{3^2}{4^2} = \frac{9}{16}$
If $z \neq 0$, then $x^{\frac{y}{z}} = (x^y)^{\frac{1}{z}} = (x^{\frac{1}{z}})^y$.	$4^{\frac{2}{3}} = (4^2)^{\frac{1}{3}} = (4^{\frac{1}{3}})^2$

Algebraic Expressions and Linear Equations

TRANSLATING WORDS INTO MATH OPERATIONS:

$x + y$	$x - y$	xy	$\dfrac{x}{y}$	x^y
x added to y x increased by y x more than y x plus y the sum of x and y the total of x and y	x decreased by y difference of x and y y fewer than x y less than x x minus y x reduced by y y subtracted from x	x multiplied by y the product of x and y x times y If $y = 2$: double x twice x If $y = 3$: triple x	x divided by y x over y the quotient of x and y the ratio of x to y If $y = 2$: half of x x halved	x to the power of y x to the yth power If $y = 2$: x squared If $y = 3$: x cubed

MANIPULATING ALGEBRAIC EXPRESSIONS:

Technique	Example
Factor to combine like terms	$3xy - 9y = 3y(x - 3)$
Divide out common factors	$\dfrac{(3xy - 9y)}{(x - 3)} = \dfrac{3y(x - 3)}{(x - 3)} = 3y(1) = 3y$
Multiply two expressions by multiplying each term of one expression by each term of the other	$(3x - 4)(9y + x) = 3x(9y + x) - 4(9y + x)$ $= 3x(9y) + 3x(x) + -4(9y) + -4(x)$ $= 27xy + 3x^2 - 36y - 4x$
Substitute constants for variables	If $x = 3$ and $y = -2$, then $3xy - x^2 + y$ can be evaluated as $3(3)(-2) - (3)^2 + (-2) = -18 - 9 - 2 = -29$.

SOLVING LINEAR EQUATIONS:

Technique	Example
Isolate a variable on one side of an equation by doing the same operations on both sides of the equation.	Solve the equation $\frac{(5x-6)}{3} = 4$ like this: (1) Multiply both sides by 3 to get $5x - 6 = 12$. (2) Add 6 to both sides to get $5x = 18$. (3) Divide both sides by 5 to get $x = \frac{18}{5}$.
To solve two equations with two variables x and y: (1) Express x in terms of y using one of the equations. (2) Substitute that expression for x to make the second equation have only the variable y. (3) Solve the second equation for y. (4) Substitute the solution for y into the first equation to solve for x.	Solve the equations A: $x - y = 2$ and B: $3x + 2y = 11$: (1) From A, $x = 2 + y$. (2) In B, substitute $2 + y$ for x to get $3(2 + y) + 2y = 11$. (3) Solve B for y: $6 + 3y + 2y = 11$ $\qquad 6 + 5y = 11$ $\qquad\quad 5y = 5$ $\qquad\qquad y = 1$. (4) Since $y = 1$, from A we find $x = 2 + 1 = 3$.
Alternative technique: (1) Multiply both sides of one equation or both equations so that the coefficients on y have the same absolute value in both equations. (2) Add or subtract the two equations to remove y and solve for x. (3) Substitute the solution for x into the first equation to find the value of y.	Solve the equations A: $x - y = 2$ and B: $3x + 2y = 11$: (1) Multiply both sides of A by 2 to get $2x - 2y = 4$. (2) Add the equation in (1) to equation B: $\qquad 2x - 2y + 3x + 2y = 4 + 11$ $\qquad\qquad 5x = 15$ $\qquad\qquad\; x = 3$. (3) Since $x = 3$, from A we find $3 - y = 2$, so $y = 1$.

Factoring, Quadratic Equations, and Inequalities

SOLVING EQUATIONS BY FACTORING:

Techniques	Example
(1) Start with a polynomial equation (2) Add or subtract expressions until 0 is on one side of the equation. (3) Write the nonzero side as a product of factors. (4) Set each factor to 0 to find a simple equation giving a solution to the original equation.	$x^3 - 2x^2 + x = -5(x-1)^2$ $x^3 - 2x^2 + x + 5(x-1)^2 = 0$ (i) $x(x^2 - 2x + 1) + 5(x-1)^2 = 0$ (ii) $x(x-1)^2 + 5(x-1)^2 = 0$ (iii) $(x+5)(x-1)^2 = 0$ $x + 5 = 0$ or $x - 1 = 0$. So, $x = -5$ or $x = 1$.

FORMULAS FOR FACTORING:

$a^2 - b^2 = (a - b)(a + b)$

$a^2 + 2ab + b^2 = (a + b)(a + b)$

$a^2 - 2ab + b^2 = (a - b)(a - b)$

THE QUADRATIC FORMULA:

For any quadratic equation $ax^2 + bx + c = 0$ with $a \neq 0$, the roots are

$$x = \frac{-b + \sqrt{b^2 - 4ac}}{2a} \text{ and } x = \frac{-b - \sqrt{b^2 - 4ac}}{2a}$$

These roots are two distinct real numbers unless $b^2 - 4ac \leq 0$.

If $b^2 - 4ac = 0$, the equation has only one root: $\frac{-b}{2a}$.

If $b^2 - 4ac < 0$, the equation has no real roots.

SOLVING INEQUALITIES:

Explanation	Example
As in solving an equation, the same number can be added to or subtracted from both sides of the inequality, or both sides can be multiplied or divided by a positive number, without changing the order of the inequality. But multiplying or dividing an inequality by a negative number reverses the order of the inequality. Thus, $6 > 2$, but $(-1)(6) < (-1)(2)$.	To solve the inequality $\frac{(5x-1)}{-2} < 3$ for x, isolate x: (1) $5x - 1 > -6$ (multiplying both sides by -2, reversing the order of the inequality) (2) $5x > -5$ (add 1 to both sides) (3) $x > -1$ (divide both sides by 5)

LINES IN THE COORDINATE PLANE:

An equation $y = mx + b$ defines a line with slope m whose y–intercept is b.

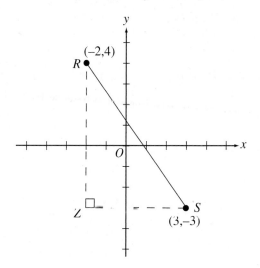

For a line through two points (x_1, y_1) and (x_2, y_2) with $x_1 \neq x_2$, the slope is $m = \frac{(y_2 - y_1)}{(x_2 - x_1)}$. Given the known

point (x_1, y_1) and the slope m, any other point (x, y) on the line satisfies the equation $m = \frac{(y - y_1)}{(x - x_1)}$.

Above, the line's slope is $\frac{(-3 - 4)}{(3 - (-2))} = \frac{7}{5}$. To find an equation of the line, we can use the point $(3, -3)$:

$$y - (-3) = \left(-\frac{7}{5}\right)(x - 3)$$

$$y + 3 = \left(-\frac{7}{5}\right)x + \frac{21}{5}$$

$$y = \left(-\frac{7}{5}\right)x + \frac{6}{5}$$

So, the y–intercept is $\frac{6}{5}$.

Find the x–intercept like this:

$$0 = \left(-\frac{7}{5}\right)x + \frac{6}{5}$$

$$\left(\frac{7}{5}\right)x = \frac{6}{5}$$

$$x = \frac{6}{7}$$

The graph shows both these intercepts.

Rates, Ratios, and Percents

FRACTIONS:

Equivalent or Equal Fractions:

Two fractions stand for the same number if dividing each fraction's numerator and denominator by their greatest common divisor makes the fractions identical.

Adding, Subtracting, Multiplying, and Dividing Fractions:

$$\frac{a}{b} + \frac{c}{d} = \frac{ad}{bd} + \frac{bc}{bd}; \frac{a}{b} - \frac{c}{d} = \frac{ad}{bd} - \frac{bc}{bd}$$

$$\frac{a}{b} \times \frac{c}{d} = \frac{ac}{bd}; \frac{a}{b} \div \frac{c}{d} = \frac{ad}{bc}$$

MIXED NUMBERS:

A mixed number of the form $a\frac{b}{c}$ equals the fraction $\frac{ac + b}{c}$.

RATE:

distance = rate × time

PROFIT:

Gross profit = Revenues − Expenses, or

Gross profit = Selling price − Cost.

INTEREST:

Simple annual interest =

(principal) × (interest rate) × (time)

Compound interest over n periods =

(principal) × (1 + interest per period)^n − principal

PERCENTS:

$$x\% = \frac{x}{100}.$$

$x\%$ of y equals $\frac{xy}{100}.$

To convert a percent to a decimal, drop the percent sign, then move the decimal point two digits left.

To convert a decimal to a percent, add a percent sign, then move the decimal point two digits right.

PERCENT INCREASE OR DECREASE:

The percent increase from x to y is $100\left(\frac{y - x}{x}\right)\%$.

The percent decrease from x to y is $100\left(\frac{x - y}{x}\right)\%$.

DISCOUNTS:

A price discounted by n percent becomes $(100 - n)$ percent of the original price.

A price discounted by n percent and then by m percent becomes $(100 - n)(100 - m)$ percent of the original price.

WORK:

$\frac{1}{r} + \frac{1}{s} = \frac{1}{h}$, where r is how long one individual takes to do an amount of work, s is how long a second individual takes to do that much work, and h is how long they take to do that much work when both are working at the same time.

MIXTURES:

	Number of units of a substance or mixture	Amount of an ingredient per unit of the substance or mixture	Total amount of that ingredient in the substance or mixture
Substance A	X	M	X × M
Substance B	Y	N	Y × N
Mixture of A and B	X + Y	$\frac{(X \times M) + (Y \times N)}{X + Y}$	(X × M) + (Y × N)

Statistics, Sets, and Counting Methods

STATISTICS:

Concept	Definition for a set of n numbers ordered from least to greatest	Example with data set $\{4, 4, 5, 7, 10\}$
Mean	The sum of the n numbers, divided by n	$\frac{(4+4+5+7+10)}{5} = \frac{30}{5} = 6$
Median	The middle number if n is odd; The mean of the two middle numbers if n is even.	5 is the middle number in $\{4, 4, 5, 7, 10\}$.
Mode	The number that appears most often in the set	4 is the only number that appears more than once in $\{4, 4, 5, 7, 10\}$.
Range	The largest number in the set minus the smallest	$10 - 4 = 6$
Standard Deviation	Calculate like this: (1) Find the arithmetic mean, (2) Find the differences between each of the n numbers and the mean, (3) Square each of the differences, (4) Find the average of the squared differences, and (5) Take the nonnegative square root of this average.	(1) The mean is 6. (2) $-2, -2, -1, 1, 4$ (3) $4, 4, 1, 1, 16$ (4) $\frac{26}{5} = 5.2$ (5) $\sqrt{5.2}$

SETS:

Concept	Notation for finite sets S and T	Example
Number of elements	$|S|$	$S = \{-5, 0, 1\}$ is a set with $|S| = 3$.
Subset	$S \subseteq T$ (S is a subset of T); $S \supseteq T$ (T is a subset of S)	$\{-5, 0, 1\}$ is a subset of $\{-5, 0, 1, 4, 10\}$.
Union	$S \cup T$	$\{3, 4\} \cup \{4, 5, 6\} = \{3, 4, 5, 6\}$
Intersection	$S \cap T$	$\{3, 4\} \cap \{4, 5, 6\} = \{4\}$
The general addition rule for two sets	$|S \cup T| = |S| + |T| - |S \cap T|$	$|\{3, 4\} \cup \{4, 5, 6\}| = |\{3, 4\}| + |\{4, 5, 6\}| - |\{3, 4\} \cap \{4, 5, 6\}| = |\{3, 4\}| + |\{4, 5, 6\}| - |\{4\}| = 2 + 3 - 1 = 4.$

COUNTING METHODS:

Concept and Equations	Examples
Multiplication Principle: The number of possible choices of 1 element apiece from the sets $A_1, A_2, \ldots, A_n$ is $\lvert A_1 \rvert \times \lvert A_2 \rvert \times \ldots \times \lvert A_n \rvert$.	The number of possible choices of 1 element apiece from the sets $S = \{-5, 0, 1\}$, $T = \{3, 4\}$, and $U = \{3, 4, 5, 6\}$ is $\lvert S \rvert \times \lvert T \rvert \times \lvert U \rvert = 3 \times 2 \times 4 = 24$.
Factorial: $n! = n \times (n-1) \times \ldots \times 1$ $0! = 1! = 1$ $n! = (n-1)!(n)$	$4! = 4 \times 3 \times 2 \times 1 = 24$ $4! = 3! \times 4$
Permutations: A set of n objects has $n!$ permutations	The set of letters A, B, and C has $3! = 6$ permutations: ABC, ACB, BAC, BCA, CAB, and CBA.
Combinations: The number of possible choices of k objects from a set of n objects is $\binom{n}{k} = \dfrac{n!}{k!(n-k)!}$.	The number of 2-element subsets of set $\{A, B, C, D, E\}$ is $\binom{5}{2} = \dfrac{5!}{2!3!} = \dfrac{120}{(2)(6)} = 10.$ The 10 subsets are: $\{A, B\}, \{A, C\}, \{A, D\}, \{A, E\}, \{B, C\}, \{B, D\}, \{B, E\}, \{C, D\}, \{C, E\},$ and $\{D, E\}.$

Probability, Sequences, and Partial Sums

PROBABILITY:

Concept	Definition, Notation, and Equations	Example: Rolling a die with 6 numbered sides once
Event	A set of outcomes of an experiment	The event of the outcome being an odd number is the set $\{1, 3, 5\}$.
Probability	The probability $P(E)$ of an event E is a number between 0 and 1, inclusive. If each outcome is equally likely, $P(E) =$ $\dfrac{\text{(the number of possible outcomes in E)}}{\text{(the total number of possible outcomes)}}$.	If the 6 outcomes are equally likely, the probability of each outcome is $\dfrac{1}{6}$. The probability that the outcome is an odd number is $P(\{1, 3, 5\}) =$ $\dfrac{|\{1, 3, 5\}|}{6} = \dfrac{3}{6} = \dfrac{1}{2}$.
Conditional Probability	The probability that E occurs if F occurs is $P(E\|F) = \dfrac{|E \cap F|}{|F|}$.	$P(\{1, 3, 5\}\|\{1, 2\}) = \dfrac{|\{1\}|}{|\{1, 2\}|} = \dfrac{1}{2}$
Not E	The set of outcomes not in event E: $P(\text{not } E) = 1 - P(E)$.	$P(\text{not}\{3\}) = \dfrac{6-1}{6} = \dfrac{5}{6}$
E and F	The set of outcomes in both E and F, that is, $E \cap F$; $P(E \text{ and } F) = P(E \cap F) = P(E\|F)P(F)$.	For $E = \{1, 3, 5\}$ and $F = \{2, 3, 5\}$: $P(E \text{ and } F) = P(E \cap F) = P(\{3, 5\}) =$ $\dfrac{|\{3, 5\}|}{6} = \dfrac{2}{6} = \dfrac{1}{3}$
E or F	The set of outcomes in E or F or both, that is, $E \cup F$; $P(E \text{ or } F) = P(E) + P(F) - P(E \text{ and } F)$.	For $E = \{1, 3, 5\}$ and $F = \{2, 3, 5\}$: $P(E \text{ or } F) = P(E) + P(F) - P(E \text{ and } F)$ $= \dfrac{3}{6} + \dfrac{3}{6} - \dfrac{2}{6} = \dfrac{4}{6} = \dfrac{2}{3}$.
Dependent and Independent Events	E is dependent on F if $P(E\|F) \neq P(E)$. E and F are independent if neither is dependent on the other. If E and F are independent, $P(E \text{ and } F) = P(E)P(F)$.	For $E = \{2, 4, 6\}$ and $F = \{5, 6\}$: $P(E\|F) = P(E) = \dfrac{1}{2}$, and $P(F\|E) = P(F) = \dfrac{1}{3}$, so E and F are independent. Thus $P(E \text{ and } F) = P(E)P(F) = \left(\dfrac{1}{2}\right)\left(\dfrac{1}{3}\right) = \dfrac{1}{6}$.

SEQUENCE:

An algebraic function whose domain contains only positive integers.

Example: Function $a(n) = n^2 + \left(\dfrac{n}{5}\right)$ with the domain of all positive integers $n = 1, 2, 3, \ldots$ is an infinite sequence a_n.

PARTIAL SUM:

The sum $\sum\limits_{i=1}^{k} a_i$ of the first k terms of series a_n is a partial sum of the series.

Example: For the function $a(n) = n^2 + \left(\dfrac{n}{5}\right)$, the partial sum of the first three terms is

$$\sum_{i=1}^{3} a_i = \left(1^2 + \dfrac{1}{5}\right) + \left(2^2 + \dfrac{2}{5}\right) + \left(3^2 + \dfrac{3}{5}\right).$$

To register for the GMAT™ exam go to www.mba.com/register

4.0   Quantitative Reasoning

4.0 Quantitative Reasoning

The Quantitative Reasoning section of the GMAT™ exam tests your math skills in the areas reviewed in Chapter 3, "Math Review": Value, Order, Factors, Algebra, Equalities, Inequalities, Rates, Ratios, Percents, Statistics, Sets, Counting, Probability, Estimation, and Series. Quantitative Reasoning questions also test how well you reason quantitatively, solve math problems, and interpret graphic data. All the math needed to answer the questions is generally taught in secondary school (or high school) math classes.

To answer a Quantitative Reasoning question, you pick one of five given answer choices. First study the question to see what information it gives and what it's asking you to do with that information. Then, scan the answer choices. If the problem seems simple, try to find the answer quickly. Then, check your answer against the choices. If your answer isn't among the choices, or if the problem is complicated, think again about what the problem is asking you to do, and try to rule out some of the choices. If you still can't narrow down the answer to a single choice, reread the question. It gives all the information you need to find the right answer. If you already know about the topic, don't use that knowledge to answer. Use only the information given.

You have 45 minutes to answer the 21 questions in the section. That's an average of about two minutes, nine seconds per question. You may run out of time if you spend too long on any one question. If you find yourself stuck on a question, it may be wise to simply pick the answer that seems best, even if you're not sure. Guessing is not usually the best way to score high on the GMAT, but making an educated guess is better than not answering.

Below are tips for solving Quantitative Reasoning questions, directions for the section, and sample questions with an answer key and explanations for the answers. These explanations also show strategies that may help you solve other Quantitative Reasoning questions.

4.1 Tips for Answering Quantitative Reasoning Questions

1. **Pace yourself.**

    Check the on-screen timer to see how much time you have left. Work carefully, but don't take too long double-checking an answer or struggling with a hard problem.

2. **Use the erasable notepad provided.**

    Solving a problem step by step on the notepad may help you avoid mistakes. If the problem doesn't show a diagram, drawing your own may be helpful.

3. **Study each question to understand what it's asking.**

    Approach word problems one step at a time. Read each sentence. When it's useful, translate the problem into math expressions.

4. **Scan all the answer choices before working on the problem.**

    By scanning the answer choices, you can avoid finding the answer in the wrong form. For example, if the choices are all fractions like $\frac{1}{4}$, you know to work out the answer as a fraction, not as a decimal like 0.25. Similarly, if the choices are all estimates, you can often take shortcuts. For example, you may be able to estimate by rounding 48% to 50% if every answer choice is an estimate.

5. **Don't waste time on a problem that's too hard for you.**

    Make your best guess. Then, move on to the next question.

4.2 Section Instructions

Go to **www.mba.com/tutorial** to read instructions for the section and get a feel for what the test center screens look like on the actual GMAT exam.

4.3 Practice Questions

Solve the problem and pick the best answer choice given.

<u>Numbers:</u> All numbers used are real numbers.

<u>Figures:</u> A figure in a Quantitative Reasoning question gives information useful in solving the problem. Figures are drawn as accurately as possible, except as noted. Lines shown as straight are straight. Lines that look jagged may also be straight. Points, angles, regions, etc., are positioned as shown. All figures are flat unless otherwise noted.

Questions 1 to 74 - Difficulty: Easy

1. Working at a constant rate, a copy machine makes 20 copies of a one-page document per minute. If the machine works at this constant rate, how many hours does it take to make 4,800 copies of a one-page document?

   (A) 4
   (B) 5
   (C) 6
   (D) 7
   (E) 8

2. If $x + y = 2$ and $x^2 + y^2 = 2$, what is the value of xy?

   (A) −2
   (B) −1
   (C)   0
   (D)   1
   (E)   2

3. The sum S of the first n consecutive positive even integers is given by $S = n(n + 1)$. For what value of n is this sum equal to 110?

   (A) 10
   (B) 11
   (C) 12
   (D) 13
   (E) 14

4. $6(87.30 + 0.65) - 5(87.30) =$

   (A)   3.90
   (B) 39.00
   (C) 90.90
   (D) 91.20
   (E) 91.85

5. What is the value of $x^2yz - xyz^2$, if $x = -2$, $y = 1$, and $z = 3$?

   (A) 20
   (B) 24
   (C) 30
   (D) 32
   (E) 48

6. A souvenir vendor purchased 1,000 shirts for a special event at a price of $5 each. The vendor sold 600 of the shirts on the day of the event for $12 each and 300 of the shirts in the week following the event for $4 each. The vendor was unable to sell the remaining shirts. What was the vendor's gross profit on the sale of these shirts?

   (A) $1,000
   (B) $2,200
   (C) $2,700
   (D) $3,000
   (E) $3,400

7. If $x > y$ and $y > z$, which of the following represents the greatest number?

    (A) $x - z$
    (B) $x - y$
    (C) $y - x$
    (D) $z - y$
    (E) $z - x$

8. To order certain plants from a catalog, it costs $3.00 per plant, plus a 5 percent sales tax, plus $6.95 for shipping and handling regardless of the number of plants ordered. If Company C ordered these plants from the catalog at the total cost of $69.95, how many plants did Company C order?

    (A) 22
    (B) 21
    (C) 20
    (D) 19
    (E) 18

9. A rug manufacturer produces rugs at a cost of $75 per rug. What is the manufacturer's gross profit from the sale of 150 rugs if $\frac{2}{3}$ of the rugs are sold for $150 per rug and the rest are sold for $200 per rug?

    (A) $10,350
    (B) $11,250
    (C) $13,750
    (D) $16,250
    (E) $17,800

10. The value of Maureen's investment portfolio has decreased by 5.8 percent since her initial investment in the portfolio. If her initial investment was $16,800, what is the current value of the portfolio?

    (A) $7,056.00
    (B) $14,280.00
    (C) $15,825.60
    (D) $16,702.56
    (E) $17,774.40

11. Company C produces toy trucks at a cost of $5.00 each for the first 100 trucks and $3.50 for each additional truck. If 500 toy trucks were produced by Company C and sold for $10.00 each, what was Company C's gross profit?

    (A) $2,250
    (B) $2,500
    (C) $3,100
    (D) $3,250
    (E) $3,500

Division	Profit or Loss (in millions of dollars)				
	1991	1992	1993	1994	1995
A	1.1	(3.4)	1.9	2.0	0.0
B	(2.3)	5.5	(4.5)	3.9	(2.9)
C	10.0	(6.6)	5.3	1.1	(3.0)

12. The annual profit or loss for the three divisions of Company T for the years 1991 through 1995 are summarized in the table shown, where losses are enclosed in parentheses. For which division and which three consecutive years shown was the division's profit or loss for the three-year period closest to $0 ?

    (A) Division A for 1991–1993
    (B) Division A for 1992–1994
    (C) Division B for 1991–1993
    (D) Division B for 1993–1995
    (E) Division C for 1992–1994

13. Of the following, which is least?

    (A) $\dfrac{0.03}{0.00071}$

    (B) $\dfrac{0.03}{0.0071}$

    (C) $\dfrac{0.03}{0.071}$

    (D) $\dfrac{0.03}{0.71}$

    (E) $\dfrac{0.03}{7.1}$

14. If the average (arithmetic mean) of 5 numbers j, $j + 5$, $2j - 1$, $4j - 2$, and $5j - 1$ is 8, what is the value of j?

(A) $\dfrac{1}{3}$

(B) $\dfrac{7}{13}$

(C) 1

(D) 3

(E) 8

15. There are five sales agents in a certain real estate office. One month Andy sold twice as many properties as Ellen, Bob sold 3 more than Ellen, Cary sold twice as many as Bob, and Dora sold as many as Bob and Ellen together. Who sold the most properties that month?

(A) Andy

(B) Bob

(C) Cary

(D) Dora

(E) Ellen

16. In a field day at a school, each child who competed in n events and scored a total of p points was given an overall score of $\dfrac{p}{n} + n$. Andrew competed in 1 event and scored 9 points. Jason competed in 3 events and scored 5, 6, and 7 points, respectively. What was the ratio of Andrew's overall score to Jason's overall score?

(A) $\dfrac{10}{23}$

(B) $\dfrac{7}{10}$

(C) $\dfrac{4}{5}$

(D) $\dfrac{10}{9}$

(E) $\dfrac{12}{7}$

17. A certain work plan for September requires that a work team, working every day, produce an average of 200 items per day. For the first half of the month, the team produced an average of 150 items per day. How many items per day must the team average during the second half of the month if it is to attain the average daily production rate required by the work plan?

(A) 225

(B) 250

(C) 275

(D) 300

(E) 350

18. A company sells radios for $15.00 each. It costs the company $14.00 per radio to produce 1,000 radios and $13.50 per radio to produce 2,000 radios. How much greater will the company's gross profit be from the production and sale of 2,000 radios than from the production and sale of 1,000 radios?

(A) $500

(B) $1,000

(C) $1,500

(D) $2,000

(E) $2,500

19. Which of the following represent positive numbers?

I. $-3 - (-5)$

II. $(-3)(-5)$

III. $-5 - (-3)$

(A) I only

(B) II only

(C) III only

(D) I and II

(E) II and III

20. A grocer has 400 pounds of coffee in stock, 20 percent of which is decaffeinated. If the grocer buys another 100 pounds of coffee of which 60 percent is decaffeinated, what percent, by weight, of the grocer's stock of coffee is decaffeinated?

(A) 28%

(B) 30%

(C) 32%

(D) 34%

(E) 40%

21. The toll T, in dollars, for a truck using a certain bridge is given by the formula $T = 1.50 + 0.50(x - 2)$, where x is the number of axles on the truck. What is the toll for an 18-wheel truck that has 2 wheels on its front axle and 4 wheels on each of its other axles?

    (A) $2.50
    (B) $3.00
    (C) $3.50
    (D) $4.00
    (E) $5.00

22. For what value of x between -4 and 4, inclusive, is the value of $x^2 - 10x + 16$ the greatest?

    (A) -4
    (B) -2
    (C) 0
    (D) 2
    (E) 4

23. If $x = -\dfrac{5}{8}$ and $y = -\dfrac{1}{2}$, what is the value of the expression $-2x - y^2$?

    (A) $-\dfrac{3}{2}$
    (B) -1
    (C) 1
    (D) $\dfrac{3}{2}$
    (E) $\dfrac{7}{4}$

24. If $x - y = R$ and $xy = S$, then $(x - 2)(y + 2) =$

    (A) $R + S - 4$
    (B) $R + 2S - 4$
    (C) $2R - S - 4$
    (D) $2R + S - 4$
    (E) $2R + S$

25. For positive integers a and b, the remainder when a is divided by b is equal to the remainder when b is divided by a. Which of the following could be a value of ab ?

    I. 24
    II. 30
    III. 36

    (A) II only
    (B) III only
    (C) I and II only
    (D) II and III only
    (E) I, II, and III

26. List S consists of the positive integers that are multiples of 9 and are less than 100. What is the median of the integers in S ?

    (A) 36
    (B) 45
    (C) 49
    (D) 54
    (E) 63

27. A rope 20.6 meters long is cut into two pieces. If the length of one piece of rope is 2.8 meters shorter than the length of the other, what is the length, in meters, of the longer piece of rope?

    (A) 7.5
    (B) 8.9
    (C) 9.9
    (D) 10.3
    (E) 11.7

28. If x and y are integers and $x - y$ is odd, which of the following must be true?

    I. xy is even.
    II. $x^2 + y^2$ is odd.
    III. $(x + y)^2$ is even.

    (A) I only
    (B) II only
    (C) III only
    (D) I and II only
    (E) I, II, and III

29. On Monday, the opening price of a certain stock was $100 per share and its closing price was $110 per share. On Tuesday the closing price of the stock was 10 percent less than its closing price on Monday, and on Wednesday the closing price of the stock was 4 percent greater than its closing price on Tuesday. What was the approximate percent change in the price of the stock from its opening price on Monday to its closing price on Wednesday?

   (A) A decrease of 6%
   (B) A decrease of 4%
   (C) A decrease of 1%
   (D) An increase of 3%
   (E) An increase of 4%

30. $1 - 0.000001 =$

   (A) (1.01)(0.99)
   (B) (1.11)(0.99)
   (C) (1.001)(0.999)
   (D) (1.111)(0.999)
   (E) (1.0101)(0.0909)

31. In a certain history class of 17 juniors and seniors, each junior has written 2 book reports and each senior has written 3 book reports. If the 17 students have written a total of 44 book reports, how many juniors are in the class?

   (A) 7
   (B) 8
   (C) 9
   (D) 10
   (E) 11

32. $|-4|(|-20|-|5|) =$

   (A) −100
   (B) −60
   (C) 60
   (D) 75
   (E) 100

33. Of the total amount that Jill spent on a shopping trip, excluding taxes, she spent 50 percent on clothing, 20 percent on food, and 30 percent on other items. If Jill paid a 4 percent tax on the clothing, no tax on the food, and an 8 percent tax on all other items, then the total tax that she paid was what percent of the total amount that she spent, excluding taxes?

   (A) 2.8%
   (B) 3.6%
   (C) 4.4%
   (D) 5.2%
   (E) 6.0%

34. How many integers x satisfy both $2 < x \leq 4$ and $0 \leq x \leq 3$?

   (A) 5
   (B) 4
   (C) 3
   (D) 2
   (E) 1

35. At the opening of a trading day at a certain stock exchange, the price per share of stock K was $8. If the price per share of stock K was $9 at the closing of the day, what was the percent increase in the price per share of stock K for that day?

   (A) 1.4%
   (B) 5.9%
   (C) 11.1%
   (D) 12.5%
   (E) 23.6%

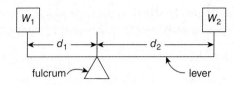

36. As shown in the diagram above, a lever resting on a fulcrum has weights of w_1 pounds and w_2 pounds, located d_1 feet and d_2 feet from the fulcrum. The lever is balanced and $w_1 d_1 = w_2 d_2$. Suppose w_1 is 50 pounds and w_2 is 30 pounds. If d_1 is 4 feet less than d_2, what is d_2, in feet?

    (A)   1.5
    (B)   2.5
    (C)   6
    (D)   10
    (E)   20

37. If r and s are positive integers such that $(2^r)(4^s) = 16$, then $2r + s =$

    (A)   2
    (B)   3
    (C)   4
    (D)   5
    (E)   6

38. Three people each contributed x dollars toward the purchase of a car. They then bought the car for y dollars, an amount less than the total number of dollars contributed. If the excess amount is to be refunded to the three people in equal amounts, each person should receive a refund of how many dollars?

    (A) $\dfrac{3x - y}{3}$

    (B) $\dfrac{x - y}{3}$

    (C) $\dfrac{x - 3y}{3}$

    (D) $\dfrac{y - 3x}{3}$

    (E) $3(x - y)$

39. Last week Jack worked 70 hours and earned $1,260. If he earned his regular hourly wage for the first 40 hours worked, $1\frac{1}{2}$ times his regular hourly wage for the next 20 hours worked, and 2 times his regular hourly wage for the remaining 10 hours worked, what was his regular hourly wage?

    (A) $7.00
    (B) $14.00
    (C) $18.00
    (D) $22.00
    (E) $31.50

40. If a and b are positive integers and $(2^a)^b = 2^3$, what is the value of $2^a \, 2^b$?

    (A)   6
    (B)   8
    (C)   16
    (D)   32
    (E)   64

41. Five machines at a certain factory operate at the same constant rate. If four of these machines, operating simultaneously, take 30 hours to fill a certain production order, how many <u>fewer</u> hours does it take all five machines, operating simultaneously, to fill the same production order?

    (A)   3
    (B)   5
    (C)   6
    (D)   16
    (E)   24

42. A certain toll station on a highway has 7 tollbooths, and each tollbooth collects $0.75 from each vehicle that passes it. From 6 o'clock yesterday morning to 12 o'clock midnight, vehicles passed each of the tollbooths at the average rate of 4 vehicles per minute. Approximately how much money did the toll station collect during that time period?

    (A) $1,500
    (B) $3,000
    (C) $11,500
    (D) $23,000
    (E) $30,000

43. How many integers between 1 and 16, inclusive, have exactly 3 different positive integer factors?
(Note: 6 is NOT such an integer because 6 has 4 different positive integer factors: 1, 2, 3, and 6.)

(A) 1
(B) 2
(C) 3
(D) 4
(E) 6

44. Stephanie has $2\frac{1}{4}$ cups of milk on hand and makes 2 batches of cookies, using $\frac{2}{3}$ cup of milk for each batch of cookies. Which of the following describes the amount of milk remaining after she makes the cookies?

(A) Less than $\frac{1}{2}$ cup

(B) Between $\frac{1}{2}$ cup and $\frac{3}{4}$ cup

(C) Between $\frac{3}{4}$ cup and 1 cup

(D) Between 1 cup and $1\frac{1}{2}$ cups

(E) More than $1\frac{1}{2}$ cups

45. The expression $n!$ is defined as the product of the integers from 1 through n. If p is the product of the integers from 100 through 299 and q is the product of the integers from 200 through 299, which of the following is equal to $\frac{p}{q}$?

(A) 99!
(B) 199!
(C) $\frac{199!}{99!}$
(D) $\frac{299!}{99!}$
(E) $\frac{299!}{199!}$

46. A school club plans to package and sell dried fruit to raise money. The club purchased 12 containers of dried fruit, each containing $16\frac{3}{4}$ pounds. What is the maximum number of individual bags of dried fruit, each containing $\frac{1}{4}$ pounds, that can be sold from the dried fruit the club purchased?

(A) 50
(B) 64
(C) 67
(D) 768
(E) 804

Height	Price
Less than 5 ft	$14.95
5 ft to 6 ft	$17.95
Over 6 ft	$21.95

47. A nursery sells fruit trees priced as shown in the chart above. In its inventory 54 trees are less than 5 feet in height. If the expected revenue from the sale of its entire stock is estimated at $2,450, approximately how much of this will come from the sale of trees that are at least 5 feet tall?

(A) $1,730
(B) $1,640
(C) $1,410
(D) $1,080
(E) $810

48. A certain bridge is 4,024 feet long. Approximately how many minutes does it take to cross this bridge at a constant speed of 20 miles per hour? (1 mile = 5,280 feet)

(A) 1
(B) 2
(C) 4
(D) 6
(E) 7

49. A purse contains 57 coins, all of which are nickels, dimes, or quarters. If the purse contains x dimes and 8 more nickels than dimes, which of the following gives the number of quarters the purse contains in terms of x ?

    (A) $2x - 49$
    (B) $2x + 49$
    (C) $2x - 65$
    (D) $49 - 2x$
    (E) $65 - 2x$

50. The annual interest rate earned by an investment increased by 10 percent from last year to this year. If the annual interest rate earned by the investment this year was 11 percent, what was the annual interest rate last year?

    (A) 1%
    (B) 1.1%
    (C) 9.1%
    (D) 10%
    (E) 10.8%

51. A total of 5 liters of gasoline is to be poured into two empty containers with capacities of 2 liters and 6 liters, respectively, such that both containers will be filled to the same percent of their respective capacities. What amount of gasoline, in liters, must be poured into the 6-liter container?

    (A) $4\frac{1}{2}$
    (B) 4
    (C) $3\frac{3}{4}$
    (D) 3
    (E) $1\frac{1}{4}$

52. What is the larger of the 2 solutions of the equation $x^2 - 4x = 96$?

    (A) 8
    (B) 12
    (C) 16
    (D) 32
    (E) 100

$$x = \frac{1}{6}gt^2$$

53. In the formula shown, if g is a constant and $x = -6$ when $t = 2$, what is the value of x when $t = 4$?

    (A) -24
    (B) -20
    (C) -15
    (D) 20
    (E) 24

54. $\dfrac{(39,897)(0.0096)}{198.76}$ is approximately

    (A) 0.02
    (B) 0.2
    (C) 2
    (D) 20
    (E) 200

55. The "prime sum" of an integer n greater than 1 is the sum of all the prime factors of n, including repetitions. For example, the prime sum of 12 is 7, since $12 = 2 \times 2 \times 3$ and $2 + 2 + 3 = 7$. For which of the following integers is the prime sum greater than 35 ?

    (A) 440
    (B) 512
    (C) 620
    (D) 700
    (E) 750

56. Each machine at a toy factory assembles a certain kind of toy at a constant rate of one toy every 3 minutes. If 40 percent of the machines at the factory are to be replaced by new machines that assemble this kind of toy at a constant rate of one toy every 2 minutes, what will be the percent increase in the number of toys assembled in one hour by all the machines at the factory, working at their constant rates?

    (A) 20%
    (B) 25%
    (C) 30%
    (D) 40%
    (E) 50%

57. When a subscription to a new magazine was purchased for m months, the publisher offered a discount of 75 percent off the regular monthly price of the magazine. If the total value of the discount was equivalent to buying the magazine at its regular monthly price for 27 months, what was the value of m?

    (A) 18
    (B) 24
    (C) 30
    (D) 36
    (E) 48

58. At a garage sale, all of the prices of the items sold were different. If the price of a radio sold at the garage sale was both the 15th highest price and the 20th lowest price among the prices of the items sold, how many items were sold at the garage sale?

    (A) 33
    (B) 34
    (C) 35
    (D) 36
    (E) 37

59. Half of a large pizza is cut into 4 equal-sized pieces, and the other half is cut into 6 equal-sized pieces. If a person were to eat 1 of the larger pieces and 2 of the smaller pieces, what fraction of the pizza would remain uneaten?

    (A) $\dfrac{5}{12}$

    (B) $\dfrac{13}{24}$

    (C) $\dfrac{7}{12}$

    (D) $\dfrac{2}{3}$

    (E) $\dfrac{17}{24}$

60. If $a = 1 + \dfrac{1}{4} + \dfrac{1}{16} + \dfrac{1}{64}$ and $b = 1 + \dfrac{1}{4}a$, then what is the value of $a - b$?

    (A) $-\dfrac{85}{256}$

    (B) $-\dfrac{1}{256}$

    (C) $-\dfrac{1}{4}$

    (D) $\dfrac{125}{256}$

    (E) $\dfrac{169}{256}$

61. In a certain learning experiment, each participant had three trials and was assigned, for each trial, a score of either –2, –1, 0, 1, or 2. The participant's final score consisted of the sum of the first trial score, 2 times the second trial score, and 3 times the third trial score. If Anne received scores of 1 and –1 for her first two trials, not necessarily in that order, which of the following could NOT be her final score?

    (A) –4
    (B) –2
    (C) 1
    (D) 5
    (E) 6

62. For all positive integers m and v, the expression $m \ominus v$ represents the remainder when m is divided by v. What is the value of $((98 \ominus 33) \ominus 17) - (98 \ominus (33 \ominus 17))$?

    (A) –10
    (B) –2
    (C) 8
    (D) 13
    (E) 17

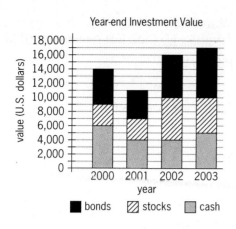

Year-end Investment Value

■ bonds ▨ stocks ▢ cash

63. The chart above shows year-end values for Darnella's investments. For just the stocks, what was the increase in value from year-end 2000 to year-end 2003 ?

   (A) $1,000
   (B) $2,000
   (C) $3,000
   (D) $4,000
   (E) $5,000

64. If the sum of the reciprocals of two consecutive odd integers is $\frac{12}{35}$, then the greater of the two integers is

   (A) 3
   (B) 5
   (C) 7
   (D) 9
   (E) 11

65. What is the sum of the odd integers from 35 to 85, inclusive?

   (A) 1,560
   (B) 1,500
   (C) 1,240
   (D) 1,120
   (E) 1,100

66. For all numbers a, b, c, and d, $\begin{vmatrix} a & b \\ c & d \end{vmatrix}$ is defined by the equation $\begin{vmatrix} a & b \\ c & d \end{vmatrix} = ad - cb$. Which of the following is equal to $\begin{vmatrix} s & t \\ 1 & 3 \end{vmatrix} - \begin{vmatrix} -t & 2 \\ s & 4 \end{vmatrix} + \begin{vmatrix} 2 & 2 \\ t & s \end{vmatrix}$?

   (A) $\begin{vmatrix} s & t \\ 1 & 5 \end{vmatrix}$

   (B) $\begin{vmatrix} s & t \\ 7 & 1 \end{vmatrix}$

   (C) $\begin{vmatrix} s & t \\ 5 & 7 \end{vmatrix}$

   (D) $\begin{vmatrix} s & -t \\ 1 & 5 \end{vmatrix}$

   (E) $\begin{vmatrix} s & -t \\ 1 & 7 \end{vmatrix}$

67. In a certain sequence, each term after the first term is one-half the previous term. If the tenth term of the sequence is between 0.0001 and 0.001, then the twelfth term of the sequence is between

   (A) 0.0025 and 0.025
   (B) 0.00025 and 0.0025
   (C) 0.000025 and 0.00025
   (D) 0.0000025 and 0.000025
   (E) 0.00000025 and 0.0000025

68. A certain drive-in movie theater has a total of 17 rows of parking spaces. There are 20 parking spaces in the first row and 21 parking spaces in the second row. In each subsequent row there are 2 more parking spaces than in the previous row. What is the total number of parking spaces in the movie theater?

   (A) 412
   (B) 544
   (C) 596
   (D) 632
   (E) 692

69. Ada and Paul received their scores on three tests. On the first test, Ada's score was 10 points higher than Paul's score. On the second test, Ada's score was 4 points higher than Paul's score. If Paul's average (arithmetic mean) score on the three tests was 3 points higher than Ada's average score on the three tests, then Paul's score on the third test was how many points higher than Ada's score?

    (A) 9
    (B) 14
    (C) 17
    (D) 23
    (E) 25

70. The price of a certain stock increased by 0.25 of 1 percent on a certain day. By what fraction did the price of the stock increase that day?

    (A) $\dfrac{1}{2,500}$
    (B) $\dfrac{1}{400}$
    (C) $\dfrac{1}{40}$
    (D) $\dfrac{1}{25}$
    (E) $\dfrac{1}{4}$

71. For each trip, a taxicab company charges $4.25 for the first mile and $2.65 for each additional mile or fraction thereof. If the total charge for a certain trip was $62.55, how many miles at most was the trip?

    (A) 21
    (B) 22
    (C) 23
    (D) 24
    (E) 25

72. When 24 is divided by the positive integer n, the remainder is 4. Which of the following statements about n must be true?

    I. n is even.
    II. n is a multiple of 5.
    III. n is a factor of 20.

    (A) III only
    (B) I and II only
    (C) I and III only
    (D) II and III only
    (E) I, II, and III

73. Terry needs to purchase some pipe for a plumbing job that requires pipes with lengths of 1 ft 4 in, 2 ft 8 in, 3 ft 4 in, 3 ft 8 in, 4 ft 8 in, 5 ft 8 in, and 9 ft 4 in. The store from which Terry will purchase the pipe sells pipe only in 10-ft lengths. If each 10-ft length can be cut into shorter pieces, what is the minimum number of 10-ft pipe lengths that Terry needs to purchase for the plumbing job?

    (Note: 1 ft = 12 in)

    (A) 3
    (B) 4
    (C) 5
    (D) 6
    (E) 7

74. What is the thousandths digit in the decimal equivalent of $\dfrac{53}{5,000}$?

    (A) 0
    (B) 1
    (C) 3
    (D) 5
    (E) 6

Questions 75 to 127 - Difficulty: **Medium**

75. If $\frac{1}{2}$ the result obtained when 2 is subtracted from $5x$ is equal to the sum of 10 and $3x$, what is the value of x?

    (A) −22
    (B) −4
    (C) 4
    (D) 18
    (E) 22

76. If Car A took n hours to travel 2 miles and Car B took m hours to travel 3 miles, which of the following expresses the time it would take Car C, traveling at the average (arithmetic mean) of those rates, to travel 5 miles?

    (A) $\dfrac{10nm}{3n+2m}$

    (B) $\dfrac{3n+2m}{10(n+m)}$

    (C) $\dfrac{2n+3m}{5nm}$

    (D) $\dfrac{10(n+m)}{2n+3m}$

    (E) $\dfrac{5(n+m)}{2n+3m}$

77. If x, y, and k are positive and x is less than y, then $\dfrac{x+k}{y+k}$ is

    (A) 1

    (B) greater than $\dfrac{x}{y}$

    (C) equal to $\dfrac{x}{y}$

    (D) less than $\dfrac{x}{y}$

    (E) less than $\dfrac{x}{y}$ or greater than $\dfrac{x}{y}$, depending on the value of k

78. Consider the following set of inequalities: $p > q$, $s > r$, $q > t$, $s > p$, and $r > q$. Between which two quantities is no relationship established?

    (A) p and r
    (B) s and t
    (C) s and q
    (D) p and t
    (E) r and t

79. Carl averaged $2m$ miles per hour on a trip that took him h hours. If Ruth made the same trip in $\frac{2}{3}h$ hours, what was her average speed in miles per hour?

    (A) $\dfrac{1}{3}mh$

    (B) $\dfrac{2}{3}mh$

    (C) m

    (D) $\dfrac{3}{2}m$

    (E) $3m$

80. Of three persons, two take relish, two take pepper, and two take salt. The one who takes no salt takes no pepper, and the one who takes no pepper takes no relish. Which of the following statements must be true?

    I.   The person who takes no salt also takes no relish.

    II. Any of the three persons who takes pepper also takes relish and salt.

    III. The person who takes no relish is not one of those who takes salt.

    (A) I only
    (B) II only
    (C) III only
    (D) I and II only
    (E) I, II, and III

81. If the smaller of 2 consecutive odd integers is a multiple of 5, which of the following could NOT be the sum of these 2 integers?

    (A) −8
    (B) 12
    (C) 22
    (D) 52
    (E) 252

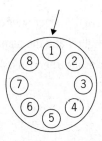

82. Eight light bulbs numbered 1 through 8 are arranged in a circle as shown above. The bulbs are wired so that every third bulb, counting in a clockwise direction, flashes until all bulbs have flashed once. If the bulb numbered 1 flashes first, which numbered bulb will flash last?

    (A) 2
    (B) 3
    (C) 4
    (D) 6
    (E) 7

Closing Prices of Stock X
During a Certain Week
(in dollars)

Monday	Tuesday	Wednesday	Thursday	Friday
21	19	22	$24\frac{1}{2}$	23

83. A certain financial analyst defines the "volatility" of a stock during a given week to be the result of the following procedure: find the absolute value of the difference in the stock's closing price for each pair of consecutive days in the week and then find the average (arithmetic mean) of these 4 values. What is the volatility of Stock X during the week shown in the table?

    (A) 0.50
    (B) 1.80
    (C) 2.00
    (D) 2.25
    (E) 2.50

84. If $y = \dfrac{|3x - 5|}{-x^2 - 3}$, for what value of x will the value of y be greatest?

    (A) −5
    (B) $-\dfrac{3}{5}$
    (C) 0
    (D) $\dfrac{3}{5}$
    (E) $\dfrac{5}{3}$

85. What values of x have a corresponding value of y that satisfies both $xy > 0$ and $xy = x + y$?

    (A) $x \le -1$
    (B) $-1 < x \le 0$
    (C) $0 < x \le 1$
    (D) $x > 1$
    (E) All real numbers

86. Employee X's annual salary is $12,000 more than half of Employee Y's annual salary. Employee Z's annual salary is $15,000 more than half of Employee X's annual salary. If Employee X's annual salary is $27,500, which of the following lists these three people in order of increasing annual salary?

    (A) Y, Z, X
    (B) Y, X, Z
    (C) Z, X, Y
    (D) X, Y, Z
    (E) X, Z, Y

$$C = \begin{cases} 0.10s, \text{ if } s \le 60{,}000 \\ 0.10s + 0.04(s - 60{,}000), \text{ if } s > 60{,}000 \end{cases}$$

87. The formula above gives the contribution C, in dollars, to a certain profit-sharing plan for a participant with a salary of s dollars. How many more dollars is the contribution for a participant with a salary of $70,000 than for a participant with a salary of $50,000 ?

    (A) $800
    (B) $1,400
    (C) $2,000
    (D) $2,400
    (E) $2,800

88. Next month, Ron and Cathy will each begin working part-time at $\frac{3}{5}$ of their respective current salaries.
    If the sum of their reduced salaries will be equal to Cathy's current salary, then Ron's current salary is what fraction of Cathy's current salary?

    (A) $\frac{1}{3}$

    (B) $\frac{2}{5}$

    (C) $\frac{1}{2}$

    (D) $\frac{3}{5}$

    (E) $\frac{2}{3}$

89. David and Ron are ordering food for a business lunch. David thinks that there should be twice as many sandwiches as there are pastries, but Ron thinks the number of pastries should be 12 more than one-fourth of the number of sandwiches. How many sandwiches should be ordered so that David and Ron can agree on the number of pastries to order?

    (A) 12
    (B) 16
    (C) 20
    (D) 24
    (E) 48

90. The cost of purchasing each box of candy from a certain mail order catalog is v dollars per pound of candy, plus a shipping charge of h dollars. How many dollars does it cost to purchase 2 boxes of candy, one containing s pounds of candy and the other containing t pounds of candy, from this catalog?

    (A) $h + stv$
    (B) $2h + stv$
    (C) $2hstv$
    (D) $2h + s + t + v$
    (E) $2h + v(s + t)$

91. If $x \ne -\dfrac{1}{2}$, then $\dfrac{6x^3 + 3x^2 - 8x - 4}{2x + 1} =$

    (A) $3x^2 + \dfrac{3}{2}x - 8$

    (B) $3x^2 + \dfrac{3}{2}x - 4$

    (C) $3x^2 - 4$

    (D) $3x - 4$

    (E) $3x + 4$

92. If $x^2 + bx + 5 = (x + c)^2$ for all numbers x, where b and c are positive constants, what is the value of b ?

    (A) $\sqrt{5}$
    (B) $\sqrt{10}$
    (C) $2\sqrt{5}$
    (D) $2\sqrt{10}$
    (E) 10

93. Last year Shannon listened to a certain public radio station 10 hours per week and contributed $35 to the station. Of the following, which is closest to Shannon's contribution per minute of listening time last year?

    (A) $0.001
    (B) $0.010
    (C) $0.025
    (D) $0.058
    (E) $0.067

94. Each of the 20 employees at Company J is to receive an end-of-year bonus this year. Agnes will receive a larger bonus than any other employee, but only $500 more than Cheryl will receive. None of the employees will receive a smaller bonus than Cheryl. If the amount of money to be distributed in bonuses at Company J this year totals $60,000, what is the largest bonus Agnes can receive?

    (A) $3,250
    (B) $3,325
    (C) $3,400
    (D) $3,475
    (E) $3,500

95. Beth, Naomi, and Juan raised a total of $55 for charity. Naomi raised $5 less than Juan, and Juan raised twice as much as Beth. How much did Beth raise?

    (A) $9
    (B) $10
    (C) $12
    (D) $13
    (E) $15

96. The set of solutions for the equation $(x^2 - 25)^2 = x^2 - 10x + 25$ contains how many real numbers?

    (A) 0
    (B) 1
    (C) 2
    (D) 3
    (E) 4

97. An aerosol can is designed so that its bursting pressure, B, in pounds per square inch, is 120% of the pressure, F, in pounds per square inch, to which it is initially filled. Which of the following formulas expresses the relationship between B and F?

    (A) $B = 1.2F$
    (B) $B = 120F$
    (C) $B = 1 + 0.2F$
    (D) $B = \dfrac{F}{1.2}$
    (E) $B = \dfrac{1.2}{F}$

98. The average (arithmetic mean) of the positive integers x, y, and z is 3. If $x < y < z$, what is the greatest possible value of z?

    (A) 5
    (B) 6
    (C) 7
    (D) 8
    (E) 9

99. The product of 3,305 and the 1-digit integer x is a 5-digit integer. The units (ones) digit of the product is 5 and the hundreds digit is y. If A is the set of all possible values of x and B is the set of all possible values of y, then which of the following gives the members of A and B?

	A	B
(A)	{1, 3, 5, 7, 9}	{0, 1, 2, 3, 4, 5, 6, 7, 8, 9}
(B)	{1, 3, 5, 7, 9}	{1, 3, 5, 7, 9}
(C)	{3, 5, 7, 9}	{1, 5, 7, 9}
(D)	{5, 7, 9}	{1, 5, 7}
(E)	{5, 7, 9}	{1, 5, 9}

100. If x and y are integers such that $2 < x \le 8$ and $2 < y \le 9$, what is the maximum value of $\dfrac{1}{x} - \dfrac{x}{y}$?

    (A) $-3\dfrac{1}{8}$
    (B) 0
    (C) $\dfrac{1}{4}$
    (D) $\dfrac{5}{18}$
    (E) 2

101. Items that are purchased together at a certain discount store are priced at $3 for the first item purchased and $1 for each additional item purchased. What is the maximum number of items that could be purchased together for a total price that is less than $30 ?

    (A) 25
    (B) 26
    (C) 27
    (D) 28
    (E) 29

102. What is the least integer z for which (0.000125)(0.0025)(0.00000125) × 10^z is an integer?

    (A)   18
    (B)   10
    (C)   0
    (D) −10
    (E) −18

103. The average (arithmetic mean) length per film for a group of 21 films is t minutes. If a film that runs for 66 minutes is removed from the group and replaced by one that runs for 52 minutes, what is the average length per film, in minutes, for the new group of films, in terms of t ?

    (A) $t + \dfrac{2}{3}$

    (B) $t - \dfrac{2}{3}$

    (C) $21t + 14$

    (D) $t + \dfrac{3}{2}$

    (E) $t - \dfrac{3}{2}$

104. A garden center sells a certain grass seed in 5-pound bags at $13.85 per bag, 10-pound bags at $20.43 per bag, and 25-pound bags at $32.25 per bag. If a customer is to buy at least 65 pounds of the grass seed, but no more than 80 pounds, what is the least possible cost of the grass seed that the customer will buy?

    (A) $94.03
    (B) $96.75
    (C) $98.78
    (D) $102.07
    (E) $105.36

105. If $x = -|w|$, which of the following must be true?

    (A) $x = -w$
    (B) $x = w$
    (C) $x^2 = w$
    (D) $x^2 = w^2$
    (E) $x^3 = w^3$

106. A certain financial institution reported that its assets totaled $2,377,366.30 on a certain day. Of this amount, $31,724.54 was held in cash. Approximately what percent of the reported assets was held in cash on that day?

    (A) 0.00013%
    (B) 0.0013%
    (C) 0.013%
    (D) 0.13%
    (E) 1.3%

$$\begin{array}{r} AB \\ + BA \\ \hline AAC \end{array}$$

107. In the correctly worked addition problem shown, where the sum of the two-digit positive integers AB and BA is the three-digit integer AAC, and A, B, and C are different digits, what is the units digit of the integer AAC ?

    (A) 9
    (B) 6
    (C) 3
    (D) 2
    (E) 0

108. The hard drive, monitor, and printer for a certain desktop computer system cost a total of $2,500. The cost of the printer and monitor together is equal to $\dfrac{2}{3}$ of the cost of the hard drive. If the cost of the printer is $100 more than the cost of the monitor, what is the cost of the printer?

    (A) $800
    (B) $600
    (C) $550
    (D) $500
    (E) $350

$$3r \le 4s + 5$$
$$|s| \le 5$$

109. Given the inequalities above, which of the following CANNOT be the value of r ?

(A) −20
(B) −5
(C) 0
(D) 5
(E) 20

110. If m is an even integer, v is an odd integer, and $m > v > 0$, which of the following represents the number of even integers less than m and greater than v ?

(A) $\dfrac{m-v}{2} - 1$

(B) $\dfrac{m-v-1}{2}$

(C) $\dfrac{m-v}{2}$

(D) $m - v - 1$

(E) $m - v$

111. A positive integer is divisible by 9 if and only if the sum of its digits is divisible by 9. If n is a positive integer, for which of the following values of k is $25 \times 10^n + k \times 10^{2n}$ divisible by 9 ?

(A) 9
(B) 16
(C) 23
(D) 35
(E) 47

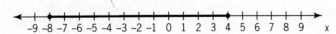

112. On the number line, the shaded interval is the graph of which of the following inequalities?

(A) $|x| \le 4$
(B) $|x| \le 8$
(C) $|x - 2| \le 4$
(D) $|x - 2| \le 6$
(E) $|x + 2| \le 6$

113. Last year members of a certain professional organization for teachers consisted of teachers from 49 different school districts, with an average (arithmetic mean) of 9.8 schools per district. Last year the average number of teachers at these schools who were members of the organization was 22. Which of the following is closest to the total number of members of the organization last year?

(A) 10^7
(B) 10^6
(C) 10^5
(D) 10^4
(E) 10^3

114. Of all the students in a certain dormitory, $\dfrac{1}{2}$ are first-year students and the rest are second-year students. If $\dfrac{4}{5}$ of the first-year students have not declared a major and if the fraction of second-year students who have declared a major is 3 times the fraction of first-year students who have declared a major, what fraction of all the students in the dormitory are second-year students who have not declared a major?

(A) $\dfrac{1}{15}$

(B) $\dfrac{1}{5}$

(C) $\dfrac{4}{15}$

(D) $\dfrac{1}{3}$

(E) $\dfrac{2}{5}$

115. If the average (arithmetic mean) of x, y, and z is $7x$ and $x \ne 0$, what is the ratio of x to the sum of y and z ?

(A) 1:21
(B) 1:20
(C) 1:6
(D) 6:1
(E) 20:1

116. Jonah drove the first half of a 100-mile trip in x hours and the second half in y hours. Which of the following is equal to Jonah's average speed, in miles per hour, for the entire trip?

    (A) $\dfrac{50}{x+y}$

    (B) $\dfrac{100}{x+y}$

    (C) $\dfrac{25}{x} + \dfrac{25}{y}$

    (D) $\dfrac{50}{x} + \dfrac{50}{y}$

    (E) $\dfrac{100}{x} + \dfrac{100}{y}$

117. If the amount of federal estate tax due on an estate valued at $1.35 million is $437,000 plus 43 percent of the value of the estate in excess of $1.25 million, then the federal tax due is approximately what percent of the value of the estate?

    A. 30%
    B. 35%
    C. 40%
    D. 45%
    E. 50%

$$7x + 6y \le 38{,}000$$
$$4x + 5y \le 28{,}000$$

118. A manufacturer wants to produce x balls and y boxes. Resource constraints require that x and y satisfy the inequalities shown. What is the maximum number of balls and boxes combined that can be produced given the resource constraints?

    (A) 5,000
    (B) 6,000
    (C) 7,000
    (D) 8,000
    (E) 10,000

119. If $\dfrac{3}{10^4} = x\%$, then $x =$

    (A) 0.3
    (B) 0.03
    (C) 0.003
    (D) 0.0003
    (E) 0.00003

120. What is the remainder when 3^{24} is divided by 5 ?

    (A) 0
    (B) 1
    (C) 2
    (D) 3
    (E) 4

121. José has a collection of 100 coins, consisting of nickels, dimes, quarters, and half-dollars. If he has a total of 35 nickels and dimes, a total of 45 dimes and quarters, and a total of 50 nickels and quarters, how many half-dollars does he have?

    (A) 15
    (B) 20
    (C) 25
    (D) 30
    (E) 35

122. David used part of $100,000 to purchase a house. Of the remaining portion, he invested $\dfrac{1}{3}$ of it at 4 percent simple annual interest and $\dfrac{2}{3}$ of it at 6 percent simple annual interest. If after a year the income from the two investments totaled $320, what was the purchase price of the house?

    (A) $96,000
    (B) $94,000
    (C) $88,000
    (D) $75,000
    (E) $40,000

123. A certain manufacturer sells its product to stores in 113 different regions worldwide, with an average (arithmetic mean) of 181 stores per region. If last year these stores sold an average of 51,752 units of the manufacturer's product per store, which of the following is closest to the total number of units of the manufacturer's product sold worldwide last year?

    (A) 10^6
    (B) 10^7
    (C) 10^8
    (D) 10^9
    (E) 10^{10}

124. Andrew started saving at the beginning of the year and had saved $240 by the end of the year. He continued to save and by the end of 2 years had saved a total of $540. Which of the following is closest to the percent increase in the amount Andrew saved during the second year compared to the amount he saved during the first year?

    (A)   11%
    (B)   25%
    (C)   44%
    (D)   56%
    (E)   125%

125. If x is a positive integer, r is the remainder when x is divided by 4, and R is the remainder when x is divided by 9, what is the greatest possible value of $r^2 + R$?

    (A)   25
    (B)   21
    (C)   17
    (D)   13
    (E)   11

126. Each of the nine digits 0, 1, 1, 4, 5, 6, 8, 8, and 9 is used once to form 3 three-digit integers. What is the greatest possible sum of the 3 integers?

    (A)   1,752
    (B)   2,616
    (C)   2,652
    (D)   2,775
    (E)   2,958

127. Given that $1^2 + 2^2 + 3^2 + \ldots + 10^2 = 385$, what is the value of $3^2 + 6^2 + 9^2 + \ldots + 30^2$?

    (A)   1,155
    (B)   1,540
    (C)   1,925
    (D)   2,310
    (E)   3,465

Questions 128 to 171 - Difficulty: Hard

128. Two numbers differ by 2 and sum to S. Which of the following is the greater of the numbers in terms of S?

    (A) $\dfrac{S}{2} - 1$

    (B) $\dfrac{S}{2}$

    (C) $\dfrac{S}{2} + \dfrac{1}{2}$

    (D) $\dfrac{S}{2} + 1$

    (E) $\dfrac{S}{2} + 2$

129. If m is an integer and $m = 10^{32} - 32$, what is the sum of the digits of m?

    (A)   257
    (B)   264
    (C)   275
    (D)   284
    (E)   292

130. In a numerical table with 10 rows and 10 columns, each entry is either a 9 or a 10. If the number of 9s in the nth row is $n - 1$ for each n from 1 to 10, what is the average (arithmetic mean) of all the numbers in the table?

    (A)   9.45
    (B)   9.50
    (C)   9.55
    (D)   9.65
    (E)   9.70

131. In 2004, the cost of 1 year-long print subscription to a certain newspaper was $4 per week. In 2005, the newspaper introduced a new rate plan for 1 year-long print subscription: $3 per week for the first 40 weeks of 2005 and $2 per week for the remaining weeks of 2005. How much less did 1 year-long print subscription to this newspaper cost in 2005 than in 2004?

    (A) $64
    (B) $78
    (C) $112
    (D) $144
    (E) $304

132. A positive integer n is a perfect number provided that the sum of all the positive factors of n, including 1 and n, is equal to $2n$. What is the sum of the reciprocals of all the positive factors of the perfect number 28 ?

    (A) $\dfrac{1}{4}$

    (B) $\dfrac{56}{27}$

    (C) 2

    (D) 3

    (E) 4

133. The infinite sequence a_1, a_2, ..., a_n, ... is such that $a_1 - 2$, $a_2 = -3$, $a_3 = 5$, $a_4 = -1$, and $a_n = a_{n-4}$ for $n > 4$. What is the sum of the first 97 terms of the sequence?

    (A) 72

    (B) 74

    (C) 75

    (D) 78

    (E) 80

134. The sequence a_1, a_2, ... a_n, ... is such that $a_n = 2a_{n-1} - x$ for all positive integers $n \geq 2$ and for a certain number x. If $a_5 = 99$ and $a_3 = 27$, what is the value of x ?

    (A) 3

    (B) 9

    (C) 18

    (D) 36

    (E) 45

135. In a certain medical survey, 45 percent of the people surveyed had the type A antigen in their blood and 3 percent had both the type A antigen and the type B antigen. Which of the following is closest to the percent of those with the type A antigen who also had the type B antigen?

    (A) 1.35%

    (B) 6.67%

    (C) 13.50%

    (D) 15.00%

    (E) 42.00%

136. On a certain transatlantic crossing, 20 percent of a ship's passengers held round-trip tickets and also took their cars aboard the ship. If 60 percent of the passengers with round-trip tickets <u>did</u> not take their cars aboard the ship, what percent of the ship's passengers held round-trip tickets?

    (A) $33\dfrac{1}{3}\%$

    (B) 40%

    (C) 50%

    (D) 60%

    (E) $66\dfrac{2}{3}\%$

137. If x and k are integers and $(12^x)(4^{2x+1}) = (2^k)(3^2)$, what is the value of k ?

    (A) 5

    (B) 7

    (C) 10

    (D) 12

    (E) 14

138. If S is the sum of the reciprocals of the 10 consecutive integers from 21 to 30, then S is between which of the following two fractions?

    (A) $\dfrac{1}{3}$ and $\dfrac{1}{2}$

    (B) $\dfrac{1}{4}$ and $\dfrac{1}{3}$

    (C) $\dfrac{1}{5}$ and $\dfrac{1}{4}$

    (D) $\dfrac{1}{6}$ and $\dfrac{1}{5}$

    (E) $\dfrac{1}{7}$ and $\dfrac{1}{6}$

139. For every even positive integer m, $f(m)$ represents the product of all even integers from 2 to m, inclusive. For example, $f(12) = 2 \times 4 \times 6 \times 8 \times 10 \times 12$. What is the greatest prime factor of $f(24)$?

    (A) 23

    (B) 19

    (C) 17

    (D) 13

    (E) 11

3, *k*, 2, 8, *m*, 3

140. The arithmetic mean of the list of numbers above is 4. If *k* and *m* are integers and *k* ≠ *m*, what is the median of the list?

(A)   2

(D)   2.5

(C)   3

(D)   3.5

(E)   4

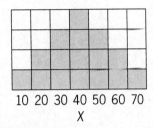

10 20 30 40 50 60 70
X

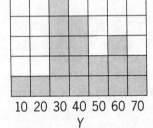

10 20 30 40 50 60 70
Y

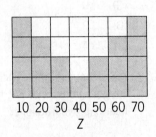

10 20 30 40 50 60 70
Z

141. If the variables, *X*, *Y*, and *Z* take on only the values 10, 20, 30, 40, 50, 60, or 70 with frequencies indicated by the shaded regions above, for which of the frequency distributions is the mean equal to the median?

(A)   *X* only

(B)   *Y* only

(C)   *Z* only

(D)   *X* and *Y*

(E)   *X* and *Z*

$$2x + y = 12$$
$$|y| \leq 12$$

142. For how many ordered pairs (*x*,*y*) that are solutions of the system above are *x* and *y* both integers?

(A)   7

(B)   10

(C)   12

(D)   13

(E)   14

143. The United States mint produces coins in 1-cent, 5-cent, 10-cent, 25-cent, and 50-cent denominations. If a jar contains exactly 100 cents worth of these coins, which of the following could be the total number of coins in the jar?

I.   91

II.   81

III.   76

(A)   I only

(B)   II only

(C)   III only

(D)   I and III only

(E)   I, II, and III

144. A certain university will select 1 of 7 candidates eligible to fill a position in the mathematics department and 2 of 10 candidates eligible to fill 2 identical positions in the computer science department. If none of the candidates is eligible for a position in both departments, how many different sets of 3 candidates are there to fill the 3 positions?

(A)   42

(B)   70

(C)   140

(D)   165

(E)   315

145. A survey of employers found that during 1993 employment costs rose 3.5 percent, where employment costs consist of salary costs and fringe-benefit costs. If salary costs rose 3 percent and fringe-benefit costs rose 5.5 percent during 1993, then fringe-benefit costs represented what percent of employment costs at the beginning of 1993 ?

(A)   16.5%

(B)   20%

(C)   35%

(D)   55%

(E)   65%

146. The subsets of the set {w, x, y} are {w}, {x}, {y}, {w, x}, {w, y}, {x, y}, {w, x, y}, and { } (the empty subset). How many subsets of the set {w, x, y, z} contain w?

    (A) Four
    (B) Five
    (C) Seven
    (D) Eight
    (E) Sixteen

147. The number $\sqrt{63 - 36\sqrt{3}}$ can be expressed as $x + y\sqrt{3}$ for some integers x and y. What is the value of xy?

    (A) −18
    (B) −6
    (C) 6
    (D) 18
    (E) 27

148. There are 10 books on a shelf, of which 4 are paperbacks and 6 are hardbacks. How many possible selections of 5 books from the shelf contain at least one paperback and at least one hardback?

    (A) 75
    (B) 120
    (C) 210
    (D) 246
    (E) 252

149. If x is to be chosen at random from the set {1, 2, 3, 4} and y is to be chosen at random from the set {5, 6, 7}, what is the probability that xy will be even?

    (A) $\frac{1}{6}$
    (B) $\frac{1}{3}$
    (C) $\frac{1}{2}$
    (D) $\frac{2}{3}$
    (E) $\frac{5}{6}$

150. The function f is defined for each positive three-digit integer n by $f(n) = 2^x 3^y 5^z$, where x, y, and z are the hundreds, tens, and units digits of n, respectively. If m and v are three-digit positive integers such that $f(m) = 9f(v)$, then m − v =

    (A) 8
    (B) 9
    (C) 18
    (C) 20
    (E) 80

151. If $10^{50} - 74$ is written as an integer in base 10 notation, what is the sum of the digits in that integer?

    (A) 424
    (B) 433
    (C) 440
    (D) 449
    (E) 467

152. A certain company that sells only cars and trucks reported that revenues from car sales in 1997 were down 11 percent from 1996 and revenues from truck sales in 1997 were up 7 percent from 1996. If total revenues from car sales and truck sales in 1997 were up 1 percent from 1996, what is the ratio of revenue from car sales in 1996 to revenue from truck sales in 1996?

    (A) 1:2
    (B) 4:5
    (C) 1:1
    (D) 3:2
    (E) 5:3

153. Becky rented a power tool from a rental shop. The rent for the tool was $12 for the first hour and $3 for each additional hour. If Becky paid a total of $27, excluding sales tax, to rent the tool, for how many hours did she rent it?

    (A) 5
    (B) 6
    (C) 9
    (D) 10
    (E) 12

154. If $4 < \dfrac{7-x}{3}$, which of the following must be true?

    I. $5 < x$

    II. $|x + 3| > 2$

    III. $-(x + 5)$ is positive.

    (A)   II only

    (B)   III only

    (C)   I and II only

    (D)   II and III only

    (E)   I, II, and III

155. On a certain day, a bakery produced a batch of rolls at a total production cost of $300. On that day, $\dfrac{4}{5}$ of the rolls in the batch were sold, each at a price that was 50 percent greater than the average (arithmetic mean) production cost per roll. The remaining rolls in the batch were sold the next day, each at a price that was 20 percent less than the price of the day before. What was the bakery's profit on this batch of rolls?

    (A) $150

    (B) $144

    (C) $132

    (D) $108

    (E) $90

156. A set of numbers has the property that for any number t in the set, $t + 2$ is in the set. If -1 is in the set, which of the following must also be in the set?

    I. -3

    II.   1

    III. 5

    (A)   I only

    (B)   II only

    (C)   I and II only

    (D)   II and III only

    (E)   I, II, and III

157. A couple decides to have 4 children. If they succeed in having 4 children and each child is equally likely to be a boy or a girl, what is the probability that they will have exactly 2 girls and 2 boys?

    (A) $\dfrac{3}{8}$

    (B) $\dfrac{1}{4}$

    (C) $\dfrac{3}{16}$

    (D) $\dfrac{1}{8}$

    (E) $\dfrac{1}{16}$

158. The closing price of Stock X changed on each trading day last month. The percent change in the closing price of Stock X from the first trading day last month to each of the other trading days last month was less than 50 percent. If the closing price on the second trading day last month was $10.00, which of the following CANNOT be the closing price on the last trading day last month?

    (A) $3.00

    (B) $9.00

    (C) $19.00

    (D) $24.00

    (E) $29.00

159. An airline passenger is planning a trip that involves three connecting flights that leave from Airports A, B, and C, respectively. The first flight leaves Airport A every hour, beginning at 8:00 a.m., and arrives at Airport B $2\dfrac{1}{2}$ hours later. The second flight leaves Airport B every 20 minutes, beginning at 8:00 a.m., and arrives at Airport C $1\dfrac{1}{6}$ hours later. The third flight leaves Airport C every hour, beginning at 8:45 a.m. What is the least total amount of time the passenger must spend between flights if all flights keep to their schedules?

    (A)   25 min

    (B)   1 hr 5 min

    (C)   1 hr 15 min

    (D)   2 hr 20 min

    (E)   3 hr 40 min

160. If n is a positive integer and n^2 is divisible by 72, then the largest positive integer that must divide n is

   (A)   6
   (B)   12
   (C)   24
   (D)   36
   (E)   48

161. A certain grocery purchased x pounds of produce for p dollars per pound. If y pounds of the produce had to be discarded due to spoilage and the grocery sold the rest for s dollars per pound, which of the following represents the gross profit on the sale of the produce?

   (A) $(x - y)s - xp$
   (B) $(x - y)p - ys$
   (C) $(s - p)y - xp$
   (D) $xp - ys$
   (E) $(x - y)(s - p)$

162. If x, y, and z are positive integers such that x is a factor of y, and x is a multiple of z, which of the following is NOT necessarily an integer?

   (A) $\dfrac{x + z}{z}$

   (B) $\dfrac{y + z}{x}$

   (C) $\dfrac{x + y}{z}$

   (D) $\dfrac{xy}{z}$

   (E) $\dfrac{yz}{x}$

163. Running at their respective constant rates, Machine X takes 2 days longer to produce w widgets than Machine Y. At these rates, if the two machines together produce $\dfrac{5}{4}w$ widgets in 3 days, how many days would it take Machine X alone to produce $2w$ widgets?

   (A)   4
   (B)   6
   (C)   8
   (D)   10
   (E)   12

164. What is the greatest positive integer n such that 5^n divides $10! - (2)(5!)^2$?

   (A)   2
   (B)   3
   (C)   4
   (D)   5
   (E)   6

165. Yesterday, Candice and Sabrina trained for a bicycle race by riding around an oval track. They both began riding at the same time from the track's starting point. However, Candice rode at a faster pace than Sabrina, completing each lap around the track in 42 seconds, while Sabrina completed each lap around the track in 46 seconds. How many laps around the track had Candice completed the next time that Candice and Sabrina were together at the starting point?

   (A)   21
   (B)   23
   (C)   42
   (D)   46
   (E)   483

166. If $n = 9! - 6^4$, which of the following is the greatest integer k such that 3^k is a factor of n ?

   (A)   1
   (B)   3
   (C)   4
   (D)   6
   (E)   8

167. The integer 120 has many factorizations. For example, $120 = (2)(60)$, $120 = (3)(4)(10)$, and $120 = (-1)(-3)(4)(10)$. In how many of the factorizations of 120 are the factors consecutive integers in ascending order?

   (A)   2
   (B)   3
   (C)   4
   (D)   5
   (E)   6

168. Jorge's bank statement showed a balance that was $0.54 greater than what his records showed. He discovered that he had written a check for $x.yz and had recorded it as $x.zy, where each of x, y, and z represents a digit from 0 though 9. Which of the following could be the value of z?

(A) 2
(B) 3
(C) 4
(D) 5
(E) 6

169. One side of a parking stall is defined by a straight stripe that consists of n painted sections of equal length with an unpainted section $\frac{1}{2}$ as long between each pair of consecutive painted sections. The total length of the stripe from the beginning of the first painted section to the end of the last painted section is 203 inches. If n is an integer and the length, in inches, of each unpainted section is an integer greater than 2, what is the value of n?

(A)   5
(B)   9
(C)   10
(D)   14
(E)   29

170. $\dfrac{2\frac{3}{5} - 1\frac{2}{3}}{\frac{2}{3} - \frac{3}{5}} =$

(A)   16
(B)   14
(C)   3
(D)   1
(E)   −1

Machine	Consecutive Minutes Machine Is Off	Units of Power When On
A	17	15
B	14	18
C	11	12

171. At a certain factory, each of Machines A, B, and C is periodically on for exactly 1 minute and periodically off for a fixed number of consecutive minutes. The table above shows that Machine A is on and uses 15 units of power every 18th minute, Machine B is on and uses 18 units of power every 15th minute, and Machine C is on and uses 12 units of power every 12th minute. The factory has a backup generator that operates only when the total power usage of the 3 machines exceeds 30 units of power. What is the time interval, in minutes, between consecutive times the backup generator begins to operate?

(A)   36
(B)   63
(C)   90
(D)   180
(E)   270

4.4 Answer Key

1.	A	32.	C	63.	B	94.	D	125.	C
2.	D	33.	C	64.	C	95.	C	126.	C
3.	A	34.	E	65.	A	96.	D	127.	E
4.	D	35.	D	66.	E	97.	A	128.	D
5.	C	36.	D	67.	C	98.	B	129.	D
6.	E	37.	D	68.	C	99.	D	130.	C
7.	A	38.	A	69.	D	100.	B	131.	A
8.	C	39.	B	70.	B	101.	C	132.	C
9.	C	40.	C	71.	C	102.	A	133.	B
10.	C	41.	C	72.	D	103.	B	134.	A
11.	C	42.	D	73.	B	104.	B	135.	B
12.	E	43.	B	74.	A	105.	D	136.	C
13.	E	44.	C	75.	A	106.	E	137.	E
14.	D	45.	C	76.	A	107.	E	138.	A
15.	C	46.	E	77.	B	108.	C	139.	E
16.	D	47.	B	78.	A	109.	E	140.	C
17.	B	48.	B	79.	E	110.	B	141.	E
18.	D	49.	D	80.	E	111.	E	142.	D
19.	D	50.	D	81.	C	112.	E	143.	D
20.	A	51.	C	82.	D	113.	D	144.	E
21.	B	52.	B	83.	D	114.	B	145.	B
22.	A	53.	A	84.	E	115.	B	146.	D
23.	C	54.	C	85.	D	116.	B	147.	A
24.	D	55.	C	86.	E	117.	B	148.	D
25.	B	56.	A	87.	D	118.	B	149.	D
26.	D	57.	D	88.	E	119.	B	150.	D
27.	E	58.	B	89.	E	120.	B	151.	C
28.	D	59.	E	90.	E	121.	E	152.	A
29.	D	60.	B	91.	C	122.	B	153.	B
30.	C	61.	E	92.	C	123.	D	154.	D
31.	A	62.	D	93.	A	124.	B	155.	C

156.	D	160.	B	164.	D	168.	E
157.	A	161.	A	165.	B	169.	C
158.	A	162.	B	166.	D	170.	B
159.	B	163.	E	167.	C	171.	C

4.5 Answer Explanations

The following discussion is intended to familiarize you with the most efficient and effective approaches to the kinds of problems common to Problem Solving questions. The particular questions in this chapter are generally representative of the kinds of problem solving questions you will encounter on the GMAT exam. Remember that it is the problem solving strategy that is important, not the specific details of a particular question.

Questions 1 to 74 - Difficulty: Easy

1. Working at a constant rate, a copy machine makes 20 copies of a one-page document per minute. If the machine works at this constant rate, how many hours does it take to make 4,800 copies of a one-page document?

   (A) 4
   (B) 5
   (C) 6
   (D) 7
   (E) 8

Arithmetic Rate

The copy machine produces 20 copies of the one-page document each minute. Because there are 60 minutes in an hour, the constant rate of 20 copies per minute is equal to $60 \times 20 = 1,200$ copies per hour. With the machine working at this rate, the amount of time that it takes to produce 4,800 copies of the document is

$$\frac{4800 \text{ } copies}{1200 \text{ } \frac{copies}{hour}} = 4 \text{ hours.}$$

The correct answer is A.

2. If $x + y = 2$ and $x^2 + y^2 = 2$, what is the value of xy ?

   (A) −2
   (B) −1
   (C) 0
   (D) 1
   (E) 2

Algebra Second-Degree Equations

$x + y = 2$	given
$y = 2 - x$	subtract x from both sides
$x^2 + (2 - x)^2 = 2$	substitute $y = 2 - x$ into $x^2 + y^2 = 2$
$2x^2 - 4x + 4 = 2$	expand and combine like terms
$2x^2 - 4x + 2 = 0$	subtract 2 from both sides
$x^2 - 2x + 1 = 0$	divide both sides by 2
$(x - 1)(x - 1) = 0$	factor
$x = 1$	set each factor equal to 0
$y = 1$	use $x = 1$ and $y = 2 - x$
$xy = 1$	multiply 1 and 1

Alternatively, the value of xy can be found by first squaring both sides of the equation $x + y = 2$.

$x + y = 2$	given
$(x + y)^2 = 4$	square both sides
$x^2 + 2xy + y^2 = 4$	expand and combine like terms
$2 + 2xy = 4$	replace $x^2 + y^2$ with 2
$2xy = 2$	subtract 2 from both sides
$xy = 1$	divide both sides by 2

The correct answer is D.

3. The sum S of the first n consecutive positive even integers is given by $S = n(n + 1)$. For what value of n is this sum equal to 110 ?

   (A) 10
   (B) 11
   (C) 12
   (D) 13
   (E) 14

Algebra Factoring

Given that the sum of the first n even numbers is $n(n + 1)$, the sum is equal to 110 when $110 = n(n + 1)$. To find the value of n in this case, we need to find the two consecutive integers whose product is 110. These integers are 10 and 11; $10 \times 11 = 110$. The smaller of these numbers is n.

The correct answer is A.

4. $6(87.30 + 0.65) - 5(87.30) =$

   (A)   3.90
   (B)   39.00
   (C)   90.90
   (D)   91.20
   (E)   91.85

Arithmetic Factors, Multiples, and Divisibility

This question is most efficiently answered by distributing the 6 over 87.30 and 0.65, and then combining the terms that contain a factor of 87.30, as follows:

$6(87.30 + 0.65) - 5(87.30) = 6\,(87.30) + 6\,(0.65)$
$- 5\,(87.30) = (6 - 5)\,87.30 + 6(0.65) = 87.30 +$
$3.90 = 91.20$

The correct answer is D.

5. What is the value of $x^2yz - xyz^2$, if $x = -2$, $y = 1$, and $z = 3$?

   (A)   20
   (B)   24
   (C)   30
   (D)   32
   (E)   48

Algebra Operations on Integers

Given that $x = -2$, $y = 1$, and $z = 3$, it follows by substitution that

$$x^2yz - xyz^2 = (-2)^2(1)(3) - (-2)(1)(3^2)$$
$$= (4)(1)(3) - (-2)(1)(9)$$
$$= 12 - (-18)$$
$$= 12 + 18$$
$$= 30$$

The correct answer is C.

6. A souvenir vendor purchased 1,000 shirts for a special event at a price of $5 each. The vendor sold 600 of the shirts on the day of the event for $12 each and 300 of the shirts in the week following the event for $4 each. The vendor was unable to sell the remaining shirts. What was the vendor's gross profit on the sale of these shirts?

   (A) $1,000
   (B) $2,200
   (C) $2,700
   (D) $3,000
   (E) $3,400

Arithmetic Applied Problems

The vendor's gross profit on the sale of the shirts is equal to the total revenue from the shirts that were sold minus the total cost for all of the shirts. The total cost for all of the shirts is equal to the number of shirts the vendor purchased multiplied by the price paid by the vendor for each shirt: $1,000 \times \$5 = \$5,000$. The total revenue from the shirts that were sold is equal to the total revenue from the 600 shirts sold for $12 each plus the total revenue from the 300 shirts that were sold for $4 each: $600 \times \$12 + 300 \times \$4 = \$7,200 + \$1,200 = \$8,400$. The gross profit is therefore $\$8,400 - \$5,000 = \$3,400$.

The correct answer is E.

7. If $x > y$ and $y > z$, which of the following represents the greatest number?

   (A) $x - z$
   (B) $x - y$
   (C) $y - x$
   (D) $z - y$
   (E) $z - x$

Algebra Inequalities

From $x > y$ and $y > z$, it follows that $x > z$. These inequalities imply the following about the differences that are given in the answer choices:

Answer choice	Difference	Algebraic sign	Reason
A	$x - z$	positive	$x > z$ implies $x - z > 0$
B	$x - y$	positive	$x > y$ implies $x - y > 0$
C	$y - x$	negative	$x - y > 0$ implies $y - x < 0$
D	$z - y$	negative	$y > z$ implies $0 > z - y$
E	$z - x$	negative	$x - z > 0$ implies $z - x < 0$

Since the expressions in A and B represent positive numbers and the expressions in C, D, and E represent negative numbers, the latter can be eliminated because every negative number is less than every positive number. To determine which of $x - z$ and $x - y$ is greater, consider the placement of points with coordinates x, y, and z on the number line.

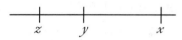

The distance between x and z (that is, $x - z$) is the sum of the distance between x and y (that is, $x - y$) and the distance between y and z (that is, $y - z$). Therefore, $(x - z) > (x - y)$, which means that $x - z$ represents the greater of the numbers represented by $(x - z)$ and $(x - y)$. Thus, $x - z$ represents the greatest of the numbers represented by the answer choices.

Alternatively,

$y > z$ given

$-y < -z$ multiply both sides by -1

$x - y < x - z$ add x to both sides

Thus, $x - z$ represents the greater of the numbers represented by $(x - z)$ and $(x - y)$. Therefore, $x - z$ represents the greatest of the numbers represented by the answer choices.

The correct answer is A.

8. To order certain plants from a catalog, it costs $3.00 per plant, plus a 5 percent sales tax, plus $6.95 for shipping and handling regardless of the number of plants ordered. If Company C ordered these plants from the catalog at the total cost of $69.95, how many plants did Company C order?

(A) 22
(B) 21
(C) 20
(D) 19
(E) 18

Algebra First-Degree Equations

Letting x represent the number of plants Company C bought from the catalog, then, in dollars, $3.00x$ is the cost of the plants, $(0.05)(3.00x)$ is the sales tax, and 6.95 is the shipping and handling fee. It follows that

$3.00x + (0.05)(3.00x) + 6.95 = 69.95$ plants + tax + shipping = total

$(3.00x)(1.05) + 6.95 = 69.95$ add like terms

$(3.00x)(1.05) = 63.00$ subtract 6.95 from both sides

$x = 20$ divide both sides by $(3.00)(1.05)$

Therefore, Company C bought 20 plants from the catalog.

The correct answer is C.

9. A rug manufacturer produces rugs at a cost of $75 per rug. What is the manufacturer's gross profit from the sale of 150 rugs if $\frac{2}{3}$ of the rugs are sold for $150 per rug and the rest are sold for $200 per rug?

(A) $10,350
(B) $11,250
(C) $13,750
(D) $16,250
(E) $17,800

Arithmetic Applied Problems; Proportions

The gross profit from the sale of 150 rugs is equal to the revenue from the sale of the rugs minus the cost of producing them. For $\frac{2}{3}$ of the 150 rugs—100 of them—the gross profit per rug is $150 – $75 = $75. For the remaining 50 rugs, the gross profit per rug is $200 − $75 = $125. The gross profit from the sale of the 150 rugs is therefore $100 × \$75 + 50 × \$125 = \$13{,}750$.

The correct answer is C.

10. The value of Maureen's investment portfolio has decreased by 5.8 percent since her initial investment in the portfolio. If her initial investment was $16,800, what is the current value of the portfolio?

(A) $7,056.00
(B) $14,280.00
(C) $15,825.60
(D) $16,702.56
(E) $17,774.40

Arithmetic Percents

Maureen's initial investment was $16,800, and it has decreased by 5.8%. Its current value is therefore (100% − 5.8%) = 94.2% of $16,800, which is equal to 0.942 × $16,800. To make the multiplication simpler, this can be expressed as $(942 × 16.8). Thus multiplying, we obtain the result of $15,825.60.

The correct answer is C.

11. Company C produces toy trucks at a cost of $5.00 each for the first 100 trucks and $3.50 for each additional truck. If 500 toy trucks were produced by Company C and sold for $10.00 each, what was Company C's gross profit?

(A) $2,250
(B) $2,500
(C) $3,100
(D) $3,250
(E) $3,500

Arithmetic Applied Problems

The company's gross profit on the 500 toy trucks is the company's revenue from selling the trucks minus the company's cost of producing the trucks. The revenue is (500)($10.00) = $5,000. The cost for the first 100 trucks is (100)($5.00) = $500, and the cost for the other 400 trucks is (400)($3.50) = $1,400 for a total cost of $500 + $1,400 = $1,900. Thus, the company's gross profit is $5,000 − $1,900 = $3,100.

The correct answer is C.

Division	Profit or Loss (in millions of dollars)				
	1991	1992	1993	1994	1995
A	1.1	(3.4)	1.9	2.0	0.6
R	(2.3)	5.5	(4.5)	3.9	(2.9)
C	10.0	(6.6)	5.3	1.1	(3.0)

12. The annual profit or loss for the three divisions of Company T for the years 1991 through 1995 are summarized in the table shown, where losses are enclosed in parentheses. For which division and which three consecutive years shown was the division's profit or loss for the three-year period closest to $0 ?

(A) Division A for 1991–1993
(B) Division A for 1992–1994
(C) Division B for 1991–1993
(D) Division B for 1993–1995
(E) Division C for 1992–1994

Arithmetic Applied Problems

For completeness, the table shows all 9 of the profit or loss amounts, in millions of dollars, for each of the 3 divisions and the 3 three-year periods.

	1991–1993	1992–1994	1993–1995
A	−0.4	0.5	4.5
B	−1.3	4.9	−3.5
C	8.7	**−0.2**	3.4

The correct answer is E.

13. Of the following, which is least?

(A) $\dfrac{0.03}{0.00071}$

(B) $\dfrac{0.03}{0.0071}$

(C) $\dfrac{0.03}{0.071}$

(D) $\dfrac{0.03}{0.71}$

(E) $\dfrac{0.03}{7.1}$

Arithmetic Operations on Rational Numbers

Since the numerator of all of the fractions in the answer choices is 0.03, the least of the fractions will be the fraction with the greatest denominator. The greatest denominator is 7.1, and so the least of the fractions is $\frac{0.03}{7.1}$.

The correct answer is E.

14. If the average (arithmetic mean) of 5 numbers $j, j + 5, 2j - 1, 4j - 2$, and $5j - 1$ is 8, what is the value of j?

(A) $\frac{1}{3}$

(B) $\frac{7}{13}$

(C) 1

(D) 3

(E) 8

Algebra First-Degree Equations

$\dfrac{j + (j + 5) + (2j - 1) + (4j - 2) + (5j - 1)}{5} = 8$	given
$j + (j + 5) + (2j - 1) + (4j - 2) + (5j - 1) = 40$	multiply both sides by 5
$13j + 1 = 40$	combine like terms
$13j = 39$	subtract 1 from both sides
$j = 3$	divide both sides by 13

The correct answer is D.

15. There are five sales agents in a certain real estate office. One month Andy sold twice as many properties as Ellen, Bob sold 3 more than Ellen, Cary sold twice as many as Bob, and Dora sold as many as Bob and Ellen together. Who sold the most properties that month?

(A) Andy

(B) Bob

(C) Cary

(D) Dora

(E) Ellen

Algebra Order

Let x represent the number of properties that Ellen sold, where $x \geq 0$. Then, since Andy sold twice as many properties as Ellen, $2x$ represents the number of properties that Andy sold. Bob sold 3 more properties than Ellen, so $(x + 3)$ represents the number of properties that Bob sold. Cary sold twice as many properties as Bob, so $2(x + 3) = (2x + 6)$ represents the number of properties that Cary sold. Finally, Dora sold as many properties as Bob and Ellen combined, so $[(x + 3) + x] = (2x + 3)$ represents the number of properties that Dora sold. The following table summarizes these results.

Agent	Properties Sold
Andy	$2x$
Bob	$x + 3$
Cary	$2x + 6$
Dora	$2x + 3$
Ellen	x

Since $x \geq 0$, clearly $2x + 6$ exceeds $x, x + 3$, $2x$, and $2x + 3$. Therefore, Cary sold the most properties.

The correct answer is C.

16. In a field day at a school, each child who competed in n events and scored a total of p points was given an overall score of $\frac{p}{n} + n$. Andrew competed in 1 event and scored 9 points. Jason competed in 3 events and scored 5, 6, and 7 points, respectively. What was the ratio of Andrew's overall score to Jason's overall score?

(A) $\frac{10}{23}$

(B) $\frac{7}{10}$

(C) $\frac{4}{5}$

(D) $\frac{10}{9}$

(E) $\frac{12}{7}$

Algebra Applied Problems; Substitution

Andrew participated in 1 event and scored

9 points, so his overall score was $\frac{9}{1} + 1 = 10$. Jason

participated in 3 events and scored $5 + 6 + 7 =$

18 points, so his overall score was $\frac{18}{3} + 3 = 9$. The

ratio of Andrew's overall score to Jason's overall

score was $\frac{10}{9}$.

The correct answer is D.

17. A certain work plan for September requires that a work team, working every day, produce an average of 200 items per day. For the first half of the month, the team produced an average of 150 items per day. How many items per day must the team average during the second half of the month if it is to attain the average daily production rate required by the work plan?

(A)   225
(B)   250
(C)   275
(D)   300
(E)   350

Arithmetic Rate Problem

The work plan requires that the team produce an average of 200 items per day in September. Because the team has only produced an average of 150 items per day in the first half of September, it has a shortfall of $200 - 150 = 50$ items per day for the first half of the month. The team must make up for this shortfall in the second half of the month, which has an equal number of days as the first half of the month. The team must therefore produce in the second half of the month an average amount per day that is 50 items greater than the required average of 200 items per day for the entire month. This amount for the second half of September is 250 items per day.

The correct answer is B.

18. A company sells radios for $15.00 each. It costs the company $14.00 per radio to produce 1,000 radios and $13.50 per radio to produce 2,000 radios. How much greater will the company's gross profit be from the production and sale of 2,000 radios than from the production and sale of 1,000 radios?

(A) $500
(B) $1,000
(C) $1,500
(D) $2,000
(E) $2,500

Arithmetic Applied Problems

If the company produces and sells 1,000 radios, its gross profit from the sale of these radios is equal to the total revenue from the sale of these radios minus the total cost. The total cost is equal to the number of radios produced multiplied by the production cost per radio: $1,000 \times \$15.00$. The total revenue is equal to the number of radios sold multiplied by the selling price: $1,000 \times \$14.00$. The gross profit in this case is therefore $1,000 \times \$15.00 - 1,000 \times \$14.00 = 1,000 \times (\$15.00 - \$14.00) = 1,000 (\$1.00) = \$1,000$. If 2,000 radios are produced and sold, the total cost is equal to $2,000 \times \$13.50$ and the total revenue is equal to $2,000 \times \$15.00$. The gross profit in this case is therefore $2,000 \times \$15.00 - 2,000 \times \$13.50 = 2,000 \times (\$15.00 - \$13.50) = 2,000 \times (\$1.50) = \$3,000$. This profit of $3,000 is $2,000 greater than the gross profit of $1,000 from producing and selling 1,000 radios.

The correct answer is D.

19. Which of the following represent positive numbers?

  I. $-3 - (-5)$
  II. $(-3)(-5)$
  III. $-5 - (-3)$

(A)   I only
(B)   II only
(C)   III only
(D)   I and II
(E)   II and III

Arithmetic Operations on Integers

Find the value of each expression to determine if it is positive.

I. $-3 - (-5) = -3 + 5 = 2$, which is positive.

II. $(-3)(-5) = 15$, which is positive.

III. $-5 - (-3) = -5 + 3 = -2$, which is not positive.

The correct answer is D.

20. A grocer has 400 pounds of coffee in stock, 20 percent of which is decaffeinated. If the grocer buys another 100 pounds of coffee of which 60 percent is decaffeinated, what percent, by weight, of the grocer's stock of coffee is decaffeinated?

    (A) 28%
    (B) 30%
    (C) 32%
    (D) 34%
    (E) 40%

Arithmetic Percents

The grocer has 400 pounds of coffee in stock, of which $(400)(20\%) = 80$ pounds is decaffeinated coffee. Therefore, if the grocer buys 100 pounds of coffee, of which $(100)(60\%) = 60$ pounds is decaffeinated coffee, then the percent of the grocer's stock of coffee that is decaffeinated would be $\dfrac{80 + 60}{400 + 100} = \dfrac{140}{500} = \dfrac{28}{100} = 28\%$.

The correct answer is A.

21. The toll T, in dollars, for a truck using a certain bridge is given by the formula $T = 1.50 + 0.50(x - 2)$, where x is the number of axles on the truck. What is the toll for an 18-wheel truck that has 2 wheels on its front axle and 4 wheels on each of its other axles?

    (A) $2.50
    (B) $3.00
    (C) $3.50
    (D) $4.00
    (E) $5.00

Algebra Operations on Rational Numbers

The 18-wheel truck has 2 wheels on its front axle and 4 wheels on each of its other axles, and so if A represents the number of axles on the truck in addition to the front axle, then $2 + 4A = 18$, from which it follows that $4A = 16$ and $A = 4$. Therefore, the total number of axles on the truck is $1 + A = 1 + 4 = 5$. Then, using $T = 1.50 + 0.50(x - 2)$, where x is the number of axles on the truck and $x = 5$, it follows that $T = 1.50 + 0.50(5 - 2) = 1.50 + 1.50 = 3.00$. Therefore, the toll for the truck is $3.00.

The correct answer is B.

22. For what value of x between -4 and 4, inclusive, is the value of $x^2 - 10x + 16$ the greatest?

    (A) -4
    (B) -2
    (C) 0
    (D) 2
    (E) 4

Algebra Second-Degree Equations

Given the expression $x^2 - 10x + 16$, a table of values can be created for the corresponding function $f(x) = x^2 - 10x + 16$ and the graph in the standard (x,y) coordinate plane can be sketched by plotting selected points:

x	$f(x)$
-4	72
-3	55
-2	40
-1	27
0	16
1	7
2	0
3	-5
4	-8
5	-9
6	-8
7	-5
8	0
9	7

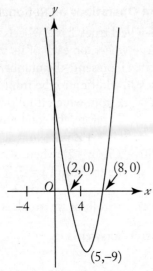

It is clear from both the table of values and the sketch of the graph that as the value of x increases from -4 to 4, the values of $x^2 - 10x + 16$ decrease. Therefore, the value of $x^2 - 10x + 16$ is greatest when $x = -4$.

Alternatively, the given expression, $x^2 - 10x + 16$, has the form $ax^2 + bx + c$, where $a = 1$, $b = -10$, and $c = 16$. The graph in the standard (x,y) coordinate plane of the corresponding function $f(x) = ax^2 + bx + c$ is a parabola with vertex at $x = -\dfrac{b}{2a}$, and so the vertex of the graph of $f(x) = x^2 - 10x + 16$ is at

$$x = -\left(\frac{-10}{2(1)}\right) = 5.$$

Because $a = 1$ and 1 is positive, this parabola opens upward and values of $x^2 - 10x + 16$ decrease as x increases from -4 to 4. Therefore, the greatest value of $x^2 - 10x + 16$ for all values of x between -4 and 4, inclusive, is at $x = -4$.

The correct answer is A.

23. If $x = -\dfrac{5}{8}$ and $y = -\dfrac{1}{2}$, what is the value of the expression $-2x - y^2$?

(A) $-\dfrac{3}{2}$

(B) -1

(C) 1

(D) $\dfrac{3}{2}$

(E) $\dfrac{7}{4}$

Algebra Fractions

If $x = -\dfrac{5}{8}$ and $y = -\dfrac{1}{2}$, then

$$-2x - y^2 = -2\left(-\frac{5}{8}\right) - \left(-\frac{1}{2}\right)^2 = \frac{5}{4} - \frac{1}{4} = \frac{4}{4} = 1.$$

The correct answer is C.

24. If $x - y = R$ and $xy = S$, then $(x - 2)(y + 2) =$

(A) $R + S - 4$
(B) $R + 2S - 4$
(C) $2R - S - 4$
(D) $2R + S - 4$
(E) $2R + S$

Algebra Simplifying Algebraic Expressions; Substitution

$$\begin{aligned}
(x - 2)(y + 2) &= xy + 2x - 2y - 4 \quad \text{multiply binomials}\\
&= xy + 2(x - y) - 4 \quad \text{distributive principle}\\
&= S + 2R - 4 \quad \text{substitution}\\
&= 2R + S - 4 \quad \text{commutative principle}
\end{aligned}$$

The correct answer is D.

25. For positive integers a and b, the remainder when a is divided by b is equal to the remainder when b is divided by a. Which of the following could be a value of ab?

I.   24
II. 30
III. 36

(A) II only
(B) III only
(C) I and II only
(D) II and III only
(E) I, II, and III

Arithmetic Properties of Integers

We are given that the remainder when a is divided by b is equal to the remainder when b is divided by a, and asked about possible values of ab. We thus need to find what our given condition implies about a and b.

We consider two cases: $a = b$ and $a \neq b$.

If $a = b$, then our given condition is trivially satisfied: the remainder when a is divided by a is equal to the remainder when a is divided by b. The condition thus allows that a be equal to b.

Now consider the case of $a \neq b$. Either a < b or $b < a$. Supposing that $a < b$, the remainder when a is divided by b is simply a. (For example, if 7 is divided by 10, then the remainder is 7.) However, according to our given condition, this remainder, a, is also the remainder when b is divided by a, which is impossible. If b is divided by a, then the remainder must be less than a. (For example, for any number that is divided by 10, the remainder cannot be 10 or greater.) Similar reasoning applies if we suppose that $b < a$. This is also impossible.

We thus see that a must be equal to b, and consider the statements I, II, and III.

I.   Factored in terms of prime numbers, $24 = 3 \times 2 \times 2 \times 2$. Because "3" occurs only once in the factorization, we see that there is no integer a such that $a \times a = 24$. Based on the reasoning above, we see that 24 cannot be a value of ab.

II. Factored in terms of prime numbers, $30 = 5 \times 3 \times 2$. Because there is no integer a such that $a \times a = 30$, we see that 30 cannot be a value of ab.

III. Because $36 = 6 \times 6$, we see that 36 is a possible value of ab (with $a = b$).

The correct answer is B.

26. List S consists of the positive integers that are multiples of 9 and are less than 100. What is the median of the integers in S?

(A)   36
(B)   45
(C)   49
(D)   54
(E)   63

Arithmetic Series and Sequences

In the set of positive integers less than 100, the greatest multiple of 9 is 99 (9×11) and the least multiple of 9 is 9 (9×1). The sequence of positive multiples of 9 that are less than 100 is therefore

the sequence of numbers $9 \times k$, where k ranges from 1 through 11. The median of the numbers k from 1 through 11 is 6. Therefore the median of the numbers $9 \times k$, where k ranges from 1 through 11, is $9 \times 6 = 54$.

The correct answer is D.

27. A rope 20.6 meters long is cut into two pieces. If the length of one piece of rope is 2.8 meters shorter than the length of the other, what is the length, in meters, of the longer piece of rope?

(A)   7.5
(B)   8.9
(C)   9.9
(D)   10.3
(E)   11.7

Algebra First-Degree Equations

If x represents the length of the longer piece of rope, then $x - 2.8$ represents the length of the shorter piece, where both lengths are in meters. The total length of the two pieces of rope is 20.6 meters so,

$$\begin{aligned} x + (x - 2.8) &= 20.6 \quad \text{given} \\ 2x - 2.8 &= 20.6 \quad \text{add like terms} \\ 2x &= 23.4 \quad \text{add 2.8 to both sides} \\ x &= 11.7 \quad \text{divide both sides by 2} \end{aligned}$$

Thus, the length of the longer piece of rope is 11.7 meters.

The correct answer is E.

28. If x and y are integers and $x - y$ is odd, which of the following must be true?

I. xy is even.
II. $x^2 + y^2$ is odd.
III. $(x + y)^2$ is even.

(A)   I only
(B)   II only
(C)   III only
(D)   I and II only
(E)   I, II, and III

Arithmetic Properties of Numbers

We are given that x and y are integers and that $x - y$ is odd, and then asked, for various operations on x and y, whether the results of the operations are odd or even. It is therefore useful to determine, given that $x - y$ is odd, whether x and y are odd or even. If both x and y are even—that is, divisible by 2—then $x - y = 2m - 2n = 2(m - n)$ for integers m and n. We thus see if both x and y are even then $x - y$ cannot be odd. And because $x - y$ *is* odd, we see that x and y cannot both be even. Similarly, if both x and y are odd, then, for integers j and k, $x = 2j + 1$ and $y = 2k + 1$. Therefore, $x - y = (2j + 1) - (2k + 1)$. The ones cancel, and we are left with $x - y = 2j - 2k = 2(j - k)$. Because $2(j - k)$ would be even, x and y cannot both be odd if $x - y$ is odd. It follows from all of this that one of x or y must be even and the other odd.

Now consider the statements I through III.

I. If one of x or y is even, then one of x or y is divisible by 2. It follows that xy is divisible by 2 and that xy is even.

II. Given that a number x or y is odd—not divisible by 2—we know that its product with itself is not divisible by 2 and is therefore odd. On the other hand, given that a number x or y is even, we know that its product with itself *is* divisible by 2 and is therefore even. The sum $x^2 + y^2$ is therefore the sum of an even number and an odd number. In such a case, the sum can be written as $(2m) + (2n + 1) = 2(m + n) + 1$, with m and n integers. It follows that $x^2 + y^2$ is not divisible by 2 and is therefore odd.

III. We know that one of x or y is even and the other is odd. We can therefore see from the discussion of statement II that $x + y$ is odd, and then also see, from the discussion of statement II, that the product of $x + y$ with itself, $(x + y)^2$, is odd.

The correct answer is D.

29. On Monday, the opening price of a certain stock was $100 per share and its closing price was $110 per share. On Tuesday the closing price of the stock was 10 percent less than its closing price on Monday, and on Wednesday the closing price of the stock was 4 percent greater than its closing price on Tuesday. What was the approximate percent change in the price of the stock from its opening price on Monday to its closing price on Wednesday?

(A) A decrease of 6%
(B) A decrease of 4%
(C) A decrease of 1%
(D) An increase of 3%
(E) An increase of 4%

Arithmetic Percents

The closing share price on Tuesday was 10% less than the closing price on Monday, $110. 10% of $110 is equal to $0.1 \times \$110 = \$11$, so the closing price on Tuesday was $\$110 - \$11 = \$99$. The closing price on Wednesday was 4% greater than this: $\$99 + (0.04 \times \$99) = \$99 + \$3.96 = \$102.96$. This value, $102.96, is 2.96% greater than $100, the opening price on Monday. The percentage change from the opening share price on Monday is therefore an increase of approximately 3%, which is the closest of the available answers to an increase of 2.96%.

The correct answer is D.

30. $1 - 0.000001 =$

(A) $(1.01)(0.99)$
(B) $(1.11)(0.99)$
(C) $(1.001)(0.999)$
(D) $(1.111)(0.999)$
(E) $(1.0101)(0.0909)$

Arithmetic Place Value

The task in this question is to find among the available answers the expression that is equal to $1 - 0.000001 = 0.999999$. In the case of answer choice C, the first of the two factors, (1.001), is equal to $1 + 0.001$. One may therefore observe that $(1.001)(0.999) = (1 + 0.001)(0.999) = 0.999 + 0.000999 = 0.999999$. Answer choice C is therefore a correct answer.

For answer choice A, $(1.01)(0.99) = (1 + 0.01)$ $(0.99) = 0.9999$. This answer choice is therefore incorrect. For answer choice B, $(1.11)(0.99) = (1 + 0.1 + 0.01)(0.99) = 0.99 + 0.099 + 0.0099 = 1.0989$. This answer choice is therefore incorrect. For answer choice D, $(1.111)(0.999) = 0.999 + 0.0999 + 0.00999 + 0.000999 = 1.109889$. This answer choice is therefore incorrect. For answer choice E, $(1.0101)(0.909) = 0.909 + 0.00909 + 0.0000909 = 0.9181809$. This answer choice is therefore incorrect.

The correct answer is C.

31. In a certain history class of 17 juniors and seniors, each junior has written 2 book reports and each senior has written 3 book reports. If the 17 students have written a total of 44 book reports, how many juniors are in the class?

    (A) 7
    (B) 8
    (C) 9
    (D) 10
    (E) 11

Algebra Simultaneous Equations

Letting j and s, respectively, represent the juniors and seniors in the class, it is given that $j + s = 17$ or $s = 17 - j$. Also, since it is given that each junior has written 2 book reports and each senior has written 3 book reports for a total of 44 book reports, it follows that $2j + 3s = 44$ or $2j + 3(17 - j) = 44$. Therefore, $j = 3(17) - 44 = 7$.

The correct answer is A.

32. $|-4|(|-20| - |5|) =$

    (A) -100
    (B) -60
    (C) 60
    (D) 75
    (E) 100

Arithmetic Absolute Value

$|-4|(|-20| - |5|) = 4(20 - 5) = 4 \times 15 = 60$

The correct answer is C.

33. Of the total amount that Jill spent on a shopping trip, excluding taxes, she spent 50 percent on clothing, 20 percent on food, and 30 percent on other items. If Jill paid a 4 percent tax on the clothing, no tax on the food, and an 8 percent tax on all other items, then the total tax that she paid was what percent of the total amount that she spent, excluding taxes?

    (A) 2.8%
    (B) 3.6%
    (C) 4.4%
    (D) 5.2%
    (E) 6.0%

Arithmetic Applied Problems

Let T represent the total amount Jill spent, excluding taxes. Jill paid a 4% tax on the clothing she bought, which accounted for 50% of the total amount she spent, and so the tax she paid on the clothing was $(0.04)(0.5T)$. Jill paid an 8% tax on the other items she bought, which accounted for 30% of the total amount she spent, and so the tax she paid on the other items was $(0.08)(0.3T)$. Therefore, the total amount of tax Jill paid was $(0.04)(0.5T) + (0.08)(0.3T) = 0.02T + 0.024T = 0.044T$. The tax as a percent of the total amount Jill spent, excluding taxes, was

$$\left(\frac{0.044T}{T} \times 100 \right)\% = 4.4\%.$$

The correct answer is C.

34. How many integers x satisfy both $2 < x \leq 4$ and $0 \leq x \leq 3$?

    (A) 5
    (B) 4
    (C) 3
    (D) 2
    (E) 1

Arithmetic Inequalities

The integers that satisfy $2 < x \leq 4$ are 3 and 4. The integers that satisfy $0 \leq x \leq 3$ are 0, 1, 2, and 3. The only integer that satisfies both $2 < x \leq 4$ and $0 \leq x \leq 3$ is 3, and so there is only one integer that satisfies both $2 < x \leq 4$ and $0 \leq x \leq 3$.

The correct answer is E.

35. At the opening of a trading day at a certain stock exchange, the price per share of stock K was $8. If the price per share of stock K was $9 at the closing of the day, what was the percent increase in the price per share of stock K for that day?

    (A) 1.4%
    (B) 5.9%
    (C) 11.1%
    (D) 12.5%
    (E) 23.6%

Arithmetic Percents

An increase from $8 to $9 represents an increase of $\left(\dfrac{9-8}{8} \times 100 \right)\% = \dfrac{100}{8}\% = 12.5\%$.

The correct answer is D.

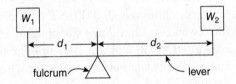

36. As shown in the diagram above, a lever resting on a fulcrum has weights of w_1 pounds and w_2 pounds, located d_1 feet and d_2 feet from the fulcrum. The lever is balanced and $w_1 d_1 = w_2 d_2$. Suppose w_1 is 50 pounds and w_2 is 30 pounds. If d_1 is 4 feet less than d_2, what is d_2, in feet?

    (A) 1.5
    (B) 2.5
    (C) 6
    (D) 10
    (E) 20

Algebra First-Degree Equations; Substitution

Given $w_1 d_1 = w_2 d_2$, $w_1 = 50$, $w_2 = 30$, and $d_1 = d_2 - 4$, it follows that $50(d_2 - 4) = 30d_2$, and so

$$50(d_2 - 4) = 30d_2 \quad \text{given}$$
$$50d_2 - 200 = 30d_2 \quad \text{distributive principle}$$
$$20d_2 = 200 \quad \text{add } 200 - 30d_2 \text{ to both sides}$$
$$d_2 = 10 \quad \text{divide both sides by 20}$$

The correct answer is D.

37. If r and s are positive integers such that $(2^r)(4^s) = 16$, then $2r + s =$

    (A) 2
    (B) 3
    (C) 4
    (D) 5
    (E) 6

Algebra Exponents

Using the rules of exponents,

$$\begin{aligned}
(2^r)(4^s) &= 16 \quad \text{given} \\
(2^r)(2^{2s}) &= 2^4 \quad 4^s = (2^2)^s = 2^{2s}, 16 = 2^4 \\
2^{r+2s} &= 2^4 \quad \text{addition property of exponents}
\end{aligned}$$

Thus, $r + 2s = 4$. However, the problem asks for the value of $2r + s$. Since r and s are positive integers, $s < 2$; otherwise, r would not be positive. Therefore, $s = 1$, and it follows that $r + (2)(1) = 4$, or $r = 2$. The value of $2r + s$ is $(2)(2) + 1 = 5$.

Alternatively, since $(2^r)(4^s) = 16$ and both r and s are positive, it follows that $s < 2$; otherwise, $4^s \geq 16$ and r would not be positive. Therefore, $s = 1$ and $(2^r)(4) = 16$. It follows that $2^r = 4$ and $r = 2$. The value of $2r + s$ is $(2)(2) + 1 = 5$.

The correct answer is D.

38. Three people each contributed x dollars toward the purchase of a car. They then bought the car for y dollars, an amount less than the total number of dollars contributed. If the excess amount is to be refunded to the three people in equal amounts, each person should receive a refund of how many dollars?

    (A) $\dfrac{3x - y}{3}$
    (B) $\dfrac{x - y}{3}$
    (C) $\dfrac{x - 3y}{3}$
    (D) $\dfrac{y - 3x}{3}$
    (E) $3(x - y)$

Algebra Applied Problems

The total to be refunded is equal to the total contributed minus the amount paid, or $3x - y$. If $3x - y$ is divided into three equal amounts, then each amount will be $\dfrac{3x - y}{3}$.

The correct answer is A.

39. Last week Jack worked 70 hours and earned $1,260. If he earned his regular hourly wage for the first 40 hours worked, $1\frac{1}{2}$ times his regular hourly wage for the next 20 hours worked, and 2 times his regular hourly wage for the remaining 10 hours worked, what was his regular hourly wage?

    (A) $7.00
    (B) $14.00
    (C) $18.00
    (D) $22.00
    (E) $31.50

Algebra First-Degree Equations

If w represents Jack's regular hourly wage, then Jack's earnings for the week can be represented by the sum of the following amounts, in dollars: $40w$ (his earnings for the first 40 hours he worked), $(20)(1.5w)$ (his earnings for the next 20 hours he worked), and $(10)(2w)$ (his earnings for the last 10 hours he worked). Therefore,

$$40w + (20)(1.5w) + (10)(2w) = 1,260 \quad \text{given}$$
$$90w = 1,260 \quad \text{add like terms}$$
$$w = 14 \quad \text{divide both sides by 90}$$

Jack's regular hourly wage was $14.00.

The correct answer is B.

40. If a and b are positive integers and $(2^a)^b = 2^3$, what is the value of $2^a\, 2^b$?

    (A) 6
    (B) 8
    (C) 16
    (D) 32
    (E) 64

Algebra Exponents

It is given that $(2^a)^b = 2^3$, or $2^{ab} = 2^3$. Therefore, $ab = 3$. Since a and b are positive integers, it follows that either $a = 1$ and $b = 3$, or $a = 3$ and $b = 1$. In either case $a + b = 4$, and so $2^a 2^b = 2^{a+b} = 2^4 = 16$.

The correct answer is C.

41. Five machines at a certain factory operate at the same constant rate. If four of these machines, operating simultaneously, take 30 hours to fill a certain production order, how many fewer hours does it take all five machines, operating simultaneously, to fill the same production order?

    (A) 3
    (B) 5
    (C) 6
    (D) 16
    (E) 24

Arithmetic Applied Problems

If 4 machines, working simultaneously, each work for 30 hours to fill a production order, it takes $(4)(30)$ machine hours to fill the order. If 5 machines are working simultaneously, it will take $\dfrac{(4)(30)}{5} = 24$ hours. Thus, 5 machines working simultaneously will take $30 - 24 = 6$ fewer hours to fill the production order than 4 machines working simultaneously.

The correct answer is C.

42. A certain toll station on a highway has 7 tollbooths, and each tollbooth collects $0.75 from each vehicle that passes it. From 6 o'clock yesterday morning to 12 o'clock midnight, vehicles passed each of the tollbooths at the average rate of 4 vehicles per minute. Approximately how much money did the toll station collect during that time period?

    (A) $1,500
    (B) $3,000
    (C) $11,500
    (D) $23,000
    (E) $30,000

Arithmetic Rate Problem

On average, 4 vehicles pass each tollbooth every minute. There are 7 tollbooths at the station, and each passing vehicle pays $0.75. Therefore, the average rate, per minute, at which money is collected by the toll station is $ $(7 \times 4 \times 0.75) =$ $ $(7 \times 4 \times \frac{3}{4}) = $ (7 \times 3) = 21. From 6 a.m. through midnight there are 18 hours. And because 18 hours is equal to 18×60 minutes, from 6 a.m. through midnight there are 1,080 minutes. The total amount of money collected by the toll station during this period is therefore $1,080 \times $21 = $22,680$, which is approximately $23,000.

The correct answer is D.

43. How many integers between 1 and 16, inclusive, have exactly 3 different positive integer factors?

    (Note: 6 is NOT such an integer because 6 has 4 different positive integer factors: 1, 2, 3, and 6.)

    (A)   1
    (B)   2
    (C)   3
    (D)   4
    (E)   6

Arithmetic Properties of Numbers

Using the process of elimination to eliminate integers that do NOT have exactly 3 different positive integer factors, the integer 1 can be eliminated since 1 has only 1 positive integer factor, namely 1 itself. Because each prime number has exactly 2 positive factors, each prime number between 1 and 16, inclusive, (namely, 2, 3, 5, 7, 11, and 13) can be eliminated. The integer 6 can also be eliminated since it was used as an example of an integer with exactly 4 positive integer factors. Check the positive integer factors of each of the remaining integers.

Integer	Positive integer factors	Number of factors
4	1, 2, 4	3
8	1, 2, 4, 8	4
9	1, 3, 9	3
10	1, 2, 5, 10	4
12	1, 2, 3, 4, 6, 12	6
14	1, 2, 7, 14	4
15	1, 3, 5, 15	4
16	1, 2, 4, 8, 16	5

Just the integers 4 and 9 have exactly 3 positive integer factors.

Alternatively, if the integer n, where $n > 1$, has exactly 3 positive integer factors, which include 1 and n, then n has exactly one other positive integer factor, say p. Since any factor of p would also be a factor of n, then p is prime, and so p is the only prime factor of n. It follows that $n = p^k$ for some integer $k > 1$. But if $k \geq 3$, then p^2 is a factor of n in addition to 1, p, and n, which contradicts the fact that n has exactly 3 positive integer factors. Therefore, $k = 2$ and $n = p^2$, which means that n is the square of a prime number. Of the integers between 1 and 16, inclusive, only 4 and 9 are the squares of prime numbers.

The correct answer is B.

44. Stephanie has $2\frac{1}{4}$ cups of milk on hand and makes 2 batches of cookies, using $\frac{2}{3}$ cup of milk for each batch of cookies. Which of the following describes the amount of milk remaining after she makes the cookies?

    (A)   Less than $\frac{1}{2}$ cup

    (B)   Between $\frac{1}{2}$ cup and $\frac{3}{4}$ cup

    (C)   Between $\frac{3}{4}$ cup and 1 cup

    (D)   Between 1 cup and $1\frac{1}{2}$ cups

    (E)   More than $1\frac{1}{2}$ cups

Arithmetic Applied Problems

In cups, the amount of milk remaining is

$2\frac{1}{4} - 2\left(\frac{2}{3}\right) = \frac{9}{4} - \frac{4}{3} = \frac{27-16}{12} = \frac{11}{12}$, which is

greater than $\frac{3}{4} = \frac{9}{12}$ and less than 1.

The correct answer is C.

45. The expression $n!$ is defined as the product of the integers from 1 through n. If p is the product of the integers from 100 through 299 and q is the product of the integers from 200 through 299, which of the following is equal to $\frac{p}{q}$?

(A)   99!

(B)   199!

(C) $\dfrac{199!}{99!}$

(D) $\dfrac{299!}{99!}$

(E) $\dfrac{299!}{199!}$

Arithmetic Series and Sequences

The number p is equal to $100 \times 101 \times 102 \times \ldots \times 299$ and the number q is equal to $200 \times 201 \times 202 \times \ldots \times 299$. The number $\frac{p}{q}$

is thus equal to $\dfrac{100 \times 101 \times 102 \times \ldots \times 299}{200 \times 201 \times 202 \times \ldots \times 299} =$

$\dfrac{100 \times 101 \times 102 \times \ldots \times 199 \times 200 \times 201 \times 202 \times \ldots \times 299}{200 \times 201 \times 202 \times \ldots \times 299}.$

Canceling $200 \times 201 \times 202 \times \ldots \times 299$ from the numerator and the denominator, we see that

$\frac{p}{q} = 100 \times 101 \times 102 \times \ldots \times 199$. Note that the

multiplication in this expression for $\frac{p}{q}$ begins

with 100 (the smallest of the numbers being multiplied), whereas the multiplication in $n! = 1 \times 2 \times 3 \times \ldots \times n$ begins with 1. Starting with 199! as our numerator, we thus need to find a denominator that will cancel the undesired elements of the multiplication (in 199!). This number is $1 \times 2 \times 3 \times \ldots \times 99 = 99!$

That is, $\frac{p}{q} = 100 \times 101 \times 102 \times \ldots \times 199 =$

$\dfrac{1 \times 2 \times 3 \times \ldots \times 99 \times 100 \times 101 \times 102 \times \ldots \times 199}{1 \times 2 \times 3 \times \ldots \times 99} = \dfrac{199!}{99!}.$

The correct answer is C.

46. A school club plans to package and sell dried fruit to raise money. The club purchased 12 containers of dried fruit, each containing $16\frac{3}{4}$ pounds. What is the maximum number of individual bags of dried fruit, each containing $\frac{1}{4}$ pounds, that can be sold from the dried fruit the club purchased?

(A)   50

(B)   64

(C)   67

(D)   768

(E)   804

Arithmetic Applied Problems; Operations with Fractions

The 12 containers, each containing $16\frac{3}{4}$ pounds

of dried fruit, contain a total of $(12)\left(16\frac{3}{4}\right) =$

$(12)\left(\frac{67}{4}\right) = (3)(67) = 201$ pounds of dried fruit,

which will make $\dfrac{201}{\frac{1}{4}} = (201)(4) = 804$ individual

bags that can be sold.

The correct answer is E.

Height	Price
Less than 5 ft	$14.95
5 ft to 6 ft	$17.95
Over 6 ft	$21.95

47. A nursery sells fruit trees priced as shown in the chart above. In its inventory 54 trees are less than 5 feet in height. If the expected revenue from the sale of its entire stock is estimated at $2,450, approximately how much of this will come from the sale of trees that are at least 5 feet tall?

(A) $1,730

(B) $1,640

(C) $1,410

(D) $1,080

(E) $810

Arithmetic Applied Problems

If the nursery sells its entire stock of trees, it will sell the 54 trees that are less than 5 feet in height at the price per tree of $14.95 shown in the chart. The expected revenue from the sale of the trees that are less than 5 feet tall is therefore $54 \times \$14.95 = \$807.30$. The revenue from the sale of the trees that are at least 5 feet tall is thus equal to the total revenue from the sale of the entire stock of trees minus $807.30. The revenue from the sale of the entire stock of trees is estimated at $2,450. Based on this estimate, the revenue from the sale of the trees that are at least 5 feet tall will be $2,450 − $807.30 = $1,642.70, which is approximately $1,640.

The correct answer is B.

48. A certain bridge is 4,024 feet long. Approximately how many minutes does it take to cross this bridge at a constant speed of 20 miles per hour? (1 mile = 5,280 feet)

(A) 1
(B) 2
(C) 4
(D) 6
(E) 7

Arithmetic Applied Problems

First, convert 4,024 feet to miles since the speed is given in miles per hour:

$$4{,}024 \text{ ft} \times \frac{1 \text{ mi}}{5{,}280 \text{ ft}} = \frac{4{,}024}{5{,}280} \text{ mi.}$$

Now, divide by 20 mph: $\frac{4{,}024}{5{,}280} \text{ mi} \div \frac{20 \text{ mi}}{1 \text{ hr}}$

$$= \frac{4{,}024 \text{ mi}}{5{,}280} \times \frac{1 \text{ hr}}{20 \text{ mi}} = \frac{4{,}024 \text{ hr}}{(5{,}280)(20)}.$$

Last, convert $\frac{4{,}024 \text{ hr}}{(5{,}280)(20)}$ to minutes:

$$\frac{4{,}024 \text{ hr}}{(5{,}280)(20)} \times \frac{60 \text{ min}}{1 \text{ hr}} = \frac{(4{,}024)(60) \text{ min}}{(5{,}280)(20)} \approx$$

$$\frac{4{,}000}{5{,}000} \times \frac{60}{20} \text{ min. Then, } \frac{4{,}000}{5{,}000} \times \frac{60}{20} \text{ min} =$$

$= 0.8 \times 3 \text{ min} \approx 2 \text{ min}$. Thus, at a constant speed of 20 miles per hour, it takes approximately 2 minutes to cross the bridge.

The correct answer is B.

49. A purse contains 57 coins, all of which are nickels, dimes, or quarters. If the purse contains x dimes and 8 more nickels than dimes, which of the following gives the number of quarters the purse contains in terms of x ?

(A) 2x + 49
(B) 2x + 49
(C) 2x − 65
(D) 49 − 2x
(E) 65 − 2x

Algebra First-Degree Equations

Letting Q be the number of quarters, there are $(x + 8)$ nickels, x dimes, and Q quarters for a total of 57 coins.

$$\begin{aligned} (x + 8) + x + Q &= 57 && \text{given} \\ 2x + 8 + Q &= 57 && \text{combine like terms} \\ Q &= 49 - 2x && \text{subtract } 2x + 8 \text{ from} \\ & && \text{both sides} \end{aligned}$$

The correct answer is D.

50. The annual interest rate earned by an investment increased by 10 percent from last year to this year. If the annual interest rate earned by the investment this year was 11 percent, what was the annual interest rate last year?

(A) 1%
(B) 1.1%
(C) 9.1%
(D) 10%
(E) 10.8%

Arithmetic Percents

If L is the annual interest rate last year, then the annual interest rate this year is 10% greater than L, or $1.1L$. It is given that $1.1L = 11\%$. Therefore, $L = \frac{11\%}{1.1} = 10\%$. (Note that if the given information had been that the investment increased by *10 percentage points*, then the equation would have been $L + 10\% = 11\%$.)

The correct answer is D.

51. A total of 5 liters of gasoline is to be poured into two empty containers with capacities of 2 liters and 6 liters, respectively, such that both containers will be filled to the same percent of their respective capacities. What amount of gasoline, in liters, must be poured into the 6-liter container?

    (A) $4\frac{1}{2}$

    (B) 4

    (C) $3\frac{3}{4}$

    (D) 3

    (E) $1\frac{1}{4}$

Algebra Ratio and Proportion

If x represents the amount, in liters, of gasoline poured into the 6-liter container, then $5 - x$ represents the amount, in liters, of gasoline poured into the 2-liter container. After the gasoline is poured into the containers, the 6-liter container will be filled to $\left(\frac{x}{6} \times 100\right)\%$ of its capacity and the 2-liter container will be filled to $\left(\frac{5-x}{2} \times 100\right)\%$ of its capacity. Because these two percents are equal,

$\frac{x}{6} = \frac{5-x}{2}$	given
$2x = 6(5-x)$	multiply both sides by 12
$2x = 30 - 6x$	use distributive property
$8x = 30$	add $6x$ to both sides
$x = 3\frac{3}{4}$	divide both sides by 8

Therefore, $3\frac{3}{4}$ liters of gasoline must be poured into the 6-liter container.

The correct answer is C.

52. What is the larger of the 2 solutions of the equation $x^2 - 4x = 96$?

    (A) 8
    (B) 12
    (C) 16
    (D) 32
    (E) 100

Algebra Second-Degree Equations

It is given that $x^2 - 4x = 96$, or $x^2 - 4x - 96 = 0$, or $(x - 12)(x + 8) = 0$. Therefore, $x = 12$ or $x = -8$, and the larger of these two numbers is 12.

Alternatively, from $x^2 - 4x = 96$ it follows that $x(x - 4) = 96$. By inspection, the left side is either the product of 12 and 8, where the value of x is 12, or the product of -8 and -12, where the value of x is -8, and the larger of these two values of x is 12.

The correct answer is B.

$$x = \frac{1}{6}gt^2$$

53. In the formula shown, if g is a constant and $x = -6$ when $t = 2$, what is the value of x when $t = 4$?

    (A) -24
    (B) -20
    (C) -15
    (D) 20
    (E) 24

Algebra Formulas

Since $x = -6$ when $t = 2$, it follows that $-6 = \left(\frac{1}{6}\right)(g)(4)$ so $g = \frac{3}{2}(-6) = -9$. Then, when $t = 4$, $x = \frac{1}{6}(-9)(16) = -24$.

The correct answer is A.

54. $\dfrac{(39{,}897)(0.0096)}{198.76}$ is approximately

    (A) 0.02
    (B) 0.2
    (C) 2
    (D) 20
    (E) 200

Arithmetic Estimation

$$\frac{(39{,}897)(0.0096)}{198.76} \approx \frac{(40{,}000)(0.01)}{200} = (200)(0.01) = 2$$

The correct answer is C.

55. The "prime sum" of an integer n greater than 1 is the sum of all the prime factors of n, including repetitions. For example, the prime sum of 12 is 7, since $12 = 2 \times 2 \times 3$ and $2 + 2 + 3 = 7$. For which of the following integers is the prime sum greater than 35 ?

    (A)   440
    (B)   512
    (C)   620
    (D)   700
    (E)   750

Arithmetic Properties of Numbers

A   Since $440 = 2 \times 2 \times 2 \times 5 \times 11$, the prime sum of 440 is $2 + 2 + 2 + 5 + 11 = 22$, which is not greater than 35.

B   Since $512 = 2^9$, the prime sum of 512 is $9(2) = 18$, which is not greater than 35.

C   Since $620 = 2 \times 2 \times 5 \times 31$, the prime sum of 620 is $2 + 2 + 5 + 31 = 40$, which is greater than 35.

Because there can be only one correct answer, D and E need not be checked. However, for completeness,

D   Since $700 = 2 \times 2 \times 5 \times 5 \times 7$, the prime sum of 700 is $2 + 2 + 5 + 5 + 7 = 21$, which is not greater than 35.

E   Since $750 = 2 \times 3 \times 5 \times 5 \times 5$, the prime sum of 750 is $2 + 3 + 5 + 5 + 5 = 20$, which is not greater than 35.

The correct answer is C.

56. Each machine at a toy factory assembles a certain kind of toy at a constant rate of one toy every 3 minutes. If 40 percent of the machines at the factory are to be replaced by new machines that assemble this kind of toy at a constant rate of one toy every 2 minutes, what will be the percent increase in the number of toys assembled in one hour by all the machines at the factory, working at their constant rates?

    (A)   20%
    (B)   25%
    (C)   30%
    (D)   40%
    (E)   50%

Arithmetic Applied Problems; Percents

Let n be the total number of machines working. Currently, it takes each machine 3 minutes to assemble 1 toy, so each machine assembles 20 toys in 1 hour and the total number of toys assembled in 1 hour by all the current machines is $20n$. It takes each new machine 2 minutes to assemble 1 toy, so each new machine assembles 30 toys in 1 hour. If 60% of the machines assemble 20 toys each hour and 40% assemble 30 toys each hour, then the total number of toys produced by the machines each hour is $(0.60n)(20) + (0.40n)(30) = 24n$. The percent increase in hourly production is $\dfrac{24n - 20n}{20n} = \dfrac{1}{5}$ or 20%.

The correct answer is A.

57. When a subscription to a new magazine was purchased for m months, the publisher offered a discount of 75 percent off the regular monthly price of the magazine. If the total value of the discount was equivalent to buying the magazine at its regular monthly price for 27 months, what was the value of m ?

    (A)   18
    (B)   24
    (C)   30
    (D)   36
    (E)   48

Algebra Percents

Let P represent the regular monthly price of the magazine. The discounted monthly price is then $0.75P$. Paying this price for m months is equivalent to paying the regular price for 27 months. Therefore, $0.75mP = 27P$, and so $0.75m = 27$. It follows that $m = \dfrac{27}{0.75} = 36$.

The correct answer is D.

58. At a garage sale, all of the prices of the items sold were different. If the price of a radio sold at the garage sale was both the 15th highest price and the 20th lowest price among the prices of the items sold, how many items were sold at the garage sale?

    (A)   33
    (B)   34
    (C)   35
    (D)   36
    (E)   37

Arithmetic **Operations with Integers**

If the price of the radio was the 15th highest price, there were 14 items that sold for prices higher than the price of the radio. If the price of the radio was the 20th lowest price, there were 19 items that sold for prices lower than the price of the radio. Therefore, the total number of items sold is $14 + 1 + 19 = 34$.

The correct answer is B.

59. Half of a large pizza is cut into 4 equal-sized pieces, and the other half is cut into 6 equal-sized pieces. If a person were to eat 1 of the larger pieces and 2 of the smaller pieces, what fraction of the pizza would remain uneaten?

(A) $\dfrac{5}{12}$

(B) $\dfrac{13}{24}$

(C) $\dfrac{7}{12}$

(D) $\dfrac{2}{3}$

(E) $\dfrac{17}{24}$

Arithmetic **Operations with Fractions**

Each of the 4 equal-sized pieces represents $\dfrac{1}{8}$ of the whole pizza since each slice is $\dfrac{1}{4}$ of $\dfrac{1}{2}$ of the pizza. Each of the 6 equal-sized pieces represents $\dfrac{1}{12}$ of the whole pizza since each slice is $\dfrac{1}{6}$ of $\dfrac{1}{2}$ of the pizza. The fraction of the pizza remaining after a person eats one of the larger pieces and 2 of the smaller pieces is $1 - \left[\dfrac{1}{8} + 2\left(\dfrac{1}{12}\right)\right] =$

$1 - \left(\dfrac{1}{8} + \dfrac{1}{6}\right) = 1 - \dfrac{6+8}{48} = 1 - \dfrac{7}{24} = \dfrac{17}{24}$.

The correct answer is E.

60. If $a = 1 + \dfrac{1}{4} + \dfrac{1}{16} + \dfrac{1}{64}$ and $b = 1 + \dfrac{1}{4}a$, then what is the value of $a - b$?

(A) $-\dfrac{85}{256}$

(B) $-\dfrac{1}{256}$

(C) $-\dfrac{1}{4}$

(D) $\dfrac{125}{256}$

(E) $\dfrac{169}{256}$

Arithmetic **Operations with Fractions**

Given that $a = 1 + \dfrac{1}{4} + \dfrac{1}{16} + \dfrac{1}{64}$, it follows that $\dfrac{1}{4}a = \dfrac{1}{4} + \dfrac{1}{16} + \dfrac{1}{64} + \dfrac{1}{256}$ and so $b = 1 + \dfrac{1}{4} + \dfrac{1}{16} + \dfrac{1}{64} + \dfrac{1}{256}$. Then $a - b = $
$\left(1 + \dfrac{1}{4} + \dfrac{1}{16} + \dfrac{1}{64}\right) - \left(1 + \dfrac{1}{4} + \dfrac{1}{16} + \dfrac{1}{64} + \dfrac{1}{256}\right) = -\dfrac{1}{256}$.

The correct answer is B.

61. In a certain learning experiment, each participant had three trials and was assigned, for each trial, a score of either –2, –1, 0, 1, or 2. The participant's final score consisted of the sum of the first trial score, 2 times the second trial score, and 3 times the third trial score. If Anne received scores of 1 and –1 for her first two trials, not necessarily in that order, which of the following could NOT be her final score?

(A) –4

(B) –2

(C) 1

(D) 5

(E) 6

Arithmetic **Applied Problems**

If x represents Anne's score on the third trial, then Anne's final score is either $1 + 2(-1) + 3x = 3x - 1$ or $-1 + 2(1) + 3x = 3x + 1$, where x can have the value –2, –1, 0, 1, or 2. The following table shows Anne's final score for each possible value of x.

x	$3x-1$	$3x+1$
-2	-7	-5
-1	-4	-2
0	-1	1
1	2	4
2	5	7

Among the answer choices, the only one not found in the table is 6.

The correct answer is E.

62. For all positive integers m and v, the expression $m \ominus v$ represents the remainder when m is divided by v. What is the value of $((98 \ominus 33) \ominus 17) - (98 \ominus (33 \ominus 17))$?

(A) -10
(B) -2
(C) 8
(D) 13
(E) 17

Arithmetic Operations with Integers

First, for $((98 \ominus 33) \ominus 17)$, determine $98 \ominus 33$, which equals 32, since 32 is the remainder when 98 is divided by 33 ($98 = 2(33) + 32$). Then, determine $32 \ominus 17$, which equals 15, since 15 is the remainder when 32 is divided by 17 ($32 = 1(17) + 15$). Thus, $((98 \ominus 33) \ominus 17) = 15$.

Next, for $(98 \ominus (33 \ominus 17))$, determine $33 \ominus 17$, which equals 16, since 16 is the remainder when 33 is divided by 17 ($33 = 1(17) + 16$). Then, determine $98 \ominus 16$, which equals 2, since 2 is the remainder when 98 is divided by 16 ($98 = 6(16) + 2$). Thus, $(98 \ominus (33 \ominus 17)) = 2$.

Finally, $((98 \ominus 33) \ominus 17 - (98 \ominus (33 \ominus 17)) = 15 - 2 = 13$.

The correct answer is D.

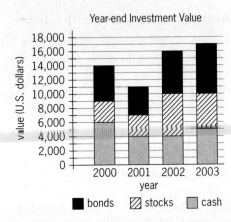

Year-end Investment Value

■ bonds   ▨ stocks   ▨ cash

63. The chart above shows year-end values for Darnella's investments. For just the stocks, what was the increase in value from year-end 2000 to year-end 2003 ?

(A) $1,000
(B) $2,000
(C) $3,000
(D) $4,000
(E) $5,000

Arithmetic Interpretation of Graphs

From the graph, the year-end 2000 value for stocks is $9,000 - 6,000 = 3,000$ and the year-end 2003 value for stocks is $10,000 - 5,000 = 5,000$. Therefore, for just the stocks, the increase in value from year-end 2000 to year-end 2003 is $5,000 - 3,000 = 2,000$.

The correct answer is B.

64. If the sum of the reciprocals of two consecutive odd integers is $\frac{12}{35}$, then the greater of the two integers is

(A) 3
(B) 5
(C) 7
(D) 9
(E) 11

Arithmetic Operations with Fractions

The sum of the reciprocals of 2 integers, a and b, is $\frac{1}{a} + \frac{1}{b} = \frac{a+b}{ab}$. Therefore, since $\frac{12}{35}$ is the sum of the reciprocals of 2 consecutive odd integers, the integers must be such that their sum is a multiple of 12 and their product is the same multiple of 35 so that the fraction reduces to $\frac{12}{35}$. Considering the simplest case where $a + b = 12$ and $ab = 35$, it is easy to see that the integers are 5 and 7 since 5 and 7 are the only factors of 35 that are consecutive odd integers. The larger of these is 7.

Algebraically, if a is the greater of the two integers, then $b = a - 2$ and

$$\frac{a + (a - 2)}{a(a - 2)} = \frac{12}{35}$$

$$\frac{2a - 2}{a(a - 2)} = \frac{12}{35}$$

$$35(2a - 2) = 12a(a - 2)$$
$$70a - 70 = 12a^2 - 24a$$
$$0 = 12a^2 - 94a + 70$$
$$0 = 2(6a - 5)(a - 7)$$

Thus, $6a - 5 = 0$, so $a = \frac{5}{6}$, or $a - 7 = 0$, so $a = 7$.

Since a must be an integer, it follows that $a = 7$.

The correct answer is C.

65. What is the sum of the odd integers from 35 to 85, inclusive?

   (A)   1,560
   (B)   1,500
   (C)   1,240
   (D)   1,120
   (E)   1,100

Arithmetic Operations on Integers

The odd integers from 35 through 85 form an arithmetic sequence with first term 35 and each subsequent term 2 more than the preceding term. Thus the sum $35 + 37 + 39 + \ldots + 85$ can be found as follows:

1st term	35	= 35		
2nd term	37	= 35	+	1(2)
3rd term	39	= 35	+	2(2)
4th term	41	= 35	+	3(2)
...	...	... ...		... ...
26th term	85	= 35	+	25(2)

$$\text{Sum} = 35(26) + (1 + 2 + 3 + \ldots + 25)(2)$$

$$= 35(26) + \frac{(25)(26)}{2}(2)$$

see note below

$$= 910 + 650$$
$$= 1,560$$

Note that if $s = 1 + 2 + 3 + \ldots + 25$, then $2s = (1 + 2 + 3 + \ldots + 25) + (25 + 24 + 23 + \ldots + 1)$, and so $2s = (1 + 25) + (2 + 24) + (3 + 23) + \ldots + (25 + 1) = (25)(26)$. Therefore, $s = \frac{(25)(26)}{2}$.

Alternatively, to determine the number of odd integers from 35 to 85, inclusive, consider that 3 of them (35, 37, and 39) have tens digit 3. Half of the integers with tens digit 4 are odd, so 5 of the odd integers between 35 and 85, inclusive, have tens digit 4. Similarly, 5 of the odd integers between 35 and 85, inclusive, have tens digit 5; 5 have tens digit 6; and 5 have tens digit 7. Finally, 3 have tens digit 8 (81, 83, and 85), and so the number of odd integers between 35 and 85, inclusive, is $3 + 5 + 5 + 5 + 5 + 3 = 26$. Now, let $S = 35 + 37 + 39 + \ldots + 85$. Then, $S = 85 + 83 + 81 + \ldots + 35$, and it follows that $2S = (35 + 85) + (37 + 83) + (39 + 81) + \ldots + (85 + 35) = (120)(26)$. Thus, $S = 35 + 37 + 39 + \ldots + 85 = \frac{(120)(26)}{2} = 1,560$.

The correct answer is A.

66. For all numbers a, b, c, and d, $\begin{vmatrix} a & b \\ c & d \end{vmatrix}$ is defined by the equation $\begin{vmatrix} a & b \\ c & d \end{vmatrix} = ad - cb$. Which of the following is equal to $\begin{vmatrix} s & t \\ 1 & 3 \end{vmatrix} - \begin{vmatrix} -t & 2 \\ s & 4 \end{vmatrix} + \begin{vmatrix} 2 & 2 \\ t & s \end{vmatrix}$?

   (A) $\begin{vmatrix} s & t \\ 1 & 5 \end{vmatrix}$

   (B) $\begin{vmatrix} s & t \\ 7 & 1 \end{vmatrix}$

   (C) $\begin{vmatrix} s & t \\ 5 & 7 \end{vmatrix}$

   (D) $\begin{vmatrix} s & -t \\ 1 & 5 \end{vmatrix}$

   (E) $\begin{vmatrix} s & -t \\ 1 & 7 \end{vmatrix}$

Algebra Formulas

First, expand the given expression using the given definition.

$$\begin{vmatrix} s & t \\ 1 & 3 \end{vmatrix} - \begin{vmatrix} -t & 2 \\ s & 4 \end{vmatrix} + \begin{vmatrix} 2 & 2 \\ t & s \end{vmatrix}$$

$$= (3s - t) - (-4t - 2s) + (2s - 2t) = 3s - t + 4t + 2s + 2s - 2t = 7s + t$$

Next, compare the result, $7s + t$, with the expanded versions of the answer choices.

A $\begin{vmatrix} s & t \\ 1 & 5 \end{vmatrix} = 5s - t$ (not correct)

B $\begin{vmatrix} s & t \\ 7 & 1 \end{vmatrix} = s - 7t$ (not correct)

C $\begin{vmatrix} s & t \\ 5 & 7 \end{vmatrix} = 7s - 5t$ (not correct)

D $\begin{vmatrix} s & -t \\ 1 & 5 \end{vmatrix} = 5s + t$ (not correct)

E $\begin{vmatrix} s & -t \\ 1 & 7 \end{vmatrix} = 7s + t$ (correct)

The correct answer is E.

67. In a certain sequence, each term after the first term is one-half the previous term. If the tenth term of the sequence is between 0.0001 and 0.001, then the twelfth term of the sequence is between

(A) 0.0025 and 0.025
(B) 0.00025 and 0.0025
(C) 0.000025 and 0.00025
(D) 0.0000025 and 0.000025
(E) 0.00000025 and 0.0000025

Arithmetic Sequences

Let a_n represent the nth term of the sequence. It is given that each term after the first term is $\frac{1}{2}$ the previous term and that $0.0001 < a_{10} < 0.001$.

Then for a_{11}, $\dfrac{0.0001}{2} < a_{11} < \dfrac{0.001}{2}$, or $0.00005 < a_{11} < 0.0005$. For a_{12}, $\dfrac{0.00005}{2} < a_{12} < \dfrac{0.0005}{2}$, or $0.000025 < a_{12} < 0.00025$. Thus, the twelfth term of the sequence is between 0.000025 and 0.00025.

The correct answer is C.

68. A certain drive-in movie theater has a total of 17 rows of parking spaces. There are 20 parking spaces in the first row and 21 parking spaces in the second row. In each subsequent row there are 2 more parking spaces than in the previous row. What is the total number of parking spaces in the movie theater?

(A) 412
(B) 544
(C) 596
(D) 632
(E) 692

Arithmetic Operations on Integers

Row	Number of parking spaces
1st row	20
2nd row	21
3rd row	21 + 1(2)
4th row	21 + 2(2)
…	… … …
17th row	21 + 15(2)

Then, letting S represent the total number of parking spaces in the theater,

$$S = 20 + (16)(21) + (1 + 2 + 3 + \ldots + 15)(2)$$

$$= 20 + 336 + \frac{(15)(16)}{2}(2) \text{ see note below}$$

$$= 356 + 240$$

$$= 596$$

Note that if $s = 1 + 2 + 3 + \ldots + 15$, then $2s = (1 + 2 + 3 + \ldots + 15) + (15 + 14 + 13 + \ldots + 1)$, and so $2s = (1 + 15) + (2 + 14) + (3 + 13) + \ldots + (15 + 1) = (15)(16)$. Therefore, $s = \dfrac{(15)(16)}{2}$.

The correct answer is C.

69. Ada and Paul received their scores on three tests. On the first test, Ada's score was 10 points higher than Paul's score. On the second test, Ada's score was 4 points higher than Paul's score. If Paul's average (arithmetic mean) score on the three tests was 3 points higher than Ada's average score on the three tests, then Paul's score on the third test was how many points higher than Ada's score?

    (A) 9
    (B) 14
    (C) 17
    (D) 23
    (E) 25

Algebra Statistics

Let a_1, a_2, and a_3 be Ada's scores on the first, second, and third tests, respectively, and let p_1, p_2, and p_3 be Paul's scores on the first, second, and third tests, respectively. Then, Ada's average score is $\frac{a_1 + a_2 + a_3}{3}$ and Paul's average score is $\frac{p_1 + p_2 + p_3}{3}$. But, Paul's average score is 3 points higher than Ada's average score, so $\frac{p_1 + p_2 + p_3}{3} = \frac{a_1 + a_2 + a_3}{3} + 3$. Also, it is given that $a_1 = p_1 + 10$ and $a_2 = p_2 + 4$, so by substitution, $\frac{p_1 + p_2 + p_3}{3} = \frac{(p_1 + 10) + (p_2 + 4) + a_3}{3} + 3$. Then, $p_1 + p_2 + p_3 = (p_1 + 10) + (p_2 + 4) + a_3 + 9$ and so $p_3 = a_3 + 23$. On the third test, Paul's score was 23 points higher than Ada's score.

The correct answer is D.

70. The price of a certain stock increased by 0.25 of 1 percent on a certain day. By what fraction did the price of the stock increase that day?

    (A) $\frac{1}{2,500}$

    (B) $\frac{1}{400}$

    (C) $\frac{1}{40}$

    (D) $\frac{1}{25}$

    (E) $\frac{1}{4}$

Arithmetic Percents

It is given that the price of a certain stock increased by 0.25 of 1 percent on a certain day. This is equivalent to an increase of $\frac{1}{4}$ of $\frac{1}{100}$, which is $\left(\frac{1}{4}\right)\left(\frac{1}{100}\right)$, and $\left(\frac{1}{4}\right)\left(\frac{1}{100}\right) = \frac{1}{400}$.

The correct answer is B.

71. For each trip, a taxicab company charges $4.25 for the first mile and $2.65 for each additional mile or fraction thereof. If the total charge for a certain trip was $62.55, how many miles at most was the trip?

    (A) 21
    (B) 22
    (C) 23
    (D) 24
    (E) 25

Arithmetic Applied Problems

Subtracting the charge for the first mile leaves a charge of $62.55 − $4.25 = $58.30 for the miles after the first mile. Divide this amount by $2.65 to find the number of miles to which $58.30 corresponds: $\frac{58.30}{2.65} = 22$ miles. Therefore, the total number of miles is at most 1 (the first mile) added to 22 (the number of miles after the first mile), which equals 23.

The correct answer is C.

72. When 24 is divided by the positive integer n, the remainder is 4. Which of the following statements about n must be true?

    I. n is even.
    II. n is a multiple of 5.
    III. n is a factor of 20.

    (A) III only
    (B) I and II only
    (C) I and III only
    (D) II and III only
    (E) I, II, and III

Arithmetic Properties of Numbers

Since the remainder is 4 when 24 is divided by the positive integer n and the remainder must be less than the divisor, it follows that $24 = qn + 4$ for some positive integer q and $4 < n$, or $qn = 20$ and $n > 4$. It follows that $n = 5$, or $n = 10$, or $n = 20$ since these are the only factors of 20 that exceed 4.

  I. n is not necessarily even. For example, n could be 5.

  II. n is necessarily a multiple of 5 since the value of n is either 5, 10, or 20.

  III. n is a factor of 20 since $20 = qn$ for some positive integer q.

The correct answer is D.

73. Terry needs to purchase some pipe for a plumbing job that requires pipes with lengths of 1 ft 4 in, 2 ft 8 in, 3 ft 4 in, 3 ft 8 in, 4 ft 8 in, 5 ft 8 in, and 9 ft 4 in. The store from which Terry will purchase the pipe sells pipe only in 10-ft lengths. If each 10-ft length can be cut into shorter pieces, what is the minimum number of 10-ft pipe lengths that Terry needs to purchase for the plumbing job?

(Note: 1 ft = 12 in)

(A) 3
(B) 4
(C) 5
(D) 6
(E) 7

Arithmetic Operations with Integers; Measurement Conversion

The 7 lengths of pipe Terry needs total 30 feet plus 8 inches, which means Terry will need to buy at least 4 pipes, each 10 feet long. Four pipes will suffice if Terry cuts pieces of the following lengths:

1st pipe: 9 feet 4 inches (with 8 inches left)

2nd pipe: 5 feet 8 inches and 3 feet 8 inches (with 8 inches left)

3rd pipe: 4 feet 8 inches, 3 feet 4 inches, and 1 foot 4 inches (with 8 inches left)

4th pipe: 2 feet 8 inches (with 7 feet 4 inches left)

The correct answer is B.

74. What is the thousandths digit in the decimal equivalent of $\dfrac{53}{5{,}000}$?

(A) 0
(B) 1
(C) 3
(D) 5
(E) 6

Arithmetic Place Value

$\dfrac{53}{5{,}000} = \dfrac{106}{10{,}000} = 0.0106$ and the thousandths digit is 0.

The correct answer is A.

Questions 75 to 127 - Difficulty: **Medium**

75. If $\frac{1}{2}$ the result obtained when 2 is subtracted from $5x$ is equal to the sum of 10 and $3x$, what is the value of x ?

(A) −22
(B) −4
(C) 4
(D) 18
(E) 22

Algebra First-Degree Equations

The result obtained when 2 is subtracted from $5x$ is $5x - 2$, and the sum of 10 and $3x$ is $10 + 3x$. Therefore, it is given that $\frac{1}{2}$ of $5x - 2$ is equal to $10 + 3x$, or $\frac{1}{2}(5x - 2) = 10 + 3x$.

$\frac{1}{2}(5x - 2) = 10 + 3x$ given

$5x - 2 = 20 + 6x$ multiply both sides by 2

$-22 = x$ subtract both $5x$ and 20 from both sides

The correct answer is A.

76. If Car A took n hours to travel 2 miles and Car B took m hours to travel 3 miles, which of the following expresses the time it would take Car C, traveling at the average (arithmetic mean) of those rates, to travel 5 miles?

(A) $\dfrac{10nm}{3n+2m}$

(B) $\dfrac{3n+2m}{10(n+m)}$

(C) $\dfrac{2n+3m}{5nm}$

(D) $\dfrac{10(n+m)}{2n+3m}$

(E) $\dfrac{5(n+m)}{2n+3m}$

Algebra Applied Problems

This is a rate problem that can be solved by several applications of the formula

$$\text{rate} \times \text{time} = \text{distance}.$$

Let r_A and r_B be the rates, respectively and in miles per hour, of Car A and Car B. Then omitting units for simplicity, for Car A this formula becomes $r_A \times n = 2$, or $r_A = \dfrac{2}{n}$, and for Car B this formula becomes $r_B \times m = 3$, or $r_B = \dfrac{3}{m}$. Thus, the average of the two rates is

$$\frac{1}{2}(r_A + r_B) = \frac{1}{2}\left(\frac{2}{n} + \frac{3}{m}\right) = \frac{1}{2}\left(\frac{2m+3n}{mn}\right) = \frac{3n+2m}{2mn}.$$

Therefore, if t is the desired time, in hours, that Car C traveled, then the above formula for Car C becomes $\dfrac{3n+2m}{2mn} \times t = 5$, or

$$t = 5 \times \frac{2mn}{3n+2m} = \frac{10mn}{3n+2m}.$$

The correct answer is A.

77. If x, y, and k are positive and x is less than y, then $\dfrac{x+k}{y+k}$ is

(A) 1

(B) greater than $\dfrac{x}{y}$

(C) equal to $\dfrac{x}{y}$

(D) less than $\dfrac{x}{y}$

(E) less than $\dfrac{x}{y}$ or greater than $\dfrac{x}{y}$, depending on the value of k

Algebra Ratios

x	$<$	y	given
kx	$<$	ky	multiply by positive k
$xy + kx$	$<$	$xy + ky$	add xy
$x(y + k)$	$<$	$y(x + k)$	factor
	$x <$	$\dfrac{y(x+k)}{y+k}$	divide by positive $y + k$
	$\dfrac{x}{y} <$	$\dfrac{x+k}{y+k}$	divide by positive y

Thus, $\dfrac{x+k}{y+k} > \dfrac{x}{y}$.

The correct answer is B.

78. Consider the following set of inequalities: $p > q$, $s > r$, $q > t$, $s > p$, and $r > q$. Between which two quantities is no relationship established?

(A) p and r

(B) s and t

(C) s and q

(D) p and t

(E) r and t

Algebra Order

Using $r > q$ and $q > t$ gives $r > t$, so a relationship is established between r and t. The correct answer is NOT E.

Using $p > q$ and $q > t$ gives $p > t$, so a relationship is established between p and t. The correct answer is NOT D.

Using $s > r$ and $r > q$ gives $s > q$, so a relationship is established between s and q. The correct answer is NOT C.

Using $s > r$, $r > q$, and $q > t$ gives $s > t$, so a relationship is established between s and t. The correct answer is NOT B.

Alternately, the diagram below shows the given relationships and does not establish a relationship between p and r.

The correct answer is A.

79. Carl averaged $2m$ miles per hour on a trip that took him h hours. If Ruth made the same trip in $\frac{2}{3}h$ hours, what was her average speed in miles per hour?

(A) $\frac{1}{3}mh$

(B) $\frac{2}{3}mh$

(C) m

(D) $\frac{3}{2}m$

(E) $3m$

Algebra Applied Problems

Using
$$\text{distance} = \text{rate} \times \text{time},$$

the distance Carl traveled on the trip was $2mh$ miles. Using $\text{rate} = \dfrac{\text{distance}}{\text{time}}$, Ruth's rate was $\dfrac{2mh}{\frac{2}{3}h} = \dfrac{3}{2}(2m) = 3m$.

The correct answer is E.

80. Of three persons, two take relish, two take pepper, and two take salt. The one who takes no salt takes no pepper, and the one who takes no pepper takes no relish. Which of the following statements must be true?

I.   The person who takes no salt also takes no relish.

II.   Any of the three persons who takes pepper also takes relish and salt.

III.   The person who takes no relish is not one of those who takes salt.

(A)   I only

(B)   II only

(C)   III only

(D)   I and II only

(E)   I, II, and III

Arithmetic Sets (Venn Diagrams)

Although this problem can be solved by the use of a Venn diagram, it is probably simpler to use ordinary reasoning. The single person who takes no salt takes no pepper, and the single person who takes no pepper takes no relish, so exactly one person does not take any of the three. Thus, each of the other two people take all three. The table below shows these results where Person 1 does not take any of the three and Persons 2 and 3 each take all three.

Person	Relish	Pepper	Salt
1	no	no	no
2	yes	yes	yes
3	yes	yes	yes

The only person who takes no salt is Person 1, who also takes no relish, so I must be true.

The only people who take pepper are Persons 2 and 3, and each of them also takes relish and salt, so II must be true.

The only person who takes no relish is Person 1, who is not a person who takes salt, so III must be true.

The correct answer is E.

81. If the smaller of 2 consecutive odd integers is a multiple of 5, which of the following could NOT be the sum of these 2 integers?

    (A)   –8
    (B)   12
    (C)   22
    (D)   52
    (E)   252

Algebra Operations with Integers

Since the smaller of the 2 consecutive odd integers is a multiple of 5, let it be represented by $5n$ for some integer n. Then the other odd integer can be represented by $5n + 2$. The sum of these two integers is $10n + 2$. The sum is -8 when $n = -1$ and $5n = (5)(-1)$ is odd. The sum is 12 when $n = 1$ and $5n = (5)(1)$ is odd. The sum is 22 when $n = 2$, but $5n = (5)(2)$ is not odd. There is no need to check the D and E because it has been determined that 22 cannot be the sum of the 2 consecutive odd integers. For completeness, the sum is 52 when $n = 5$ and $5n = (5)(5)$ is odd. The sum is 252 when $n = 25$ and $5n = (5)(25)$ is odd.

The correct answer is C.

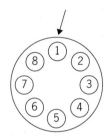

82. Eight light bulbs numbered 1 through 8 are arranged in a circle as shown above. The bulbs are wired so that every third bulb, counting in a clockwise direction, flashes until all bulbs have flashed once. If the bulb numbered 1 flashes first, which numbered bulb will flash last?

    (A)   2
    (B)   3
    (C)   4
    (D)   6
    (E)   7

Arithmetic Properties of Integers

The easiest way to do this problem might be by just counting every third bulb going clockwise around the circle starting at Bulb 1, which flashes, skipping 2 bulbs and getting to Bulb 4, which flashes, skipping 2 bulbs and getting to Bulb 7, which flashes, skipping 2 bulbs and getting to Bulb 2, which flashes, skipping 2 bulbs and getting to Bulb 5, which flashes, skipping 2 bulbs and getting to Bulb 8, which flashes, skipping 2 bulbs and getting to Bulb 3, which flashes, and finally skipping 2 bulbs and getting to Bulb 6, which flashes. Now, all 8 bulbs have flashed once and the last one to flash was Bulb 6.

The correct answer is D.

Closing Prices of Stock X
During a Certain Week
(in dollars)

Monday	Tuesday	Wednesday	Thursday	Friday
21	19	22	$24\frac{1}{2}$	23

83. A certain financial analyst defines the "volatility" of a stock during a given week to be the result of the following procedure: find the absolute value of the difference in the stock's closing price for each pair of consecutive days in the week and then find the average (arithmetic mean) of these 4 values. What is the volatility of Stock X during the week shown in the table?

    (A)   0.50
    (B)   1.80
    (C)   2.00
    (D)   2.25
    (E)   2.50

Arithmetic Statistics

The volatility of Stock X during the week is the average of the 4 values associated with the 4 pairs of consecutive days during the week.

$$\frac{(\text{Mon}\ \&\ \text{Tue})+(\text{Tue}\ \&\ \text{Wed})+(\text{Wed}\ \&\ \text{Thu})+(\text{Thu}\ \&\ \text{Fri})}{4}$$

$$=\frac{|19-21|+|22-19|+|24.5-22|+|23-24.5|}{4}$$

$$=\frac{|-2|+|3|+|2.5|+|-1.5|}{4}=\frac{2+3+2.5+1.5}{4}=\frac{9}{4}=2.25$$

The correct answer is D.

84. If $y=\dfrac{|3x-5|}{-x^2-3}$, for what value of x will the value of y be greatest?

(A) -5

(B) $-\dfrac{3}{5}$

(C) 0

(D) $\dfrac{3}{5}$

(E) $\dfrac{5}{3}$

Algebra Functions; Absolute Value

Since the absolute value of any real number is greater than or equal to zero, it follows that $|3x-5|\ge 0$. Also, for any real number x we have $x^2\ge 0$, and hence $-x^2\le 0$. Subtracting 3 from both sides of the last inequality gives $-x^2-3\le -3$. Therefore, the numerator of the expression for y is greater than or equal to zero and the denominator of the expression for y is negative. It follows that the value of y cannot be greater than 0. However, the value of y is equal to 0 when $|3x-5|=0$, or $3x-5=0$, or $x=\dfrac{5}{3}$. Therefore, the value of x for which the value of y is greatest (i.e., when $y=0$) is $x=\dfrac{5}{3}$.

The correct answer is E.

85. What values of x have a corresponding value of y that satisfies both $xy>0$ and $xy=x+y$?

(A) $x\le -1$

(B) $-1<x\le 0$

(C) $0<x\le 1$

(D) $x>1$

(E) All real numbers

Algebra Equations; Inequalities

First, use $xy=x+y$ to solve for y in terms of x.

$$\begin{array}{lll} xy & = & x+y \quad\text{given}\\ xy-y & = & x \quad\text{subtract } y \text{ from both sides}\\ y(x-1) & = & x \quad\text{factor}\\ y & = & \dfrac{x}{x-1} \quad\text{divide both sides by } x-1 \end{array}$$

Note that the division by $x-1$ requires $x\ne 1$, and thus $x=1$ needs to be considered separately. However, if $x=1$, then $xy=x+y$ becomes $y=1+y$, which is not true for any value of y.

Using $y=\dfrac{x}{x-1}$, it follows that the inequality $xy>0$ is equivalent to $\dfrac{x^2}{x-1}>0$. Since $x^2\ge 0$ for each value of x, the quotient $\dfrac{x^2}{x-1}$ can only be positive when $x\ne 0$ and $x-1$ is positive, or when $x>1$.

Alternatively, the correct answer can be found by eliminating the incorrect answers, which can be accomplished by considering the endpoints of the intervals given in the answer choices.

Case 1: If $x=-1$, then $xy=x+y$ becomes $-y=-1+y$, or $y=\dfrac{1}{2}$. However, in this case $xy=(-1)\left(\dfrac{1}{2}\right)$ is negative, and thus $xy>0$ is not true. Therefore, the answer cannot be A or E.

Case 2: If $x=0$, then $xy=0$, and thus $xy>0$ is not true. Therefore, the answer cannot be B or E.

Case 3: If $x=1$, then $xy=x+y$ becomes $y=1+y$, which is not true for any value of y. Therefore, the answer cannot be C or E.

Since the answer cannot be A, B, C, or E, it follows that the answer is D.

The correct answer is D.

86. Employee X's annual salary is $12,000 more than half of Employee Y's annual salary. Employee Z's annual salary is $15,000 more than half of Employee X's annual salary. If Employee X's annual salary is $27,500, which of the following lists these three people in order of increasing annual salary?

   (A) Y, Z, X
   (B) Y, X, Z
   (C) Z, X, Y
   (D) X, Y, Z
   (E) X, Z, Y

Algebra First-Degree Equations

Letting x, y, and z represent the annual salary, in dollars, of Employee X, Employee Y, and Employee Z, respectively, the following information is given:

(1) $x = 12,000 + \dfrac{y}{2}$

(2) $z = 15,000 + \dfrac{x}{2}$

(3) $x = 27,500$

From (1) and (3), it follows that $27,500 = 12,000 + \dfrac{y}{2}$ or $y = 2(27,500 - 12,000) = 31,000$.
From (2) and (3), it follows that $z = 15,000 + \dfrac{27,500}{2} = 28,750$. Therefore, $x < z < y$.

The correct answer is E.

87. $C = \begin{cases} 0.10s, \text{ if } s \le 60,000 \\ 0.10s + 0.04(s - 60,000), \text{ if } s > 60,000 \end{cases}$

   The formula above gives the contribution C, in dollars, to a certain profit-sharing plan for a participant with a salary of s dollars. How many more dollars is the contribution for a participant with a salary of $70,000 than for a participant with a salary of $50,000 ?

   (A) $800
   (B) $1,400
   (C) $2,000
   (D) $2,400
   (E) $2,800

Algebra Applied Problems; Formulas

For a participant with a salary of $70,000,
$C = 0.1(\$70,000) + 0.04(\$70,000 - \$60,000) = \$7,000 + \$400 = \$7,400$. For a participant with a salary of $50,000, $C = 0.1(\$50,000) = \$5,000$. The difference is $\$7,400 - \$5,000 = \$2,400$.

The correct answer is D.

88. Next month, Ron and Cathy will each begin working part-time at $\dfrac{3}{5}$ of their respective current salaries. If the sum of their reduced salaries will be equal to Cathy's current salary, then Ron's current salary is what fraction of Cathy's current salary?

   (A) $\dfrac{1}{3}$

   (B) $\dfrac{2}{5}$

   (C) $\dfrac{1}{2}$

   (D) $\dfrac{3}{5}$

   (E) $\dfrac{2}{3}$

Algebra First-Degree Equations

Letting R and C, respectively, represent Ron's and Cathy's current salaries, it is given that $\dfrac{3}{5}R + \dfrac{3}{5}C = C$. It follows that $\dfrac{3}{5}R = \dfrac{2}{5}C$ and

$$R = \dfrac{5}{3}\left(\dfrac{2}{5}C\right) = \dfrac{2}{3}C.$$

The correct answer is E.

89. David and Ron are ordering food for a business lunch. David thinks that there should be twice as many sandwiches as there are pastries, but Ron thinks the number of pastries should be 12 more than one-fourth of the number of sandwiches. How many sandwiches should be ordered so that David and Ron can agree on the number of pastries to order?

   (A) 12
   (B) 16
   (C) 20
   (D) 24
   (E) 48

Algebra Simultaneous Equations

Let S be the number of sandwiches that should be ordered and let P be the number of pastries that should be ordered. Then David desires $S = 2P$ and Ron desires $P = 12 + \frac{1}{4}S$.

$S = 2P$	given
$S = 2(12 + \frac{1}{4}S)$ $\quad P = 12 + \frac{1}{4}S$	
$S = 24 + \frac{1}{2}S$	distributive law
$\frac{1}{2}S = 24$	subtract $\frac{1}{2}S$ from both sides
$S = 48$	multiply both sides by 2

The correct answer is E.

90. The cost of purchasing each box of candy from a certain mail order catalog is v dollars per pound of candy, plus a shipping charge of h dollars. How many dollars does it cost to purchase 2 boxes of candy, one containing s pounds of candy and the other containing t pounds of candy, from this catalog?

   (A) $h + stv$

   (B) $2h + stv$

   (C) $2hstv$

   (D) $2h + s + t + v$

   (E) $2h + v(s + t)$

Algebra Formulas

The cost, in dollars, to purchase the 2 boxes of candy is the sum of 2 shipping charges and the cost of $s + t$ pounds of candy.

$$\text{cost} = (2 \text{ shipping charges}) + (v)(s + t)$$
$$\text{cost} = 2(h) + (v)(s + t)$$
$$\text{cost} = 2h + v(s + t)$$

The correct answer is E.

91. If $x \neq -\frac{1}{2}$, then $\dfrac{6x^3 + 3x^2 - 8x - 4}{2x + 1} =$

   (A) $3x^2 + \frac{3}{2}x - 8$

   (B) $3x^2 + \frac{3}{2}x - 4$

   (C) $3x^2 - 4$

   (D) $3x - 4$

   (E) $3x + 4$

Algebra Factoring

$$\frac{6x^3 + 3x^2 - 8x - 4}{2x + 1} = \frac{(6x^3 + 3x^2) - (8x + 4)}{2x + 1} \quad \text{group}$$

$$= \frac{3x^2(2x + 1) - 4(2x + 1)}{2x + 1} \quad \text{factor}$$

$$= \frac{(3x^2 - 4)(2x + 1)}{2x + 1} \quad \text{factor}$$

$$= 3x^2 - 4 \quad \text{cancel since } x \neq \frac{1}{2}$$

Alternatively, sometimes it is easier or quicker to test one-variable expressions for equality by substituting a convenient value for the variable and eliminating answer choices for which the value of the expression in that answer choice does not equal the value of the given expression. For example, choose $x = 0$, since calculations for $x = 0$ are minimal. Then, as shown in the table below, $\dfrac{6x^3 + 3x^2 - 8x - 4}{2x + 1} = \dfrac{-4}{1} = -4$, but $3x^2 + \frac{3}{2}x - 8 = -8$ and $3x + 4 = 4$, neither of which equals -4, so answer choices A and E can be eliminated. Another convenient value to choose for x is 1. There is no need to evaluate answer choices A and E at 1 since they have already been eliminated. As shown, when $x = 1$, $\dfrac{6x^3 + 3x^2 - 8x - 4}{2x + 1} = -1$, but $3x^2 + \frac{3}{2}x - 4 = \frac{1}{2} \neq -1$, so answer choice B can be eliminated. A third convenient value for x is -1. There is no need to evaluate answer choices A, B, and E at -1 since they have already been eliminated. As shown, when $x = -1$, $\dfrac{6x^3 + 3x^2 - 8x - 4}{2x + 1} = -1$, but $3x - 4 = -7 \neq -1$, so answer choice D can be eliminated. Note that, if $x = -1$ had been chosen initially, A, B, D, and E would have been eliminated immediately since $3x^2 + \dfrac{3}{2}x - 8 = -6\dfrac{1}{2} \neq -1$,

$3x^2 + \dfrac{3}{2}x - 4 = -2\dfrac{1}{2} \neq -1$, $3x - 4 = -7 \neq -1$, and

$3x + 4 = 1 \neq -1$.

		$x = 0$	$x = 1$	$x = -1$
	$\dfrac{6x^3 + 3x^2 - 8x - 4}{2x + 1}$	-4	-1	-1
A	$3x^2 + \dfrac{3}{2}x - 8$	-8		
B	$3x^2 + \dfrac{3}{2}x - 4$	-4	$\dfrac{1}{2}$	
C	$3x^2 - 4$	-4	-1	-1
D	$3x - 4$	-4	-1	-7
E	$3x + 4$	4		

The correct answer is C.

92. If $x^2 + bx + 5 = (x + c)^2$ for all numbers x, where b and c are positive constants, what is the value of b ?

(A) $\sqrt{5}$
(B) $\sqrt{10}$
(C) $2\sqrt{5}$
(D) $2\sqrt{10}$
(E) 10

Algebra Second-Degree Equations

Given that $x^2 + bx + 5 = (x + c)^2$, since $(x + c)^2 = x^2 + 2cx + c^2$, it follows that $5 = c^2$ and $b = 2c$. The possible values of c are $-\sqrt{5}$ and $\sqrt{5}$, but since c is positive, $c = \sqrt{5}$ and $b = 2c = 2\sqrt{5}$.

The correct answer is C.

93. Last year Shannon listened to a certain public radio station 10 hours per week and contributed $35 to the station. Of the following, which is closest to Shannon's contribution per minute of listening time last year?

(A) $0.001
(B) $0.010
(C) $0.025
(D) $0.058
(E) $0.067

Arithmetic Measurement Conversion

Since there are 52 weeks in 1 year and 60 minutes in 1 hour, 10 hours per week is equivalent to $(10)(52)(60) = 31{,}200$ minutes per year. Shannon's $35 contribution is then $\dfrac{35}{31{,}200}$ dollars per minute, which is closest to $0.001 per minute.

The correct answer is A.

94. Each of the 20 employees at Company J is to receive an end-of-year bonus this year. Agnes will receive a larger bonus than any other employee, but only $500 more than Cheryl will receive. None of the employees will receive a smaller bonus than Cheryl. If the amount of money to be distributed in bonuses at Company J this year totals $60,000, what is the largest bonus Agnes can receive?

(A) $3,250
(B) $3,325
(C) $3,400
(D) $3,475
(E) $3,500

Algebra Applied Problems

Since the total amount of the bonuses is fixed, the largest possible bonus that Agnes can receive will occur when the total amount received by the 19 employees other than Agnes is the smallest possible. Let A be the bonus, in dollars, that Agnes receives. Then, in dollars, Cheryl will receive $(A - 500)$, and each of the remaining 18 employees will receive between $(A - 500)$ and A. Therefore, the total amount received by the 19 employees other than Agnes is smallest when each of these 19 employees receives $(A - 500)$ dollars.

$19(A - 500) + A$	$=$	$60{,}000$	total of 20 bonuses is $60,000
$19A - 9{,}500 + A$	$=$	$60{,}000$	distributive law
$20A - 9{,}500$	$=$	$60{,}000$	combine like terms
$20A$	$=$	$69{,}500$	add 9,500 to both sides
A	$=$	$3{,}475$	divide both sides by 20

The correct answer is D.

95. Beth, Naomi, and Juan raised a total of $55 for charity. Naomi raised $5 less than Juan, and Juan raised twice as much as Beth. How much did Beth raise?

    (A) $9
    (B) $10
    (C) $12
    (D) $13
    (E) $15

Algebra Simultaneous Equations

Let B, N, and J be the amounts raised, respectively and in dollars, by Beth, Naomi, and Juan.

$$
\begin{array}{lll}
B + N + J & = & 55 \\
N & = & J - 5 \\
J & = & 2B \\
J & = & 55 - B - N \\
J & = & 55 - B - (J - 5) \\
2B & = & 55 - B - (2B - 5) \\
B & = & 12
\end{array}
$$

given
given
given
subtract $B + N$ from both sides of first equation
$N = J - 5$
$J = 2B$
solve for B

The correct answer is C.

96. The set of solutions for the equation $(x^2 - 25)^2 = x^2 - 10x + 25$ contains how many real numbers?

    (A) 0
    (B) 1
    (C) 2
    (D) 3
    (E) 4

Algebra Second-Degree Equations

$$
\begin{array}{ll}
(x^2 - 25)^2 = x^2 - 10x + 25 & \text{given} \\
(x + 5)^2 (x - 5)^2 = (x - 5)^2 & \text{factor} \\
(x + 5)^2 (x - 5)^2 - (x - 5)^2 = 0 & \text{subtract } (x - 5)^2 \\
(x - 5)^2 [(x + 5)^2 - 1] = 0 & \text{factor} \\
(x - 5)^2 [(x + 5) - 1] & \\
\quad [(x + 5) + 1] = 0 & \text{factor} \\
(x - 5)^2 (x + 4)(x + 6) = 0 & \text{subtraction, addition}
\end{array}
$$

Thus the solution set of $(x^2 - 25)^2 = x^2 - 10x + 25$ contains 3 real numbers: 5, −4, and −6.

The correct answer is D.

97. An aerosol can is designed so that its bursting pressure, B, in pounds per square inch, is 120% of the pressure, F, in pounds per square inch, to which it is initially filled. Which of the following formulas expresses the relationship between B and F?

    (A) $B = 1.2F$
    (B) $B = 120F$
    (C) $B = 1 + 0.2F$
    (D) $B - \dfrac{F}{1.2}$
    (E) $B = \dfrac{1.2}{F}$

Algebra Formulas; Percents

We are given that B is 120% of F, so $B = (120\%)F$, or $B = 1.2F$. Note that both B and F are given in pounds per square inch, so there are no unit conversions involved.

The correct answer is A.

98. The average (arithmetic mean) of the positive integers x, y, and z is 3. If $x < y < z$, what is the greatest possible value of z?

    (A) 5
    (B) 6
    (C) 7
    (D) 8
    (E) 9

Algebra Inequalities

It is given that $\dfrac{x + y + z}{3} = 3$, or $x + y + z = 9$, or $z = 9 + (-x - y)$. It follows that the greatest possible value of z occurs when $-x - y = -(x + y)$ has the greatest possible value, which occurs when $x + y$ has the least possible value. Because x and y are different positive integers, the least possible value of $x + y$ occurs when $x = 1$ and $y = 2$. Therefore, the greatest possible value of z is $9 - 1 - 2 = 6$.

The correct answer is B.

99. The product of 3,305 and the 1-digit integer x is a 5-digit integer. The units (ones) digit of the product is 5 and the hundreds digit is y. If A is the set of all possible values of x and B is the set of all possible values of y, then which of the following gives the members of A and B?

	A	B
(A)	{1, 3, 5, 7, 9}	{0, 1, 2, 3, 4, 5, 6, 7, 8, 9}
(B)	{1, 3, 5, 7, 9}	{1, 3, 5, 7, 9}
(C)	{3, 5, 7, 9}	{1, 5, 7, 9}
(D)	{5, 7, 9}	{1, 5, 7}
(E)	{5, 7, 9}	{1, 5, 9}

Arithmetic Properties of Numbers

Since the products of 3,305 and 1, 3,305 and 2, and 3,305 and 3 are the 4-digit integers 3,305, 6,610, and 9,915, respectively, it follows that x must be among the 1-digit integers 4, 5, 6, 7, 8, and 9. Also, since the units digit of the product of 3,305 and x is 5, it follows that x cannot be 4 (product has units digit 0), 6 (product has units digit 0), or 8 (product has units digit 0). Therefore, $A = \{5, 7, 9\}$. The possibilities for y will be the hundreds digits of the products $(3,305)(5) = 16,525$, $(3,305)(7) = 23,135$, and $(3,305)(9) = 29,745$. Thus, y can be 5, 1, or 7, and so $B = \{1, 5, 7\}$.

The correct answer is D.

100. If x and y are integers such that $2 < x \le 8$ and $2 < y \le 9$, what is the maximum value of $\dfrac{1}{x} - \dfrac{x}{y}$?

(A) $-3\dfrac{1}{8}$

(B) 0

(C) $\dfrac{1}{4}$

(D) $\dfrac{5}{18}$

(E) 2

Algebra Inequalities

Because x and y are both positive, the maximum value of $\dfrac{1}{x} - \dfrac{x}{y}$ will occur when the value of $\dfrac{1}{x}$ is maximum and the value of $\dfrac{x}{y}$ is minimum. The value of $\dfrac{1}{x}$ is maximum when the value of

x is minimum or when $x = 3$. The value of $\dfrac{x}{y}$ is minimum when the value of x is minimum (or when $x = 3$) and the value of y is maximum (or when $y = 9$). Thus, the maximum value of $\dfrac{1}{x} - \dfrac{x}{y}$ is $\dfrac{1}{3} - \dfrac{3}{9} = 0$.

The correct answer is B.

101. Items that are purchased together at a certain discount store are priced at $3 for the first item purchased and $1 for each additional item purchased. What is the maximum number of items that could be purchased together for a total price that is less than $30?

(A) 25

(B) 26

(C) 27

(D) 28

(E) 29

Arithmetic Applied Problems

After the first item is purchased, $29.99 − $3.00 = $26.99 remains to purchase the additional items. Since the price for each of the additional items is $1.00, a maximum of 26 additional items could be purchased. Therefore, a maximum of $1 + 26 = 27$ items could be purchased for less than $30.00.

The correct answer is C.

102. What is the least integer z for which $(0.000125)(0.0025)(0.00000125) \times 10^z$ is an integer?

(A) 18

(B) 10

(C) 0

(D) −10

(E) −18

Arithmetic Decimals

Considering each of the three decimal numbers in parentheses separately, we know that 0.000125×10^6 is the integer 125, 0.0025×10^4 is the integer 25, and 0.00000125×10^8 is the integer 125. We thus know that $(0.000125) \times 10^6 \times (0.0025) \times 10^4 \times (0.00000125) \times 10^8 = (0.000125)(0.0025)(0.00000125) \times 10^6 \times 10^4 \times 10^8 = (0.000125)(0.0025)(0.00000125) \times$

$10^{6+4+8} = (0.000125)(0.0025)(0.00000125) \times 10^{18}$ is the integer $125 \times 25 \times 125$. We therefore know that if $z = 18$, then $(0.000125)(0.0025)(0.00000125) \times 10^z$ is an integer.

Now, if the product $125 \times 25 \times 125$ were divisible by 10, then for at least one integer z less than 18, $(0.000125)(0.0025)(0.00000125) \times 10^z$ would be an integer. However, each of the three numbers being multiplied in the product $125 \times 25 \times 125$ is odd (not divisible by 2). We thus know that $125 \times 25 \times 125$ is not divisible by 2 and is therefore odd. Because only even numbers are divisible by 10, we know that $125 \times 25 \times 125$ is not divisible by 10. We thus know that 18 is the *least* integer z such that $(0.000125)(0.0025)(0.00000125) \times 10^z$ is an integer.

Note that it is not necessary to perform the multiplication $125 \times 25 \times 125$.

The correct answer is A.

103. The average (arithmetic mean) length per film for a group of 21 films is t minutes. If a film that runs for 66 minutes is removed from the group and replaced by one that runs for 52 minutes, what is the average length per film, in minutes, for the new group of films, in terms of t?

(A) $t + \dfrac{2}{3}$

(B) $t - \dfrac{2}{3}$

(C) $21t + 14$

(D) $t + \dfrac{3}{2}$

(E) $t - \dfrac{3}{2}$

Arithmetic Statistics

Let S denote the sum of the lengths, in minutes, of the 21 films in the original group. Since the average length is t minutes, it follows that $\dfrac{S}{21} = t$.

If a 66-minute film is replaced by a 52-minute film, then the sum of the lengths of the 21 films in the resulting group is $S - 66 + 52 = S - 14$. Therefore, the average length of the resulting 21 films is $\dfrac{S - 14}{21} = \dfrac{S}{21} - \dfrac{14}{21} = t - \dfrac{2}{3}$.

The correct answer is B.

104. A garden center sells a certain grass seed in 5-pound bags at $13.85 per bag, 10-pound bags at $20.43 per bag, and 25-pound bags at $32.25 per bag. If a customer is to buy at least 65 pounds of the grass seed, but no more than 80 pounds, what is the least possible cost of the grass seed that the customer will buy?

(A) $94.03

(B) $96.75

(C) $98.78

(D) $102.07

(E) $105.36

Arithmetic Applied Problems

Let x represent the amount of grass seed, in pounds, the customer is to buy. It follows that $65 \leq x \leq 80$. Since the grass seed is available in only 5-pound, 10-pound, and 25-pound bags, then the customer must buy either 65, 70, 75, or 80 pounds of grass seed. Because the seed is more expensive per pound for smaller bags, the customer should minimize the number of the smaller bags and maximize the number of 25-pound bags to incur the least possible cost for the grass seed. The possible purchases are given in the table below.

x	Number of 25-pound bags	Number of 10-pound bags	Number of 5-pound bags	Total cost
65	2	1	1	$98.78
70	2	2	0	$105.36
75	3	0	0	$96.75
80	3	0	1	$110.60

The least possible cost is then $3(\$32.25) = \$96.75$.

The correct answer is B.

105. If $x = -|w|$, which of the following must be true?

(A) $x = -w$

(B) $x = w$

(C) $x^2 = w$

(D) $x^2 = w^2$

(E) $x^3 = w^3$

Algebra Absolute Value

Squaring both sides of $x = -|w|$ gives
$x^2 = (-|w|)^2$, or $x^2 = |w|^2 = w^2$.

Alternatively, if (x, w) is equal to either of the pairs $(-1,1)$ or $(-1,-1)$, then $x = -|w|$ is true. However, each of the answer choices except $x^2 = w^2$ is false for at least one of these two pairs.

The correct answer is D.

106. A certain financial institution reported that its assets totaled $2,377,366.30 on a certain day. Of this amount, $31,724.54 was held in cash. Approximately what percent of the reported assets was held in cash on that day?

   (A)   0.00013%
   (B)   0.0013%
   (C)   0.013%
   (D)   0.13%
   (E)   1.3%

Arithmetic Percents; Estimation

The requested percent can be estimated by converting the values into scientific notation.

$$\frac{31,724.54}{2,377,366.30} \quad \text{value as fraction}$$

$$= \frac{3.172454 \times 10^4}{2.37736630 \times 10^6} \quad \begin{array}{l}\text{convert to scientific}\\\text{notation}\end{array}$$

$$= \frac{3.172454}{2.37736630} \times \frac{10^4}{10^6} \quad \begin{array}{l}\text{arithmetic property of}\\\text{fractions}\end{array}$$

$$= \frac{3.172454}{2.37736630} \times 10^{-2} \quad \text{subtract exponents}$$

$$\approx \frac{3}{2} \times 10^{-2} \quad \text{approximate}$$

$$= 1.5 \times 10^{-2} \quad \text{convert to decimal fraction}$$

$$= 0.015 \quad \text{multiply}$$

$$= 1.5\% \quad \text{convert to percent}$$

A more detailed computation would show that 1.3% is a better approximation. However, in order to select the best value from the values given as answer choices, the above computation is sufficient.

The correct answer is E.

$$
\begin{array}{r}
AB \\
+\ BA \\
\hline
AAC
\end{array}
$$

107. In the correctly worked addition problem shown, where the sum of the two-digit positive integers AB and BA is the three-digit integer AAC, and A, B, and C are different digits, what is the units digit of the integer AAC ?

   (A)   9
   (B)   6
   (C)   3
   (D)   2
   (E)   0

Arithmetic Place Value

Determine the value of C.

It is given that $(10A + B) + (10B + A) = 100A + 10A + C$ or $11A + 11B = 110A + C$. Thus, $11B - 99A = C$, or $11(B - 9A) = C$. Therefore, C is divisible by 11, and 0 is the only digit that is divisible by 11.

The correct answer is E.

108. The hard drive, monitor, and printer for a certain desktop computer system cost a total of $2,500. The cost of the printer and monitor together is equal to $\frac{2}{3}$ of the cost of the hard drive. If the cost of the printer is $100 more than the cost of the monitor, what is the cost of the printer?

   (A) $800
   (B) $600
   (C) $550
   (D) $500
   (E) $350

Algebra Simultaneous Equations

Letting d, m, and p, respectively, represent the cost of the hard drive, monitor, and printer, the following equations are given:

(1) $d + m + p = 2,500$

(2) $p + m = \frac{2}{3}d$

(3) $p = m + 100$

Using (2) and substituting $\frac{2}{3}d$ for $m + p$ in (1) gives $\frac{5}{3}d = 2,500$, from which $d = 1,500$. Then from (1), $p + m = 1,000$, but $m = p - 100$ from (2), so $2p - 100 = 1,000$, $2p = 1,100$, and $p = 550$.

The correct answer is C.

$$3r \le 4s + 5$$
$$|s| \le 5$$

109. Given the inequalities above, which of the following CANNOT be the value of r?

(A)　−20
(B)　−5
(C)　0
(D)　5
(E)　20

Algebra Inequalities

Since $|s| \le 5$, it follows that $-5 \le s \le 5$. Therefore, $-20 \le 4s \le 20$, and hence $-15 \le 4s + 5 \le 25$. Since $3r \le 4s + 5$ (given) and $4s + 5 \le 25$ (end of previous sentence), it follows that $3r \le 25$. Among the answer choices, $3r \le 25$ is false only for $r = 20$.

The correct answer is E.

110. If m is an even integer, v is an odd integer, and $m > v > 0$, which of the following represents the number of even integers less than m and greater than v?

(A)　$\frac{m-v}{2} - 1$

(B)　$\frac{m-v-1}{2}$

(C)　$\frac{m-v}{2}$

(D)　$m - v - 1$

(E)　$m - v$

Arithmetic Properties of Numbers

Since there is only one correct answer, one method of solving the problem is to choose values for m and v and determine which of the expressions gives the correct number for these values. For example, if $m = 6$ and $v = 1$, then there are 2 even integers less than 6 and greater than 1, namely the even integers 2 and 4. As the table

below shows, $\frac{m-v-1}{2}$ is the only expression given that equals 2.

$$\frac{m-v}{2} - 1 = 1.5$$
$$\frac{m-v-1}{2} = 2$$
$$\frac{m-v}{2} = 2.5$$
$$m - v - 1 = 4$$
$$m - v = 5$$

To solve this problem it is not necessary to show that $\frac{m-v-1}{2}$ always gives the correct number of even integers. However, one way this can be done is by the following method, first shown for a specific example and then shown in general. For the specific example, suppose $v = 15$ and $m = 144$. Then a list—call it the first list—of the even integers greater than v and less than m is 16, 18, 20, …, 140, 142. Now subtract 14 (chosen so that the second list will begin with 2) from each of the integers in the first list to form a second list, which has the same number of integers as the first list: 2, 4, 6, …, 128. Finally, divide each of the integers in the second list (all of which are even) by 2 to form a third list, which also has the same number of integers as the first list: 1, 2, 3, …, 64. Since the number of integers in the third list is 64, it follows that the number of integers in the first list is 64. For the general situation, the first list is the following list of even integers: $v + 1$, $v + 3$, $v + 5$, …, $m - 4$, $m - 2$. Now subtract the even integer $v - 1$ from (i.e., add $-v + 1$ to) each of the integers in the first list to obtain the second list: 2, 4, 6, …, $m - v - 3$, $m - v - 1$. (Note, for example, that $m - 4 - (v - 1) = m - v - 3$.) Finally, divide each of the integers (all of which are even) in the second list by 2 to obtain the third list: 1, 2, 3, …, $\frac{m-v-3}{2}$, $\frac{m-v-1}{2}$. Since the number of integers in the third list is $\frac{m-v-1}{2}$, it follows that the number of integers in the first list is $\frac{m-v-1}{2}$.

The correct answer is B.

111. A positive integer is divisible by 9 if and only if the sum of its digits is divisible by 9. If n is a positive integer, for which of the following values of k is $25 \times 10^n + k \times 10^{2n}$ divisible by 9 ?

    (A)   9
    (B)   16
    (C)   23
    (D)   35
    (E)   47

Arithmetic Properties of Numbers

Since n can be any positive integer, let $n = 2$. Then $25 \times 10^n = 2{,}500$, so its digits consist of the digits 2 and 5 followed by two digits of 0. Also, $k \times 10^{2n} = k \times 10{,}000$, so its digits consist of the digits of k followed by four digits of 0. Therefore, the digits of $(25 \times 10^n) + (k \times 10^{2n})$ consist of the digits of k followed by the digits 2 and 5, followed by two digits of 0. The table below shows this for $n = 2$ and $k = 35$:

$$25 \times 10^n = \quad 2{,}500$$
$$35 \times 10^{2n} = 350{,}000$$
$$(25 \times 10^n) + (35 \times 10^{2n}) = 352{,}500$$

Thus, when $n = 2$, the sum of the digits of $(25 \times 10^n) + (k \times 10^{2n})$ will be $2 + 5 = 7$ plus the sum of the digits of k. Of the answer choices, this sum of digits is divisible by 9 only for $k = 47$, which gives $2 + 5 + 4 + 7 = 18$. It can also be verified that, for each positive integer n, the only such answer choice is $k = 47$, although this additional verification is not necessary to obtain the correct answer.

The correct answer is E.

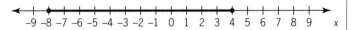

112. On the number line, the shaded interval is the graph of which of the following inequalities?

    (A) $|x| \leq 4$
    (B) $|x| \leq 8$
    (C) $|x - 2| \leq 4$
    (D) $|x - 2| \leq 6$
    (E) $|x + 2| \leq 6$

Algebra Inequalities; Absolute Value

The midpoint of the interval from –8 to 4, inclusive, is $\dfrac{-8+4}{2} = -2$ and the length of the interval from –8 to 4, inclusive, is $4 - (-8) = 12$, so the interval consists of all numbers within a distance of $\dfrac{12}{2} = 6$ from –2. Using an inequality involving absolute values, this can be described by $|x - (-2)| \leq 6$, or $|x + 2| \leq 6$.

Alternatively, the inequality $-8 \leq x \leq 4$ can be written as the conjunction $-8 \leq x$ and $x \leq 4$. Rewrite this conjunction so that the lower value, –8, and the upper value, 4, are shifted to values that have the same magnitude. This can be done by adding 2 to each side of each inequality, which gives $-6 \leq x + 2$ and $x + 2 \leq 6$. Thus, $x + 2$ lies between –6 and 6, inclusive, and it follows that $|x + 2| \leq 6$.

The correct answer is E.

113. Last year members of a certain professional organization for teachers consisted of teachers from 49 different school districts, with an average (arithmetic mean) of 9.8 schools per district. Last year the average number of teachers at these schools who were members of the organization was 22. Which of the following is closest to the total number of members of the organization last year?

    (A) 10^7
    (B) 10^6
    (C) 10^5
    (D) 10^4
    (E) 10^3

Arithmetic Statistics

There are 49 school districts and an average of 9.8 schools per district, so the number of schools is $(49)(9.8) \approx (50)(10) = 500$. There are approximately 500 schools and an average of 22 teachers at each school, so the number of teachers is approximately $(500)(22) \approx (500)(20) = 10{,}000 = 10^4$.

The correct answer is D.

114. Of all the students in a certain dormitory, $\frac{1}{2}$ are first-year students and the rest are second-year students. If $\frac{4}{5}$ of the first-year students have <u>not</u> declared a major and if the fraction of second-year students who have declared a major is 3 times the fraction of first-year students who have declared a major, what fraction of all the students in the dormitory are second-year students who have <u>not</u> declared a major?

(A) $\frac{1}{15}$

(B) $\frac{1}{5}$

(C) $\frac{4}{15}$

(D) $\frac{1}{3}$

(E) $\frac{2}{5}$

Arithmetic Applied Problems

Consider the table below in which T represents the total number of students in the dormitory. Since $\frac{1}{2}$ of the students are first-year students and the rest are second-year students, it follows that $\frac{1}{2}$ of the students are second-year students, and so the totals for the first-year and second-year columns are both $0.5T$. Since $\frac{4}{5}$ of the first-year students have not declared a major, it follows that the middle entry in the first-year column is $\frac{4}{5}(0.5T) = 0.4T$ and the first entry in the first-year column is $0.5T - 0.4T = 0.1T$. Since the fraction of second-year students who have declared a major is 3 times the fraction of first-year students who have declared a major, it follows that the first entry in the second-year column is $3(0.1T) = 0.3T$ and the second entry in the second-year column is $0.5T - 0.3T = 0.2T$. Thus, the fraction of students that are second-year students who have not declared a major is $\frac{0.2T}{T} = 0.2 = \frac{1}{5}$.

	First-year	Second-year	Total
Declared major	$0.1T$	$0.3T$	$0.4T$
Not declared major	$0.4T$	$0.2T$	$0.6T$
Total	$0.5T$	$0.5T$	T

The correct answer is B.

115. If the average (arithmetic mean) of x, y, and z is 7x and $x \neq 0$, what is the ratio of x to the sum of y and z ?

(A) 1:21

(B) 1:20

(C) 1:6

(D) 6:1

(E) 20:1

Algebra Ratio and Proportion

Given that the average of x, y, and z is $7x$, it follows that $\frac{x + y + z}{3} = 7x$, or $x + y + z = 21x$, or $y + z = 20x$. Dividing both sides of the last equation by $20(y + z)$ gives $\frac{1}{20} = \frac{x}{y + z}$, so the ratio of x to the sum of y and z is 1:20.

The correct answer is B.

116. Jonah drove the first half of a 100-mile trip in y hours and the second half in y hours. Which of the following is equal to Jonah's average speed, in miles per hour, for the entire trip?

(A) $\frac{50}{x + y}$

(B) $\frac{100}{x + y}$

(C) $\frac{25}{x} + \frac{25}{y}$

(D) $\frac{50}{x} + \frac{50}{y}$

(E) $\frac{100}{x} + \frac{100}{y}$

Algebra Applied Problems

Using average speed $= \dfrac{\text{total distance}}{\text{total time}}$, it follows that Jonah's average speed for his entire 100-mile trip is $\dfrac{100}{x + y}$.

The correct answer is B.

117. If the amount of federal estate tax due on an estate valued at $1.35 million is $437,000 plus 43 percent of the value of the estate in excess of $1.25 million, then the federal tax due is approximately what percent of the value of the estate?

(A) 30%
(B) 35%
(C) 40%
(D) 45%
(E) 50%

Arithmetic Percents; Estimation

The amount of tax divided by the value of the estate is

$$\frac{[0.437 + (0.43)(1.35 - 1.25)] \; \text{million}}{1.35 \; \text{million}} \quad \text{value as fraction}$$

$$= \frac{0.437 + (0.43)(0.1)}{1.35} \quad \text{arithmetic}$$

$$= \frac{0.48}{1.35} = \frac{48}{135} \quad \text{arithmetic}$$

By long division, $\dfrac{48}{135}$ is approximately 35.6, so the closest answer choice is 35%.

Alternatively, $\dfrac{48}{135}$ can be estimated by

$\dfrac{48}{136} = \dfrac{6}{17} \approx \dfrac{6}{18} = \dfrac{1}{3} \approx 33\%$, so the closest answer choice is 35%. Note that $\dfrac{48}{135}$ is greater than $\dfrac{48}{136}$, and $\dfrac{6}{17}$ is greater than $\dfrac{6}{18}$, so the correct value is greater than 33%, which rules out 30% being the closest.

The correct answer is B.

$$7x + 6y \le 38{,}000$$
$$4x + 5y \le 28{,}000$$

118. A manufacturer wants to produce x balls and y boxes. Resource constraints require that x and y satisfy the inequalities shown. What is the maximum number of balls and boxes combined that can be produced given the resource constraints?

(A) 5,000
(B) 6,000
(C) 7,000
(D) 8,000
(E) 10,000

Algebra Inequalities

We are to determine the maximum value of $x + y$ given the inequalities above. Note that if $A \le B$ and $C \le D$, then we can "add inequalities" to obtain $A + C \le B + D$, since (roughly speaking) the sum of two smaller numbers is less than the sum of two larger numbers. Adding the inequalities shown above gives $(7x + 6y) + (4x + 5y) \le 38{,}000 + 28{,}000$, or $11x + 11y \le 66{,}000$. Dividing both sides of this last inequality by 11 gives $x + y \le 6{,}000$. Therefore, the values of $x + y$ are at most 6,000, and hence the maximum value of $x + y$ is *at most* 6,000.

The fact that the maximum value of $x + y$ is *equal* to 6,000 follows from the fact that the system of simultaneous equations $7x + 6y = 38{,}000$ and $4x + 5y = 28{,}000$ has a solution, which in turn follows from the fact that these two equations correspond to a pair of nonparallel lines in the standard (x, y) coordinate plane. In particular, the pair $x = 2{,}000$ and $y = 4{,}000$ satisfy both the two inequalities and the equation $x + y = 6{,}000$.

The correct answer is B.

119. If $\dfrac{3}{10^4} = x\%$, then $x =$

(A) 0.3
(B) 0.03
(C) 0.003
(D) 0.0003
(E) 0.00003

Arithmetic Percents

Given that $\dfrac{3}{10^4} = x\,\%$, and writing $x\,\%$ as $\dfrac{x}{100}$, it

follows that $\dfrac{3}{10^4} = \dfrac{x}{100}$. Multiplying both sides by

100 gives $x = \dfrac{300}{10^4} = \dfrac{300}{10{,}000} = \dfrac{3}{100} = 0.03$.

The correct answer is B.

120. What is the remainder when 3^{24} is divided by 5 ?

   (A)   0
   (B)   1
   (C)   2
   (D)   3
   (E)   4

Arithmetic Properties of Numbers

A pattern in the units digits of the numbers
$3, 3^2 = 9, 3^3 = 27, 3^4 = 81, 3^5 = 243$, etc., can
be found by observing that the units digit of
a product of two integers is the same as the
units digit of the product of the units digit
of the two integers. For example, the units
digit of $3^5 = 3 \times 3^4 = 3 \times 81$ is 3 since the
units digit of 3×1 is 3, and the units digit of
$3^6 = 3 \times 3^5 = 3 \times 243$ is 9 since the units digit of
3×3 is 9. From this it follows that the units digit
of the powers of 3 follow the pattern 3, 9, 7, 1, 3, 9,
7, 1, etc., with a units digit of 1 for $3^4, 3^8, 3^{12}, \ldots,$
$3^{24}, \ldots$. Therefore, the units digit of 3^{24} is 1. Thus,
3^{24} is 1 more than a multiple of 10, and hence
3^{24} is 1 more than a multiple of 5, and so the
remainder when 3^{24} is divided by 5 is 1.

The correct answer is B.

121. José has a collection of 100 coins, consisting of
   nickels, dimes, quarters, and half-dollars. If he has a
   total of 35 nickels and dimes, a total of 45 dimes and
   quarters, and a total of 50 nickels and quarters, how
   many half-dollars does he have?

   (A)   15
   (B)   20
   (C)   25
   (D)   30
   (E)   35

Algebra Simultaneous Equations

Letting n, d, q, and h, respectively, represent the
numbers of nickels, dimes, quarters, and half-
dollars José has, determine the value of h.

The following are given:

   (1) $n + d + q + h = 100$
   (2) $n + d = 35$
   (3) $d + q = 45$
   (4) $n + q = 50$

Adding (2), (3), and (4) gives $2n + 2d + 2q = 130$
or $n + d + q = 65$. Subtracting this equation from
(1) gives $h = 100 - 65 = 35$.

The correct answer is E.

122. David used part of $100,000 to purchase a house. Of
   the remaining portion, he invested $\dfrac{1}{3}$ of it at 4 percent
   simple annual interest and $\dfrac{2}{3}$ of it at 6 percent simple
   annual interest. If after a year the income from the
   two investments totaled $320, what was the purchase
   price of the house?

   (A) $96,000
   (B) $94,000
   (C) $88,000
   (D) $75,000
   (E) $40,000

Algebra Applied Problems; Percents

Let x be the amount, in dollars, that David used
to purchase the house. Then David invested
$(100{,}000 - x)$ dollars, $\dfrac{1}{3}$ at 4% simple annual
interest and $\dfrac{2}{3}$ at 6% simple annual interest. After
one year the total interest, in dollars, on this
investment was $\dfrac{1}{3}(100{,}000 - x)(0.04) +$
$\dfrac{2}{3}(100{,}000 - x)(0.06) = 320$. Solve this equation
to find the value of x.

$$\frac{1}{3}(100{,}000-x)(0.04)+$$

$$\frac{2}{3}(100{,}000-x)(0.06)=320 \quad \text{given}$$

$(100{,}000-x)(0.04)+$
$2(100{,}000-x)(0.06)=960$ multiply both sides by 3

$4{,}000-0.04x+$
$12{,}000-0.12x=960$ distributive property

$16{,}000-0.16x=960$ combine like terms

$16{,}000-960=0.16x$ add $0.16x-960$ to both sides

$100{,}000-6{,}000=x$ divide both sides by 0.16

$94{,}000=x$

Therefore, the purchase price of the house was $94,000.

The correct answer is B.

123. A certain manufacturer sells its product to stores in 113 different regions worldwide, with an average (arithmetic mean) of 181 stores per region. If last year these stores sold an average of 51,752 units of the manufacturer's product per store, which of the following is closest to the total number of units of the manufacturer's product sold worldwide last year?

(A) 10^6
(B) 10^7
(C) 10^8
(D) 10^9
(E) 10^{10}

Arithmetic Estimation

$(113)(181)(51{,}752)\approx(100)(200)(50{,}000)$
$$=10^2\times(2\times10^2)\times(5\times10^4)$$
$$=(2\times5)\times10^{2+2+4}$$
$$=10^1\times10^8=10^9$$

The correct answer is D.

124. Andrew started saving at the beginning of the year and had saved $240 by the end of the year. He continued to save and by the end of 2 years had saved a total of $540. Which of the following is closest to the percent increase in the amount Andrew saved during the second year compared to the amount he saved during the first year?

(A) 11%
(B) 25%
(C) 44%
(D) 56%
(E) 125%

Arithmetic Percents

Andrew saved $240 in the first year and $540 − $240 = $300 in the second year. The percent increase in the amount Andrew saved in the second year compared to the amount he saved in the first year is $\left(\frac{300-240}{240}\times100\right)\% =$
$\left(\frac{60}{240}\times100\right)\%=\left(\frac{1}{4}\times100\right)\%=25\%.$

The correct answer is B.

125. If x is a positive integer, r is the remainder when x is divided by 4, and R is the remainder when x is divided by 9, what is the greatest possible value of r^2+R?

(A) 25
(B) 21
(C) 17
(D) 13
(E) 11

Arithmetic Properties of Integers

If r is the remainder when the positive integer x is divided by 4, then $0\le r<4$, so the maximum value of r is 3. If R is the remainder when the positive integer x is divided by 9, then $0\le R<9$, so the maximum value of R is 8. Thus, the maximum value of r^2+R is $3^2+8=17$.

The correct answer is C.

126. Each of the nine digits 0, 1, 1, 4, 5, 6, 8, 8, and 9 is used once to form 3 three-digit integers. What is the greatest possible sum of the 3 integers?

    (A) 1,752
    (B) 2,616
    (C) 2,652
    (D) 2,775
    (E) 2,958

Arithmetic Place Value

To create 3 three-digit numbers using each of the digits 0, 1, 1, 4, 5, 6, 8, 8, and 9 and having the maximum possible sum, the greatest three digits must be in hundreds place, the next greatest three in tens place, and the three smallest digits in units place. The sum will then be $(9 + 8 + 8)(100) + (4 + 5 + 6)(10) + (0 + 1 + 1) = 25(100) + 15(10) + 2 = 2,500 + 150 + 2 = 2,652$.

The correct answer is C.

127. Given that $1^2 + 2^2 + 3^2 + \ldots + 10^2 = 385$, what is the value of $3^2 + 6^2 + 9^2 + \ldots + 30^2$?

    (A) 1,155
    (B) 1,540
    (C) 1,925
    (D) 2,310
    (E) 3,465

Arithmetic Series and Sequences

We can use the fact that each term of the second series is $3^2 = 9$ times greater than the corresponding term of the first series to find the sum of the second series.

$3^2 + 6^2 + 9^2 + \ldots + 30^2$
$= (3 \cdot 1)^2 + (3 \cdot 2)^2 + (3 \cdot 3)^2 + \ldots + (3 \cdot 10)^2$
$= (3^2 \cdot 1^2) + (3^2 \cdot 2^2) + (3^2 \cdot 3^2) + \ldots + (3^2 \cdot 10^2)$
$= 3^2(1^2 + 2^2 + 3^2 + \ldots + 10^2) = 9(385) = 3,465$

The correct answer is E.

Questions 128 to 171 - Difficulty: Hard

128. Two numbers differ by 2 and sum to S. Which of the following is the greater of the numbers in terms of S?

    (A) $\dfrac{S}{2} - 1$

    (B) $\dfrac{S}{2}$

    (C) $\dfrac{S}{2} + \dfrac{1}{2}$

    (D) $\dfrac{S}{2} + 1$

    (E) $\dfrac{S}{2} + 2$

Algebra First-Degree Equations

Let x represent the greater of the two numbers that differ by 2. Then, $x - 2$ represents the lesser of the two numbers. The two numbers sum to S, so $x + (x - 2) = S$. It follows that $2x - 2 = S$, or $2x = S + 2$, or $x = \dfrac{S}{2} + 1$.

The correct answer is D.

129. If m is an integer and $m = 10^{32} - 32$, what is the sum of the digits of m?

    (A) 257
    (B) 264
    (C) 275
    (D) 284
    (E) 292

Arithmetic Arithmetic Operations

When written in standard base 10 notation, 10^{32} is the digit 1 followed by 32 digits of 0. Now consider the following subtractions and the digit pattern they suggest, a pattern which is easily seen to continue.

$$
\begin{aligned}
100 &- 32 = 68 \\
1,000 &- 32 = 968 \\
10,000 &- 32 = 9,968 \\
100,000 &- 32 = 99,968 \\
1,000,000 &- 32 = 999,968
\end{aligned}
$$

Using this digit pattern, $m = 10^{32} - 32$ in standard base 10 notation consists of $32 - 2 = 30$ occurrences of the digit 9 followed by the digits 6 and 8. Therefore, the sum of the digits of m is $30(9) + 6 + 8 = 270 + 14 = 284$.

The correct answer is D.

130. In a numerical table with 10 rows and 10 columns, each entry is either a 9 or a 10. If the number of 9s in the nth row is $n - 1$ for each n from 1 to 10, what is the average (arithmetic mean) of all the numbers in the table?

    (A) 9.45
    (B) 9.50
    (C) 9.55
    (D) 9.65
    (E) 9.70

Arithmetic Operations with Integers

There are $(10)(10) = 100$ entries in the table. In rows 1, 2, 3, …, 10, the number of 9s is 0, 1, 2, …, 9, respectively, giving a total of $0 + 1 + 2 + … + 9 = 45$ entries with a 9. This leaves a total of $100 - 45 = 55$ entries with a 10. Therefore, the sum of the 100 entries is $45(9) + 55(10) = 405 + 550 = 955$, and the average of the 100 entries is $\dfrac{955}{100} = 9.55$

The correct answer is C.

131. In 2004, the cost of 1 year-long print subscription to a certain newspaper was $4 per week. In 2005, the newspaper introduced a new rate plan for 1 year-long print subscription: $3 per week for the first 40 weeks of 2005 and $2 per week for the remaining weeks of 2005. How much less did 1 year-long print subscription to this newspaper cost in 2005 than in 2004 ?

    (A) $64
    (B) $78
    (C) $112
    (D) $144
    (E) $304

Arithmetic Applied Problems

The cost, in dollars, of 1 year-long print subscription in 2004 was $52(4) = 208$ and the cost, in dollars, of 1 year-long print subscription in 2005 was $40(3) + 12(2) = 120 + 24 = 144$. Therefore, the cost in 2005 was less than the cost in 2004 by $208 - 144 = 64$ dollars.

The correct answer is A.

132. A positive integer n is a perfect number provided that the sum of all the positive factors of n, including 1 and n, is equal to $2n$. What is the sum of the reciprocals of all the positive factors of the perfect number 28 ?

    (A) $\dfrac{1}{4}$

    (B) $\dfrac{56}{27}$

    (C) 2

    (D) 3

    (E) 4

Arithmetic Properties of Numbers

The factors of 28 are 1, 2, 4, 7, 14, and 28. Therefore, the sum of the reciprocals of the factors of 28 is $\dfrac{1}{1} + \dfrac{1}{2} + \dfrac{1}{4} + \dfrac{1}{7} + \dfrac{1}{14} + \dfrac{1}{28} =$

$\dfrac{28}{28} + \dfrac{14}{28} + \dfrac{7}{28} + \dfrac{4}{28} + \dfrac{2}{28} + \dfrac{1}{28} =$

$\dfrac{28 + 14 + 7 + 4 + 2 + 1}{28} = \dfrac{56}{28} = 2.$

The correct answer is C.

133. The infinite sequence a_1, a_2, … , a_n, … is such that $a_1 = 2$, $a_2 = -3$, $a_3 = 5$, $a_4 = -1$, and $a_n = a_{n-4}$ for $n > 4$. What is the sum of the first 97 terms of the sequence?

    (A) 72
    (B) 74
    (C) 75
    (D) 78
    (E) 80

Arithmetic Sequences and Series

Because $a_n = a_{n-4}$ for $n > 4$, it follows that the terms of the sequence repeat in groups of 4 terms:

Values for n	Values for a_n
1, 2, 3, 4	2, –3, 5, –1
5, 6, 7, 8	2, –3, 5, –1
9, 10, 11, 12	2, –3, 5, –1
13, 14, 15, 16	2, –3, 5, –1

Thus, since $97 = 24(4) + 1$, the sum of the first 97 terms can be grouped into 24 groups of 4 terms each, with one remaining term, which allows the sum to be easily found:

$$(a_1 + a_2 + a_3 + a_4) + (a_5 + a_6 + a_7 + a_8) + \ldots +$$
$$(a_{93} + a_{94} + a_{95} + a_{96}) + a_{97}$$

$$= (2 - 3 + 5 - 1) + (2 - 3 + 5 - 1) + \ldots +$$
$$(2 - 3 + 5 - 1) + 2$$

$$= 24(2 - 3 + 5 - 1) + 2 = 24(3) + 2 = 74$$

The correct answer is B.

134. The sequence a_1, a_2, ... , a_n, ... is such that $a_n = 2a_{n-1} - x$ for all positive integers $n \geq 2$ and for a certain number x. If $a_5 = 99$ and $a_3 = 27$, what is the value of x ?

    (A)   3
    (B)   9
    (C)   18
    (D)   36
    (E)   45

Algebra Sequences and Series

An expression for a_5 that involves x can be obtained using $a_3 = 27$ and applying the equation $a_n = 2a_{n-1} - x$ twice, once for $n = 4$ and once for $n = 5$.

$a_4 = 2a_3 - x$	using $a_n = 2a_{n-1} - x$ for $n = 4$
$= 2(27) - x$	using $a_3 = 27$
$a_5 = 2a_4 - x$	using $a_n = 2a_{n-1} - x$ for $n = 5$
$= 2[2(27) - x] - x$	using $a_4 = 2(27) - x$
$= 4(27) - 3x$	combine like terms

Therefore, using $a_5 = 99$, we have

$99 = 4(27) - 3x$	given
$3x = 4(27) - 99$	adding $(3x - 99)$ to both sides
$x = 4(9) - 33$	dividing both sides by 3
$x = 3$	arithmetic

The correct answer is A.

135. In a certain medical survey, 45 percent of the people surveyed had the type A antigen in their blood and 3 percent had both the type A antigen and the type B antigen. Which of the following is closest to the percent of those with the type A antigen who also had the type B antigen?

    (A)   1.35%
    (B)   6.67%
    (C)   13.50%
    (D)   15.00%
    (E)   42.00%

Arithmetic Applied Problems; Percents

Let n be the total number of people surveyed. Then, the proportion of the people who had type A who also had type B is $\dfrac{(3\%)n}{(45\%)n} = \dfrac{3}{45} = \dfrac{1}{15}$, which as a percent is approximately 6.67%. Note that by using $\dfrac{1}{15} = \dfrac{1}{3} \times \dfrac{1}{5}$, which equals $\dfrac{1}{3}$ of 20%, we can avoid dividing by a 2-digit integer.

The correct answer is B.

136. On a certain transatlantic crossing, 20 percent of a ship's passengers held round-trip tickets and also took their cars aboard the ship. If 60 percent of the passengers with round-trip tickets did <u>not</u> take their cars aboard the ship, what percent of the ship's passengers held round-trip tickets?

    (A) $33\frac{1}{3}$%
    (B)   40%
    (C)   50%
    (D)   60%
    (E) $66\frac{2}{3}$%

Arithmetic Percents

Since the number of passengers on the ship is immaterial, let the number of passengers on the ship be 100 for convenience. Let x be the number of passengers that held round-trip tickets. Then, since 20 percent of the passengers held a round-trip ticket and took their cars aboard the ship, $0.20(100) = 20$ passengers held round-trip tickets and took their cars aboard the ship. The remaining passengers with round-trip tickets did not take their cars aboard, and they represent $0.6x$ (that is, 60 percent of the passengers with round-trip tickets). Thus $0.6x + 20 = x$, from which it follows that $20 = 0.4x$, and so $x = 50$. The percent of passengers with round-trip tickets is, then,

$$\frac{50}{100} = 50\%.$$

The correct answer is C.

137. If x and k are integers and $(12^x)(4^{2x+1}) = (2^k)(3^2)$, what is the value of k?

(A) 5
(B) 7
(C) 10
(D) 12
(E) 14

Arithmetic Exponents

Rewrite the expression on the left so that it is a product of powers of 2 and 3.

$$(12^x)(4^{2x+1}) = [(3 \cdot 2^2)^x][(2^2)^{2x+1}]$$
$$= (3^x)[(2^2)^x][2^{2(2x+1)}]$$
$$= (3^x)(2^{2x})(2^{4x+2})$$
$$= (3^x)(2^{6x+2})$$

Then, since $(12^x)(4^{2x+1}) = (2^k)(3^2)$, it follows that $(3^x)(2^{6x+2}) = (2^k)(3^2) = (3^2)(2^k)$, so $x = 2$ and $k = 6x + 2$. Substituting 2 for x gives $k = 6(2) + 2 = 14$.

The correct answer is E.

138. If S is the sum of the reciprocals of the 10 consecutive integers from 21 to 30, then S is between which of the following two fractions?

(A) $\frac{1}{3}$ and $\frac{1}{2}$
(B) $\frac{1}{4}$ and $\frac{1}{3}$
(C) $\frac{1}{5}$ and $\frac{1}{4}$
(D) $\frac{1}{6}$ and $\frac{1}{5}$
(E) $\frac{1}{7}$ and $\frac{1}{6}$

Arithmetic Estimation

The value of $\frac{1}{21} + \frac{1}{22} + \frac{1}{23} + \ldots + \frac{1}{30}$ is LESS than $\frac{1}{20} + \frac{1}{20} + \frac{1}{20} + \ldots + \frac{1}{20}$ (10 numbers added), which equals $10\left(\frac{1}{20}\right) = \frac{1}{2}$, and GREATER than $\frac{1}{30} + \frac{1}{30} + \frac{1}{30} + \ldots + \frac{1}{30}$ (10 numbers added), which equals $10\left(\frac{1}{30}\right) = \frac{1}{3}$. Therefore, the value of $\frac{1}{21} + \frac{1}{22} + \frac{1}{23} + \ldots + \frac{1}{30}$ is between $\frac{1}{3}$ and $\frac{1}{2}$.

The correct answer is A.

139. For every even positive integer m, $f(m)$ represents the product of all even integers from 2 to m, inclusive. For example, $f(12) = 2 \times 4 \times 6 \times 8 \times 10 \times 12$. What is the greatest prime factor of $f(24)$?

(A) 23
(B) 19
(C) 17
(D) 13
(E) 11

Arithmetic Properties of Numbers

Rewriting $f(24) = 2 \times 4 \times 6 \times 8 \times 10 \times 12 \times 14 \times \ldots \times 20 \times 22 \times 24$ as $2 \times 4 \times 2(3) \times 8 \times 2(5) \times 12 \times 2(7) \times \ldots \times 20 \times 2(11) \times 24$ shows that all of the prime numbers from 2 through 11 are factors of $f(24)$. The next prime number is 13, but 13 is not a factor of $f(24)$ because none of the even integers from 2 through 24 has 13 as a factor. Therefore, the largest prime factor of $f(24)$ is 11.

The correct answer is E.

$$3, k, 2, 8, m, 3$$

140. The arithmetic mean of the list of numbers above is 4. If k and m are integers and $k \neq m$ what is the median of the list?

(A)   2
(B)   2.5
(C)   3
(D)   3.5
(E)   4

Arithmetic Statistics

Since the arithmetic mean $= \dfrac{\text{sum of values}}{\text{number of values}}$, then $\dfrac{3+k+2+8+m+3}{6} = 4$, and so $\dfrac{16+k+m}{6} = 4$, $16 + k + m = 24$, $k + m = 8$. Since $k \neq m$, then either $k < 4$ and $m > 4$ or $k > 4$ and $m < 4$. Because k and m are integers, either $k \le 3$ and $m \ge 5$ or $k \ge 5$ and $m \le 3$.

Case (i):   If $k \le 2$, then $m \ge 6$ and the six integers in ascending order are k, 2, 3, 3, m, 8 or k, 2, 3, 3, 8, m. The two middle integers are both 3 so the median is $\dfrac{3+3}{2} = 3$.

Case (ii):   If $k = 3$, then $m = 5$ and the six integers in ascending order are 2, k, 3, 3, m, 8. The two middle integers are both 3 so the median is $\dfrac{3+3}{2} = 3$.

Case (iii):   If $k = 5$, then $m = 3$ and the six integers in ascending order are 2, m, 3, 3, k, 8. The two middle integers are both 3 so the median is $\dfrac{3+3}{2} = 3$.

Case (iv):   If $k \ge 6$, then $m \le 2$ and the six integers in ascending order are m, 2, 3, 3, k, 8 or m, 2, 3, 3, 8, k. The two middle integers are both 3 so the median is $\dfrac{3+3}{2} = 3$.

The correct answer is C.

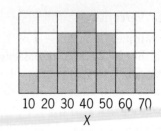

X

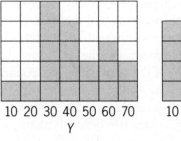

Y

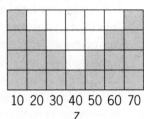

Z

141. If the variables X, Y, and Z take on only the values 10, 20, 30, 40, 50, 60, or 70 with frequencies indicated by the shaded regions above, for which of the frequency distributions is the mean equal to the median?

(A) X only
(B) Y only
(C) Z only
(D) X and Y
(E) X and Z

Arithmetic Statistics

The frequency distributions for both X and Z are symmetric about 40, and thus both X and Z have mean = median = 40. Therefore, any answer choice that does not include both X and Z can be eliminated. This leaves only answer choice E.

The correct answer is E.

$$2x + y = 12$$
$$|y| \le 12$$

142. For how many ordered pairs (x, y) that are solutions of the system above are x and y both integers?

(A)   7
(B)   10
(C)   12
(D)   13
(E)   14

Algebra Absolute Value

From $|y| \le 12$, if y must be an integer, then y must be in the set

$$S = \{\pm 12, \pm 11, \pm 10, \dots, \pm 3, \pm 2, \pm 1, 0\}.$$

Since $2x + y = 12$, then $x = \dfrac{12 - y}{2}$. If x must be
an integer, then $12 - y$ must be divisible by 2; that
is, $12 - y$ must be even. Since 12 is even, $12 - y$
is even if and only if y is even. This eliminates
all odd integers from S, leaving only the even
integers $\pm 12, \pm 10, \pm 8, \pm 6, \pm 4, \pm 2,$ and 0. Thus,
there are 13 possible integer y-values, each with
a corresponding integer x-value and, therefore,
there are 13 ordered pairs (x, y), where x and y are
both integers, that solve the system.

The correct answer is D.

143   The United States mint produces coins in 1-cent,
5-cent, 10-cent, 25-cent, and 50-cent denominations. If
a jar contains exactly 100 cents worth of these coins,
which of the following could be the total number of
coins in the jar?

   I.   91
   II.   81
   III. 76

   (A)   I only
   (B)   II only
   (C)   III only
   (D)   I and III only
   (E)   I, II, and III

Arithmetic Operations with Integers

Letting p, n, d, q, and h, respectively, represent
the numbers of pennies (1-cent coins), nickels
(5-cent coins), dimes (10-cent coins), quarters
(25-cent coins), and half-dollars (50-cent
coins) with a total worth of 100 cents, it
follows that $p + 5n + 10d + 25q + 50h = 100$.
Then $p = 100 - (5n + 10d + 25q + 50h) =$
$5(20 - n - 2d - 5q - 10h)$, so p must be a
multiple of 5.

   I.   If the jar contained 90 pennies and 1 dime,
        the total number of coins would be
        $90 + 1 = 91$ and the coins would be worth
        $90 + 10 = 100$ cents.

   II. For the jar to contain 81 coins with a
        total worth of 100 cents, there could be
        80 pennies, but then the one coin remaining
        would have to amount to 20 cents to make
        the coins' total worth 100 cents. This is not

possible since none of the coins is a 20-cent
coin. If there were 75 pennies, then the
remaining 6 coins would have to amount to
25 cents. This is not possible because 6 coins
of the next smallest denomination would
be worth 30 cents. If there were 70 pennies,
then the remaining 11 coins would have
to amount to 30 cents. This is not possible
because 11 coins of the next smallest
denomination would be worth 55 cents.
Continuing in this manner shows that it is
not possible for the jar to contain 81 coins
with a total worth of 100 cents.

   III. If the jar contained 70 pennies and 6 nickels,
         the total number of coins would be
         $70 + 6 = 76$ and the coins would be worth
         $70 + 30 = 100$ cents.

The correct answer is D.

144.   A certain university will select 1 of 7 candidates
eligible to fill a position in the mathematics department
and 2 of 10 candidates eligible to fill 2 identical
positions in the computer science department. If none
of the candidates is eligible for a position in both
departments, how many different sets of 3 candidates
are there to fill the 3 positions?

   (A)   42
   (B)   70
   (C)   140
   (D)   165
   (E)   315

Arithmetic Elementary Combinatorics

To fill the position in the math department,
1 candidate will be selected from a group of
7 eligible candidates, and so there are 7 sets of
1 candidate each to fill the position in the math
department. To fill the positions in the computer
science department, any one of the 10 eligible
candidates can be chosen for the first position
and any of the remaining 9 eligible candidates
can be chosen for the second position, making
a total of $10 \times 9 = 90$ sets of 2 candidates to fill
the computer science positions. But, this number
includes the set in which Candidate A was
chosen to fill the first position and Candidate B
was chosen to fill the second position as well as
the set in which Candidate B was chosen for the

first position and Candidate A was chosen for the second position. These sets are not different essentially since the positions are identical and in both sets Candidates A and B are chosen to fill the 2 positions. Therefore, there are $\frac{90}{2} = 45$ sets of 2 candidates to fill the computer science positions. Then, using the multiplication principle, there are $7 \times 45 = 315$ different sets of 3 candidates to fill the 3 positions.

The correct answer is E.

145. A survey of employers found that during 1993 employment costs rose 3.5 percent, where employment costs consist of salary costs and fringe-benefit costs. If salary costs rose 3 percent and fringe-benefit costs rose 5.5 percent during 1993, then fringe-benefit costs represented what percent of employment costs at the beginning of 1993 ?

    (A) 16.5%
    (B) 20%
    (C) 35%
    (D) 55%
    (E) 65%

Algebra; Arithmetic First-Degree Equations; Percents

Let E represent employment costs, S represent salary costs, and F represent fringe-benefit costs. Then $E = S + F$. An increase of 3 percent in salary costs and a 5.5 percent increase in fringe-benefit costs resulted in a 3.5 percent increase in employment costs. Therefore $1.03S + 1.055F = 1.035E$. But, $E = S + F$, so $1.03S + 1.055F = 1.035(S + F) = 1.035S + 1.035F$.

Combining like terms gives $(1.055 - 1.035)F = (1.035 - 1.03)S$ or

$0.02F = 0.005S$. Then, $S = \frac{0.02}{0.005}F = 4F$. Thus, since $E = S + F$, it follows that $E = 4F + F = 5F$.

Then, F as a percent of E is $\frac{F}{E} = \frac{F}{5F} = \frac{1}{5} = 20\%$.

The correct answer is B.

146. The subsets of the set $\{w, x, y\}$ are $\{w\}$, $\{x\}$, $\{y\}$, $\{w, x\}$, $\{w, y\}$, $\{x, y\}$, $\{w, x, y\}$, and $\{\ \}$ (the empty subset). How many subsets of the set $\{w, x, y, z\}$ contain w ?

    (A) Four
    (B) Five
    (C) Seven
    (D) Eight
    (E) Sixteen

Arithmetic Sets

As shown in the table, the subsets of $\{w, x, y, z\}$ can be organized into two columns, those subsets of $\{w, x, y, z\}$ that do not contain w (left column) and the corresponding subsets of $\{w, x, y, z\}$ that contain w (right column), and each of these collections has the same number of sets. Therefore, there are 8 subsets of $\{w, x, y, z\}$ that contain w.

subsets not containing w	subsets containing w
$\{\ \}$	$\{w\}$
$\{x\}$	$\{w, x\}$
$\{y\}$	$\{w, y\}$
$\{z\}$	$\{w, z\}$
$\{x, y\}$	$\{w, x, y\}$
$\{x, z\}$	$\{w, x, z\}$
$\{y, z\}$	$\{w, y, z\}$
$\{x, y, z\}$	$\{w, x, y, z\}$

The correct answer is D.

147. The number $\sqrt{63 - 36\sqrt{3}}$ can be expressed as $x + y\sqrt{3}$ for some integers x and y. What is the value of xy ?

    (A) −18
    (B) −6
    (C) 6
    (D) 18
    (E) 27

Algebra Operations on Radical Expressions

Squaring both sides of $\sqrt{63 - 36\sqrt{3}} = x + y\sqrt{3}$ gives $63 - 36\sqrt{3} = x^2 + 2xy\sqrt{3} + 3y^2 = (x^2 + 3y^2) + (2xy)\sqrt{3}$, which implies that $-36 = 2xy$, or $xy = -18$. Indeed, if $-36 \neq 2xy$, or equivalently, if $36 + 2xy \neq 0$, then we could write

$\sqrt{3}$ as a quotient of the two integers $63 - x^2 - 3y^2$ and $36 + 2xy$, which is not possible because $\sqrt{3}$ is an irrational number. To be more explicit, $63 - 36\sqrt{3} = x^2 + 2xy\sqrt{3} + 3y^2$ implies $63 - x^2 - 3y^2 = (36 + 2xy)\sqrt{3}$, and if $36 + 2xy \neq 0$, then we could divide both sides of the equation $63 - x^2 - 3y^2 = (36 + 2xy)\sqrt{3}$ by $36 + 2xy$ to get $\dfrac{63 - x^2 - 3y^2}{36 + 2xy} = \sqrt{3}$.

The correct answer is A.

148. There are 10 books on a shelf, of which 4 are paperbacks and 6 are hardbacks. How many possible selections of 5 books from the shelf contain at least one paperback and at least one hardback?

(A) 75
(B) 120
(C) 210
(D) 246
(E) 252

Arithmetic Elementary Combinatorics

The number of selections of 5 books containing at least one paperback and at least one hardback is equal to $T - N$, where T is the total number of selections of 5 books and N is the number of selections that do not contain both a paperback and a hardback. The value of T is

$$\binom{10}{5} = \frac{10!}{5!(10-5)!} = \frac{(6)(7)(8)(9)(10)}{(1)(2)(3)(4)(5)}$$
$$= (7)(2)(9)(2) = 252.$$

To find the value of N, first note that no selection of 5 books can contain all paperbacks, since there are only 4 paperback books. Thus, the value of N is equal to the number of selections of 5 books that contain all hardbacks, which is equal to 6 since there are 6 ways that a single hardback can be left out when choosing the 5 hardback books. It follows that the number of selections of 5 books containing at least one paperback and at least one hardback is $T - N = 252 - 6 = 246$.

The correct answer is D.

149. If x is to be chosen at random from the set {1, 2, 3, 4} and y is to be chosen at random from the set {5, 6, 7}, what is the probability that xy will be even?

(A) $\dfrac{1}{6}$

(B) $\dfrac{1}{3}$

(C) $\dfrac{1}{2}$

(D) $\dfrac{2}{3}$

(E) $\dfrac{5}{6}$

Arithmetic; Algebra Probability; Concepts of Sets

By the principle of multiplication, since there are 4 elements in the first set and 3 elements in the second set, there are $(4)(3) = 12$ possible products of xy, where x is chosen from the first set and y is chosen from the second set. These products will be even EXCEPT when both x and y are odd. Since there are 2 odd numbers in the first set and 2 odd numbers in the second set, there are $(2)(2) = 4$ products of x and y that are odd. This means that the remaining $12 - 4 = 8$ products are even. Thus, the probability that xy is even is $\dfrac{8}{12} = \dfrac{2}{3}$.

The correct answer is D.

150. The function f is defined for each positive three-digit integer n by $f(n) = 2^x\, 3^y\, 5^z$, where x, y, and z are the hundreds, tens, and units digits of n, respectively. If m and v are three-digit positive integers such that $f(m) = 9f(v)$, then $m - v =$

(A) 8
(B) 9
(C) 18
(D) 20
(E) 80

Algebra Place Value

Let the hundreds, tens, and units digits of m be A, B, and C, respectively; and let the hundreds, tens, and units digits of v be a, b, and c, respectively. From $f(m) = 9f(v)$ it follows that $2^A 3^B 5^C = 9(2^a 3^b 5^c) = 3^2(2^a 3^b 5^c) = 2^a 3^{b+2} 5^c$. Therefore, $A = a$, $B = b + 2$, and $C = c$. Now calculate $m - v$.

$$
\begin{aligned}
m - v &= (100A + 10B + C) \\
&\quad - (100a + 10b + c) &\text{place value property} \\
&= (100a + 10(b + 2) + c) &\text{obtained above} \\
&\quad - (100a + 10b + c) \\
&= 10(b + 2) - 10b &\text{combine like terms} \\
&= 10b + 20 - 10b &\text{distributive property} \\
&= 20 &\text{combine like terms}
\end{aligned}
$$

The correct answer is D.

151. If $10^{50} - 74$ is written as an integer in base 10 notation, what is the sum of the digits in that integer?

    (A) 424
    (B) 433
    (C) 440
    (D) 449
    (E) 467

Arithmetic Properties of Numbers

$10^2 - 74$	=	$100 - 74$	=	26
$10^3 - 74$	=	$1,000 - 74$	=	926
$10^4 - 74$	=	$10,000 - 74$	=	9,926
$10^5 - 74$	=	$100,000 - 74$	=	99,926
$10^6 - 74$	=	$1,000,000 - 74$	=	999,926

From the table above it is clear that $10^{50} - 74$ in base 10 notation will be 48 digits of 9 followed by the digits 2 and 6. Therefore, the sum of the digits of $10^{50} - 74$ is equal to $48(9) + 2 + 6 = 440$.

The correct answer is C.

152. A certain company that sells only cars and trucks reported that revenues from car sales in 1997 were down 11 percent from 1996 and revenues from truck sales in 1997 were up 7 percent from 1996. If total revenues from car sales and truck sales in 1997 were up 1 percent from 1996, what is the ratio of revenue from car sales in 1996 to revenue from truck sales in 1996 ?

    (A) 1:2
    (B) 4:5
    (C) 1:1
    (D) 3:2
    (E) 5:3

Algebra; Arithmetic First-Degree Equations; Percents

Let C_{96} and C_{97} represent revenues from car sales in 1996 and 1997, respectively, and let T_{96} and T_{97} represent revenues from truck sales in 1996 and 1997, respectively. A decrease of 11 percent in revenue from car sales from 1996 to 1997 can be represented as $(1 - 0.11)C_{96} = C_{97}$, and a 7 percent increase in revenue from truck sales from 1996 to 1997 can be represented as $(1 + 0.07)T_{96} = T_{97}$. An overall increase of 1 percent in revenue from car and truck sales from 1996 to 1997 can be represented as $C_{97} + T_{97} = (1 + 0.01)(C_{96} + T_{96})$. Then, by substitution of expressions for C_{97} and T_{97} that were derived above, $(1 - 0.11)C_{96} + (1 + 0.07)T_{96} = (1 + 0.01)(C_{96} + T_{96})$ and so $0.89C_{96} + 1.07T_{96} = 1.01(C_{96} + T_{96})$ or $0.89C_{96} + 1.07T_{96} = 1.01C_{96} + 1.01T_{96}$. Then, combining like terms gives $(1.07 - 1.01)T_{96} = (1.01 - 0.89)C_{96}$ or $0.06T_{96} = 0.12C_{96}$. Thus $\dfrac{C_{96}}{T_{96}} = \dfrac{0.06}{0.12} = \dfrac{1}{2}$. The ratio of revenue from car sales in 1996 to revenue from truck sales in 1996 is 1:2.

The correct answer is A.

153. Becky rented a power tool from a rental shop. The rent for the tool was $12 for the first hour and $3 for each additional hour. If Becky paid a total of $27, excluding sales tax, to rent the tool, for how many hours did she rent it?

    (A) 5
    (B) 6
    (C) 9
    (D) 10
    (E) 12

Arithmetic Applied Problems

Becky paid a total of $27 to rent the power tool. She paid $12 to rent the tool for the first hour and $27 - $12 = $15 to rent the tool for the additional hours at the rate of $3 per additional hour. It follows that she rented the tool for $\dfrac{15}{3} = 5$ additional hours and a total of $1 + 5 = 6$ hours.

The correct answer is B.

154. If $4 < \dfrac{7-x}{3}$, which of the following must be true?

   I. $5 < x$

   II. $|x+3| > 2$

   III. $-(x+5)$ is positive.

(A)   II only

(B)   III only

(C)   I and II only

(D)   II and III only

(E)   I, II, and III

Algebra Inequalities

Given that $4 < \dfrac{7-x}{3}$, it follows that $12 < 7 - x$. Then, $5 < -x$ or, equivalently, $x < -5$.

   I. If $4 < \dfrac{7-x}{3}$, then $x < -5$. If $5 < x$ were true then, by combining $5 < x$ and $x < -5$, it would follow that $5 < -5$, which cannot be true. Therefore, it is not the case that, if $4 < \dfrac{7-x}{3}$, then Statement I must be true. In fact, Statement I is never true.

   II. If $4 < \dfrac{7-x}{3}$, then $x < -5$, and it follows that $x + 3 < -2$. Since $-2 < 0$, then $x + 3 < 0$ and $|x+3| = -(x+3)$. If $x + 3 < -2$, then $-(x+3) > 2$ and by substitution, $|x+3| > 2$. Therefore, Statement II must be true for every value of x such that $x < -5$. Therefore, Statement II must be true if $4 < \dfrac{7-x}{3}$.

   III. If $4 < \dfrac{7-x}{3}$, then $x < -5$ and $x + 5 < 0$. But if $x + 5 < 0$, then it follows that $-(x+5) > 0$ and so $-(x+5)$ is positive. Therefore Statement III must be true if $4 < \dfrac{7-x}{3}$.

The correct answer is D.

155. On a certain day, a bakery produced a batch of rolls at a total production cost of $300. On that day, $\dfrac{4}{5}$ of the rolls in the batch were sold, each at a price that was 50 percent greater than the average (arithmetic mean) production cost per roll. The remaining rolls in the batch were sold the next day, each at a price that was 20 percent less than the price of the day before. What was the bakery's profit on this batch of rolls?

(A) $150

(B) $144

(C) $132

(D) $108

(E) $90

Arithmetic Applied Problems

Let n be the number of rolls in the batch and p be the average production price, in dollars, per roll. Then the total cost of the batch is $np = 300$ dollars, and the total revenue from selling the rolls in the batch is $\left(\dfrac{4}{5}n\right)(1.5p) + \left(\dfrac{1}{5}n\right)(0.8)(1.5p) =$ $\left(\dfrac{4}{5}n\right)\left(\dfrac{3}{2}p\right) + \left(\dfrac{1}{5}n\right)\left(\dfrac{4}{5}\right)\left(\dfrac{3}{2}p\right) = \left(\dfrac{6}{5} + \dfrac{6}{25}\right)np$ $= \left(\dfrac{36}{25}\right)np$. Therefore, the profit from selling the rolls in the batch is $\left(\dfrac{36}{25}\right)np - np = \left(\dfrac{11}{25}\right)np =$ $\left(\dfrac{11}{25}\right)(300)$ dollars $= 132$ dollars.

The correct answer is C.

156. A set of numbers has the property that for any number t in the set, $t + 2$ is in the set. If -1 is in the set, which of the following must also be in the set?

   I. -3

   II. 1

   III. 5

(A)   I only

(B)   II only

(C)   I and II only

(D)   II and III only

(E)   I, II, and III

Arithmetic Properties of Numbers

It is given that -1 is in the set and, if t is in the set, then $t + 2$ is in the set.

   I. Since $\{-1, 1, 3, 5, 7, 9, 11, \ldots\}$ contains -1 and satisfies the property that if t is in the set, then $t + 2$ is in the set, it is not true that -3 must be in the set.

II. Since −1 is in the set, −1 + 2 = 1 is in the set. Therefore, it must be true that 1 is in the set.

III. Since −1 is in the set, −1 + 2 = 1 is in the set. Since 1 is in the set, 1 + 2 = 3 is in the set. Since 3 is in the set, 3 + 2 = 5 is in the set. Therefore, it must be true that 5 is in the set.

The correct answer is D.

157. A couple decides to have 4 children. If they succeed in having 4 children and each child is equally likely to be a boy or a girl, what is the probability that they will have exactly 2 girls and 2 boys?

(A) $\frac{3}{8}$

(B) $\frac{1}{4}$

(C) $\frac{3}{16}$

(D) $\frac{1}{8}$

(E) $\frac{1}{16}$

Arithmetic Probability

Representing the birth order of the 4 children as a sequence of 4 letters, each of which is B for boy and G for girl, there are 2 possibilities (B or G) for the first letter, 2 for the second letter, 2 for the third letter, and 2 for the fourth letter, making a total of $2^4 = 16$ sequences. The table below categorizes some of these 16 sequences.

# of boys	# of girls	Sequences	# of sequences
0	4	GGGG	1
1	3	BGGG, GBGG, GGBG, GGGB	4
3	1	GBBB, BGBB, BBGB, BBBG	4
4	0	BBBB	1

The table accounts for 1 + 4 + 4 + 1 = 10 sequences. The other 6 sequences will have 2Bs and 2Gs. Therefore the probability that the couple will have exactly 2 boys and 2 girls is $\frac{6}{16} = \frac{3}{8}$.

For the mathematically inclined, if it is assumed that a couple has a fixed number of children, that the probability of having a girl each time is p, and that the sex of each child is independent of the sex of the other children, then the number of girls, r, born to a couple with n children is a random variable having the binomial probability distribution. The probability of having exactly x girls born to a couple with n children is given by the formula $\binom{n}{x} p^x (1-p)^{n-x}$. For the problem at hand, it is given that each child is equally likely to be a boy or a girl, and so $p = \frac{1}{2}$. Thus, the probability of having exactly 2 girls born to a couple with 4 children is

$$\binom{4}{2}\left(\frac{1}{2}\right)^2\left(\frac{1}{2}\right)^2 = \frac{4!}{2!2!}\left(\frac{1}{2}\right)^2\left(\frac{1}{2}\right)^2 = (6)\left(\frac{1}{4}\right)\left(\frac{1}{4}\right) = \frac{6}{16} = \frac{3}{8}.$$

The correct answer is A.

158. The closing price of Stock X changed on each trading day last month. The percent change in the closing price of Stock X from the first trading day last month to each of the other trading days last month was less than 50 percent. If the closing price on the second trading day last month was $10.00, which of the following CANNOT be the closing price on the last trading day last month?

(A) $3.00

(B) $9.00

(C) $19.00

(D) $24.00

(E) $29.00

Arithmetic Applied Problems; Percents

Let P be the first-day closing price, in dollars, of the stock. It is given that the second-day closing price was $(1 + n\%)P = 10$, so $P = \frac{10}{1 + n\%}$, for some value of n such that $-50 < n < 50$. Therefore, P is between $\frac{10}{1 + 0.50} \approx 6.67$ and $\frac{10}{1 - 0.50} = 20$. Hence, if Q is the closing price, in dollars, of the stock on the last day, then Q is between

$(0.50)(6.67) \approx 3.34$ (50% decrease from the lowest possible first-day closing price) and $(1.50)(20) = 30$ (50% increase from the greatest possible first-day closing price). The only answer choice that gives a number of dollars not between 3.34 and 30 is the first answer choice.

The correct answer is A.

159. An airline passenger is planning a trip that involves three connecting flights that leave from Airports A, B, and C, respectively. The first flight leaves Airport A every hour, beginning at 8:00 a.m., and arrives at Airport B $2\frac{1}{2}$ hours later. The second flight leaves Airport B every 20 minutes, beginning at 8:00 a.m., and arrives at Airport C $1\frac{1}{6}$ hours later. The third flight leaves Airport C every hour, beginning at 8:45 a.m. What is the least total amount of time the passenger must spend between flights if all flights keep to their schedules?

(A)   25 min
(B)   1 hr 5 min
(C)   1 hr 15 min
(D)   2 hr 20 min
(E)   3 hr 40 min

Arithmetic Operations on Rational Numbers

Since the flight schedules at each of Airports A, B, and C are the same hour after hour, assume that the passenger leaves Airport A at 8:00 and arrives at Airport B at 10:30. Since flights from Airport B leave at 20-minute intervals beginning on the hour, the passenger must wait 10 minutes at Airport B for the flight that leaves at 10:40 and arrives at Airport C $1\frac{1}{6}$ hours or 1 hour 10 minutes later. Thus, the passenger arrives at Airport C at 11:50. Having arrived too late for the 11:45 flight from Airport C, the passenger must wait 55 minutes for the 12:45 flight. Thus, the least total amount of time the passenger must spend waiting between flights is $10 + 55 = 65$ minutes, or 1 hour 5 minutes.

The correct answer is B.

160. If n is a positive integer and n^2 is divisible by 72, then the largest positive integer that must divide n is

(A)   6
(B)   12
(C)   24
(D)   36
(E)   48

Arithmetic Properties of Numbers

Since n^2 is divisible by 72, $n^2 = 72k$ for some positive integer k. Since $n^2 = 72k$, then $72k$ must be a perfect square. Since $72k = (2^3)(3^2)k$, then $k = 2m^2$ for some positive integer m in order for $72k$ to be a perfect square. Then, $n^2 = 72k = (2^3)(3^2)(2m^2) = (2^4)(3^2)m^2 = [(2^2)(3)(m)]^2$, and $n = (2^2)(3)(m)$. The positive integers that MUST divide n are 1, 2, 3, 4, 6, and 12. Therefore, the largest positive integer that must divide n is 12.

The correct answer is B.

161. A certain grocery purchased x pounds of produce for p dollars per pound. If y pounds of the produce had to be discarded due to spoilage and the grocery sold the rest for s dollars per pound, which of the following represents the gross profit on the sale of the produce?

(A) $(x - y)s - xp$
(B) $(x - y)p - ys$
(C) $(s - p)y - xp$
(D) $xp - ys$
(E) $(x - y)(s - p)$

Algebra Simplifying Algebraic Expressions; Applied Problems

Since the grocery bought x pounds of produce for p dollars per pound, the total cost of the produce was xp dollars. Since y pounds of the produce was discarded, the grocery sold $x - y$ pounds of produce at the price of s dollars per pound, yielding a total revenue of $(x - y)s$ dollars. Then, the grocery's gross profit on the sale of the produce is its total revenue minus its total cost or $(x - y)s - xp$ dollars.

The correct answer is A.

162. If x, y, and z are positive integers such that x is a factor of y, and x is a multiple of z, which of the following is NOT necessarily an integer?

(A) $\dfrac{x+z}{z}$

(B) $\dfrac{y+z}{x}$

(C) $\dfrac{x+y}{z}$

(D) $\dfrac{xy}{z}$

(E) $\dfrac{yz}{x}$

Arithmetic Properties of Numbers

Since the positive integer x is a factor of y, then $y = kx$ for some positive integer k. Since x is a multiple of the positive integer z, then $x = mz$ for some positive integer m.

Substitute these expressions for x and/or y into each answer choice to find the one expression that is NOT necessarily an integer.

A $\dfrac{x+z}{z} = \dfrac{mz+z}{z} = \dfrac{(m+1)z}{z} = m+1$, which MUST be an integer

B $\dfrac{y+z}{x} = \dfrac{y}{x}+\dfrac{z}{x} = \dfrac{kx}{x}+\dfrac{z}{mz} = k+\dfrac{1}{m}$, which NEED NOT be an integer

Because only one of the five expressions need not be an integer, the expressions given in C, D, and E need not be tested. However, for completeness,

C $\dfrac{x+y}{z} = \dfrac{mz+kx}{z} = \dfrac{mz+k(mz)}{z} = \dfrac{mz(1+k)}{z}$
$= m(1+k)$, which MUST be an integer

D $\dfrac{xy}{z} = \dfrac{(mz)y}{z} = my$, which MUST be an integer

E $\dfrac{yz}{x} = \dfrac{(kx)(z)}{x} = kz$, which MUST be an integer

The correct answer is B.

163. Running at their respective constant rates, Machine X takes 2 days longer to produce w widgets than Machine Y. At these rates, if the two machines together produce $\frac{5}{4}w$ widgets in 3 days, how many days would it take Machine X alone to produce 2w widgets?

(A) 4
(B) 6
(C) 8
(D) 10
(E) 12

Algebra Applied Problems

If x, where $x > 2$, represents the number of days Machine X takes to produce w widgets, then Machine Y takes $x-2$ days to produce w widgets. It follows that Machines X and Y can produce $\frac{w}{x}$ and $\frac{w}{x-2}$ widgets, respectively, in 1 day and together they can produce $\frac{w}{x}+\frac{w}{x-2}$ widgets in 1 day. Since it is given that, together, they can produce $\frac{5}{4}w$ widgets in 3 days, it follows that, together, they can produce $\frac{1}{3}\left(\frac{5}{4}w\right)=\frac{5}{12}w$ widgets in 1 day. Thus,

$$\frac{w}{x}+\frac{w}{x-2}=\frac{5}{12}w$$
$$\left(\frac{1}{x}+\frac{1}{x-2}\right)w=\frac{5}{12}w$$
$$\left(\frac{1}{x}+\frac{1}{x-2}\right)=\frac{5}{12}$$
$$12x(x-2)\left(\frac{1}{x}+\frac{1}{x-2}\right)=12x(x-2)\left(\frac{5}{12}\right)$$
$$12[(x-2)+x]=5x(x-2)$$
$$12(2x-2)=5x(x-2)$$
$$24x-24=5x^2-10x$$
$$0=5x^2-34x+24$$
$$0=(5x-4)(x-6)$$
$$x=\frac{4}{5}\text{ or }6$$

Therefore, since $x > 2$, it follows that $x = 6$. Machine X takes 6 days to produce w widgets and $2(6) = 12$ days to produce $2w$ widgets.

The correct answer is E.

164. What is the greatest positive integer n such that 5^n divides $10! - (2)(5!)^2$?

    (A)   2
    (B)   3
    (C)   4
    (D)   5
    (E)   6

Arithmetic Properties of Numbers; Exponents

The greatest positive integer n such that 5^n divides a given integer is the number of factors of 5 in the prime factorization of the given integer. By repeated identification of common factors, the indicated difference can be factored sufficiently to determine the number of factors of 5 in its prime factorization. In the computations that follow, we have used the equalities $10! = (5!)(6)(7)(8)(9)(10)$ and $5! = (2)(3)(4)(5)$.

$10! - (2)(5!)^2$
$= (5! \cdot 6 \cdot 7 \cdot 8 \cdot 9 \cdot 10) - (2 \cdot 5! \cdot 5!)$
$= (5!)(6 \cdot 7 \cdot 8 \cdot 9 \cdot 10 - 2 \cdot 5!)$
$= (5!)(6 \cdot 7 \cdot 8 \cdot 9 \cdot 10 - 2 \cdot 2 \cdot 3 \cdot 4 \cdot 5)$
$= (5!)(2^4)(3 \cdot 7 \cdot 9 \cdot 10 - 3 \cdot 5)$
$= (5!)(2^4)(3)(7 \cdot 9 \cdot 10 - 5)$
$= (5!)(2^4)(3)(5)(7 \cdot 9 \cdot 2 - 1)$
$= (5!)(2^4)(3)(5)(63 \cdot 2 - 1)$
$= (5!)(2^4)(3)(5)(126 - 1)$
$= (5!)(2^4)(3)(5)(125)$

Since there is exactly 1 factor of 5 in $5! = (2)(3)(4)(5)$, no factors of 5 in either 2^4 or 3, exactly 1 factor of 5 in 5, and exactly 3 factors of 5 in $125 = 5^3$, it follows that there are $1 + 1 + 3 = 5$ factors of 5 in $10! - (2)(5!)^2 = (5!)(2^4)(3)(5)(125)$.

The correct answer is D.

165. Yesterday, Candice and Sabrina trained for a bicycle race by riding around an oval track. They both began riding at the same time from the track's starting point.

However, Candice rode at a faster pace than Sabrina, completing each lap around the track in 42 seconds, while Sabrina completed each lap around the track in 46 seconds. How many laps around the track had Candice completed the next time that Candice and Sabrina were together at the starting point?

    (A)   21
    (B)   23
    (C)   42
    (D)   46
    (E)   483

Arithmetic Applied Problems; Properties of Integers

Let C and S be the number of laps around the track, respectively, whenever Candice and Sabrina were together again at the starting point. Since Candice completes each lap in 42 seconds, Candice had been riding for a total of $42C$ seconds, and since Sabrina completes each lap in 46 seconds, Sabrina had been riding for a total of $46S$ seconds. Because they had been riding for the same total amount of time, we have $42C = 46S$, or $21C = 23S$, where C and S are positive integers.

Because 23 is a prime number that divides the product of 21 and C (note that 23 divides $23S$ and $23S = 21C$), it follows that 23 divides 21 (not true) or 23 divides C, and hence 23 divides C. Also, because 3 is a prime number that divides the product of 23 and S (note that 3 divides $21C$ and $21C = 23S$), it follows that 3 divides 23 (not true) or 3 divides S, and hence 3 divides S. Finally, because 7 is a prime number that divides the product of 23 and S (note that 7 divides $21C$ and $21C = 23S$), it follows that 7 divides 23 (not true) or 7 divides S, and hence 7 divides S

It follows that C is a multiple of 23 and S is a multiple of both 3 and 7. The least positive integer values for C and S with this property are $C = 23$ and $S = 3 \times 7 = 21$. Therefore, the next time after beginning that Candice and Sabrina were together at the starting point, Candice had completed 23 laps and Sabrina had completed 21 laps.

The correct answer is B.

166. If $n = 9! - 6^4$, which of the following is the greatest integer k such that 3^k is a factor of n?

(A)　1

(B)　3

(C)　4

(D)　6

(E)　8

Arithmetic Properties of Integers

The following charts isolate and count the occurrences of 2 and of 3 in the factorizations of $9! = (9)(8)(7)(6)(5)(4)(3)(2)$ and $6^4 = (6)(6)(6)(6)$.

9!	=	(9)	(8)	(7)	(6)	(5)	(4)	(3)	(2)
Occurrences of 2		0	3	0	1	0	2	0	1
Occurrences of 3		2	0	0	1	0	0	1	0

6^4	=	(6)	(6)	(6)	(6)
Occurrences of 2		1	1	1	1
Occurrences of 3		1	1	1	1

So, $9! - 6^4 = (2^7 \cdot 3^4 \cdot 5 \cdot 7) - (2^4 \cdot 3^4) = (2^4 \cdot 3^4)$ $(2^3 \cdot 5 \cdot 7 - 1) = (2^4 \cdot 3^4)(279) = (2^4 \cdot 3^4)(3^2 \cdot 31) =$ $2^4 \cdot 3^6 \cdot 31$, where 31 is prime. Therefore $k = 6$.

Alternatively, express $n = 9! - 6^4$ as $(9)(8)(7)(6)$ $(5)(4)(3)(2)(1) - 6^4 = [(9)(8)](7)(6)(5)(4)[(3)(2)]$ $(1) - 6^4$. Then factor $(9)(8)$ as $(36)(2) = (6^2)(2)$ and multiply $(3)(2)$ to get 6. Factoring 6^4 from $n = (6^2)(2)(7)(6)(5)(4)(6)(1) - 6^4$ gives $n = 6^4[(2)(7)(5)(4)(1) - 1] = 6^4(279)$. It follows that 6^4 has 4 factors of 3 and 279 has 2 additional factors of 3 since $279 = (3^2)(31)$, so the greatest integer k such that 3^k is a factor of n is $4 + 2 = 6$.

The correct answer is D.

167. The integer 120 has many factorizations. For example, $120 = (2)(60)$, $120 = (3)(4)(10)$, and $120 = (-1)(-3)(4)$ (10). In how many of the factorizations of 120 are the factors consecutive integers in ascending order?

(A)　2

(B)　3

(C)　4

(D)　5

(E)　6

Arithmetic Properties of Integers

All of the positive factors of 120 listed in ascending order are 1, 2, 3, 4, 5, 6, 8, 10, 12, 15, 20, 24, 30, 40, 60, and 120. The negative factors of 120 listed in ascending order are $-120, -60,$ $-40, -30, -24, -20, -15, -12, -10, -8, -6, -5, -4,$ $-3, -2,$ and -1. Examining these lists for groups of consecutive factors whose product is 120 gives $(1)(2)(3)(4)(5)$, $(2)(3)(4)(5)$, $(4)(5)(6)$, and $(-5)(-4)(-3)(-2)$.

The correct answer is C.

168. Jorge's bank statement showed a balance that was $0.54 greater than what his records showed. He discovered that he had written a check for $x.yz and had recorded it as $x.zy, where each of x, y, and z represents a digit from 0 though 9. Which of the following could be the value of z?

(A)　2

(B)　3

(C)　4

(D)　5

(E)　6

Arithmetic Place Value

Since the amount Jorge recorded for the check ($x.zy) was $0.54 more than the actual amount of the check ($x.yz), it follows that $x.zy - $x.yz = $0.54. This is equivalent to $x + \dfrac{z}{10} + \dfrac{y}{100} - (x + \dfrac{y}{10} + \dfrac{z}{100}) = \dfrac{54}{100}$. Then $\dfrac{10z + y}{100} - \dfrac{10y + z}{100} = \dfrac{54}{100}$ or, equivalently, $10z + y - (10y + z) = 54$. It follows that $9z - 9y = 54$ or $z - y = 6$. Since y and z are digits, the possible values of y and z, respectively, are 0 and 6, 1 and 7, 2 and 8, and 3 and 9. Of the possible values of z, only 6 is given as one of the answer choices.

The correct answer is E.

169. One side of a parking stall is defined by a straight stripe that consists of n painted sections of equal length with an unpainted section $\dfrac{1}{2}$ as long between each pair of consecutive painted sections. The total length of the stripe from the beginning of the first

painted section to the end of the last painted section is 203 inches. If n is an integer and the length, in inches, of each unpainted section is an integer greater than 2, what is the value of n?

(A) 5
(B) 9
(C) 10
(D) 14
(E) 29

Algebra Applied Problems

2k inches   k inches

The figure above is a schematic diagram of the parking stall's painted sections, where each painted section has length $2k$ inches and each unpainted section has length k inches. Since there is a total of n painted sections and a total of $(n-1)$ unpainted sections, it follows that $n(2k) + (n-1)k = 203$, or $(3n-1)k = 203$. Also, since n and k are positive integers with $n \geq 2$, and $203 = (7)(29)$ is the only factorization of 203 with integer factors greater than or equal to 2, we have two cases.

Case 1: $3n - 1 = 7$ and $k = 29$. In this case we have $n = \dfrac{8}{3}$.

Case 2: $3n - 1 = 29$ and $k = 7$. In this case we have $n = 10$.

Because $\dfrac{8}{3}$ is not an integer, we discard Case 1, and hence $n = 10$.

The correct answer is C.

170. $\dfrac{2\frac{3}{5} - 1\frac{2}{3}}{\frac{2}{3} - \frac{3}{5}} =$

(A) 16
(B) 14
(C) 3
(D) 1
(E) −1

Arithmetic Operations on Rational Numbers

Work the problem:

$$\frac{2\frac{3}{5} - 1\frac{2}{3}}{\frac{2}{3} - \frac{3}{5}} =$$

$$\frac{\frac{13}{5} - \frac{5}{3}}{\frac{2}{3} - \frac{3}{5}} = \frac{\frac{39-25}{15}}{\frac{10-9}{15}} = \frac{\frac{14}{15}}{\frac{1}{15}} = \frac{14}{15} \times \frac{15}{1} = 14$$

The correct answer is B.

Machine	Consecutive Minutes Machine Is Off	Units of Power When On
A	17	15
B	14	18
C	11	12

171. At a certain factory, each of Machines A, B, and C is periodically on for exactly 1 minute and periodically off for a fixed number of consecutive minutes. The table above shows that Machine A is on and uses 15 units of power every 18th minute, Machine B is on and uses 18 units of power every 15th minute, and Machine C is on and uses 12 units of power every 12th minute. The factory has a backup generator that operates only when the total power usage of the 3 machines exceeds 30 units of power. What is the time interval, in minutes, between consecutive times the backup generator begins to operate?

(A) 36
(B) 63
(C) 90
(D) 180
(E) 270

Arithmetic Applied Problems

The given table shows that the backup generator will not operate when only one of the machines is operating, since none of the machines uses more than 30 units of power. The table below shows the power usage when more than one machine is operating at the same time.

Machines	Units of power when on	Backup generator
A & B	15 + 18 = 33	On
B & C	18 + 12 = 30	Off
C & A	12 + 15 = 27	Off
A & B & C	15 + 18 + 12 = 45	On

Thus, the backup generator will be on whenever Machines A and B are both on, this being true regardless of whether Machine C is on. We are given that Machine A is on for 1 minute every 18 minutes and Machine B is on for 1 minute every 15 minutes. Therefore, if Machines A and B are both on for a certain minute, then the following are the minutes when these machines are again on.

Minutes when Machine A is on: 1st, 19th, 37th, 55th, 73rd, **91st**, 109th, ...

Minutes when Machine B is on: 1st, 16th, 31st, 46th, 61st, 76th, **91st**, 106th, ...

Therefore, the next time Machines A and B are both on is the 91st minute, which is 90 minutes after the first minute.

Alternatively, Machine A is on every $18 = (2)(3^2)$ minutes and Machine B is on every $15 = (3)(5)$ minutes, so the machines are both on every $(2)(3^2)(5) = 90$ minutes (least common multiple of 18 and 15).

The correct answer is C.

5.0 GMAT™ Official Guide Quantitative Review Question Index

5.0 GMAT™ Official Guide Quantitative Review Question Index

The Quantitative Review Question Index is organized by GMAT™ section, difficulty level, and then by mathematical concept. The question number, page number, and answer explanation page number are listed so that questions within the book can be quickly located.

Quantitative Reasoning – Chapter 4 – Page 68

Difficulty	Concept	Question #	Page	Answer Explanation Page
Easy	Absolute Value	32	76	109
Easy	Applied Problems	6	72	100
Easy	Applied Problems	11	73	102
Easy	Applied Problems	12	73	102
Easy	Applied Problems	18	74	104
Easy	Applied Problems	33	76	109
Easy	Applied Problems	38	77	110
Easy	Applied Problems	41	77	111
Easy	Applied Problems	44	78	112
Easy	Applied Problems	47	78	113
Easy	Applied Problems	48	78	114
Easy	Applied Problems	61	80	117
Easy	Applied Problems	71	82	121
Easy	Applied Problems; Operations with Fractions	46	78	113
Easy	Applied Problems; Percents	56	79	116
Easy	Applied Problems; Proportions	9	73	101
Easy	Applied Problems; Substitution	16	74	103
Easy	Estimation	54	79	115
Easy	Exponents	37	77	110
Easy	Exponents	40	77	111
Easy	Factoring	3	72	99
Easy	Factors, Multiples, and Divisibility	4	72	100

(Continued)

Difficulty	Concept	Question #	Page	Answer Explanation Page
Easy	First-Degree Equations	8	73	101
Easy	First-Degree Equations	14	74	103
Easy	First-Degree Equations	27	75	107
Easy	First-Degree Equations	39	77	111
Easy	First-Degree Equations	49	79	114
Easy	First-Degree Equations; Substitution	36	77	110
Easy	Formulas	53	79	115
Easy	Formulas	66	81	119
Easy	Fractions	23	75	106
Easy	Inequalities	7	73	100
Easy	Inequalities	34	76	109
Easy	Interpretation of Graphs	63	81	118
Easy	Operations on Integers	5	72	100
Easy	Operations on Integers	19	74	104
Easy	Operations on Integers	65	81	119
Easy	Operations on Integers	68	81	120
Easy	Operations on Rational Numbers	13	73	102
Easy	Operations on Rational Numbers	21	75	105
Easy	Operations with Fractions	59	80	117
Easy	Operations with Fractions	60	80	117
Easy	Operations with Fractions	64	81	118
Easy	Operations with Integers	58	80	116
Easy	Operations with Integers	62	80	118
Easy	Operations with Integers; Measurement Conversion	73	82	122
Easy	Order	15	74	103
Easy	Percents	10	73	102
Easy	Percents	20	74	105
Easy	Percents	29	76	108
Easy	Percents	35	76	110

Difficulty	Concept	Question #	Page	Answer Explanation Page
Easy	Percents	50	79	114
Easy	Percents	57	80	116
Easy	Percents	70	82	121
Easy	Place Value	30	76	108
Easy	Place Value	74	82	122
Easy	Properties of Integers	25	75	106
Easy	Properties of Numbers	28	75	107
Easy	Properties of Numbers	43	78	112
Easy	Properties of Numbers	55	79	116
Easy	Properties of Numbers	72	82	121
Easy	Rate	1	72	99
Easy	Rate Problem	17	74	104
Easy	Rate Problem	42	77	111
Easy	Ratio and Proportion	51	79	115
Easy	Second-Degree Equations	2	72	99
Easy	Second-Degree Equations	22	75	105
Easy	Second-Degree Equations	52	79	115
Easy	Sequences	67	81	120
Easy	Series and Sequences	26	75	107
Easy	Series and Sequences	45	78	113
Easy	Simplifying Algebraic Expressions; Substitution	24	75	106
Easy	Simultaneous Equations	31	76	109
Easy	Statistics	69	82	121
Medium	Absolute Value	105	87	132
Medium	Applied Problems	76	83	123
Medium	Applied Problems	79	83	124
Medium	Applied Problems	94	86	129
Medium	Applied Problems	101	87	131
Medium	Applied Problems	104	87	132

(Continued)

Difficulty	Concept	Question #	Page	Answer Explanation Page
Medium	Applied Problems	114	88	136
Medium	Applied Problems	116	89	136
Medium	Applied Problems; Formulas	87	85	127
Medium	Applied Problems; Percents	122	89	138
Medium	Decimals	102	87	131
Medium	Equations; Inequalities	85	84	126
Medium	Estimation	123	89	139
Medium	Factoring	91	85	128
Medium	First-Degree Equations	75	83	122
Medium	First-Degree Equations	86	85	127
Medium	First-Degree Equations	88	85	127
Medium	Formulas	90	85	128
Medium	Formulas; Percents	97	86	130
Medium	Functions; Absolute Value	84	84	126
Medium	Inequalities	98	86	130
Medium	Inequalities	100	86	131
Medium	Inequalities	109	88	134
Medium	Inequalities	118	89	137
Medium	Inequalities; Absolute Value	112	88	135
Medium	Measurement Conversion	93	86	129
Medium	Operations with Integers	81	84	125
Medium	Order	78	83	123
Medium	Percents	119	89	137
Medium	Percents	124	90	139
Medium	Percents; Estimation	106	87	133
Medium	Percents; Estimation	117	89	137
Medium	Place Value	107	87	133
Medium	Place Value	126	90	140
Medium	Properties of Integers	82	84	125
Medium	Properties of Integers	125	90	139

Difficulty	Concept	Question #	Page	Answer Explanation Page
Medium	Properties of Numbers	99	86	131
Medium	Properties of Numbers	110	88	134
Medium	Properties of Numbers	111	88	135
Medium	Properties of Numbers	120	89	138
Medium	Ratio and Proportion	115	88	136
Medium	Ratios	77	83	123
Medium	Second-Degree Equations	92	85	129
Medium	Second-Degree Equations	96	86	130
Medium	Series and Sequences	127	90	140
Medium	Sets (Venn Diagrams)	80	83	124
Medium	Simultaneous Equations	89	85	127
Medium	Simultaneous Equations	95	86	130
Medium	Simultaneous Equations	108	87	133
Medium	Simultaneous Equations	121	89	138
Medium	Statistics	83	84	125
Medium	Statistics	103	87	132
Medium	Statistics	113	88	135
Hard	Absolute Value	142	92	144
Hard	Applied Problems	131	90	141
Hard	Applied Problems	153	93	148
Hard	Applied Problems	155	94	149
Hard	Applied Problems	163	95	152
Hard	Applied Problems	169	96	154
Hard	Applied Problems	171	96	155
Hard	Applied Problems; Percents	135	91	142
Hard	Applied Problems; Percents	158	94	150
Hard	Applied Problems; Properties of Integers	165	95	153
Hard	Arithmetic Operations	129	90	140

(Continued)

Difficulty	Concept	Question #	Page	Answer Explanation Page
Hard	Elementary Combinatorics	144	92	145
Hard	Elementary Combinatorics	148	93	147
Hard	Estimation	138	91	143
Hard	Exponents	137	91	143
Hard	First-Degree Equations	128	90	140
Hard	First-Degree Equations; Percents	145	92	146
Hard	First-Degree Equations; Percents	152	93	148
Hard	Inequalities	154	94	149
Hard	Operations on Radical Expressions	147	93	146
Hard	Operations on Rational Numbers	159	94	151
Hard	Operations on Rational Numbers	170	96	155
Hard	Operations with Integers	130	90	141
Hard	Operations with Integers	143	92	145
Hard	Percents	136	91	142
Hard	Place Value	150	93	147
Hard	Place Value	168	96	154
Hard	Probability	157	94	150
Hard	Probability; Concepts of Sets	149	93	147
Hard	Properties of Integers	132	91	141
Hard	Properties of Integers	139	91	143
Hard	Properties of Numbers	151	93	148
Hard	Properties of Numbers	156	94	149
Hard	Properties of Numbers	160	95	151
Hard	Properties of Numbers	162	95	152
Hard	Properties of Numbers	166	95	154
Hard	Properties of Numbers	167	95	154
Hard	Properties of Numbers; Exponents	164	95	153
Hard	Sequences and Series	133	91	141
Hard	Sequences and Series	134	91	142

Difficulty	Concept	Question #	Page	Answer Explanation Page
Hard	Sets	146	93	146
Hard	Simplifying Algebraic Expressions; Applied Problems	161	95	151
Hard	Statistics	140	92	144
Hard	Statistics	141	92	144

To register for the GMAT™ exam go to www.mba.com/register

Appendix A   Answer Sheet

Quantitative Reasoning Answer Sheet

1.	36.	71.	106.	141.
2.	37.	72.	107.	142.
3.	38.	73.	108.	143.
4.	39.	74.	109.	144.
5.	40.	75.	110.	145.
6.	41.	76.	111.	146.
7.	42.	77.	112.	147.
8.	43.	78.	113.	148.
9.	44.	79.	114.	149.
10.	45.	80.	115.	150.
11.	46.	81.	116.	151.
12.	47.	82.	117.	152.
13.	48.	83.	118.	153.
14.	49.	84.	119.	154.
15.	50.	85.	120.	155.
16.	51.	86.	121.	156.
17.	52.	87.	122.	157.
18.	53.	88.	123.	158.
19.	54.	89.	124.	159.
20.	55.	90.	125.	160.
21.	56.	91.	126.	161.
22.	57.	92.	127.	162.
23.	58.	93.	128.	163.
24.	59.	94.	129.	164.
25.	60.	95.	130.	165.
26.	61.	96.	131.	166.
27.	62.	97.	132.	167.
28.	63.	98.	133.	168.
29.	64.	99.	134.	169.
30.	65.	100.	135.	170.
31.	66.	101.	136.	171.
32.	67.	102.	137.	
33.	68.	103.	138.	
34.	69.	104.	139.	
35.	70.	105.	140.	

Notes

Notes

Notes

Focus Edition

Power Up Your Prep
with Official Practice Exams

Research shows that first-time
GMAT test takers can **increase their
scores by up to 75 points** after taking
all Official Practice Exams!

Benefit from:

◎ The same scoring algorithm as the
real GMAT Focus, with questions that
adapt in difficulty as you improve

◎ Scaled section scores and
a total score that aligns to
the actual test

◎ Detailed score performance
report, including time management

**Get your Official Practice at
mba.com/gmatprep**

**Graduate
Management
Admission
Council**